Verne C. Smith

INCIDENT AT HARPER'S FERRY

PRIMARY SOURCE MATERIALS
FOR TEACHING THE THEORY AND TECHNIQUE
OF THE INVESTIGATIVE ESSAY

Incident at

Harper's Ferry

Edited by Edward Stone

OHIO UNIVERSITY

PRENTICE-HALL, INC.

Englewood Cliffs, N. J. 1956

Dedicated to

THE LATE   PHILIP WILLIAMS, JR.,   OF VIRGINIA

colleague - benefactor - friend

Ut te postremo donarem munere mortis

FOREWORD

What happened at Harper's Ferry? This book does not answer that question; it is designed rather to provide you with the best means possible of answering it yourself—the facts. Presented here is a selection of contemporaneous accounts and opinion so widely varied in its coverage that a casual reader's initial reaction may well be one of bewilderment to the sharp disparities between the accounts of Reporter A and Raider B, between the speeches of Senator C and Reverend D. No attempt is made here to synthesize or "interpret" these primary sources; that is up to you, be your point of departure the Research Paper, a program in American history and government, or another of the many purposes which these data might serve.

Indeed, this very conflict and diversity of reactions to John Brown's raid are the substance of its undiminished fascination; this abortive, ill-fated act of a handful of men touched off a controversy whose blaze illumined a cleavage of passion and principle that was so soon to find its resolution in a bloody Civil War. *Incident at Harper's Ferry* offers a hundred or more authentic, often hard-to-come-by, sources—books, magazines, newspapers, speeches, sermons, letters, affidavits, songs, and poems —from the hands of actual participants in the raid, those directly subject to its effects, and eyewitnesses to the events surrounding a figure who became a legend of his time. "Bleeding" Kansas, a military problem "starring" celebrities-to-be, a famous law trial, and a presidential election feature in the patchwork of John Brown's story.

Such a collection of materials could serve many interests, academic and otherwise, but its ideal use (and one kept in mind in the preparation of this volume) might well be as an exercise in the Research Paper. Although its inclusion somewhere in the college English course is usually considered indispensable, the Research Paper has seldom been other than a source of vexation to both instructor and student. One reason for the difficulty is that current custom has students do their research on (1) any subject congenial only to them, or (2) any subject congenial only to the instructor. Either way, there's trouble. What instructor's range is so broad as to enable him to guide effectively and grade intelligently twenty-five different projects in each of his classes, on topics anywhere from Aardvarks to Zoroastrianism? Consider, on the other hand, the equally lamentable plight of the pre-Business student required to elucidate upon the subtleties of Gertrude Stein. Here, we suggest, is one escape from the dilemma. This intensely dramatic and historically significant incident is subject matter of such universal interest as to provide a common ground between student and student, between student and instructor.

Another problem of the Research Paper that cries out for solution is that of materials. How often has the tedious chore of compiling a bibliography simply been transferred to the reference librarian, who must then unearth the drought or disorderly deluge (depending upon the subject and the library) of scrambled primary and secondary sources? How often then has a pastiche or an indiscriminate skimming of these been palmed off as an act of scholarship? The more realistic your view, the larger would be your estimate; in any case, we could fairly say, *"Too* often." In this text, however, are carefully selected materials from a wide assortment of strictly contemporary reportage, opinion, and testimony of this historic moment uncolored by knowledge of the holocaust that was to follow in its wake. Each word is the fresh, undistilled reaction of one of those actually involved; no predigested interpretations of the modern historian are offered as a substitute for original thought.

Another discouraging feature of the Research Paper usually submitted is that, being the first, it is seriously flawed; and, being also the last (on its particular topic, at least), there is no effective remedy short of actually rewriting it, a generally impracticable and always agonizing "reappraisal." To avoid the waste, through misunderstanding and lack of experience, of the effort expended in the full-length paper, topics for preliminary 100-word to 500-word research exercises are provided at the end of each chapter or division of chapter so that the student can "warm up" and learn the craft of research through trial and error before plunging into the deep water to answer, in its larger sense, our question, *"What happened* at Harper's Ferry?"

As for the conventional procedures of literary etiquette and formality (quoting, paraphrasing, footnoting and such), the separate items can easily be documented as if they had not been collected into one volume. The instructor can demonstrate these techniques without breaking stride as he teaches his subject matter.

For here, at last, the *subject matter* as well as the technique of scholarship can be brought into the classroom, whatever the department or the student's major, and *taught,* instead of having to be pursued individually by night. That it *must* be taught is well known to teachers in many American history and culture programs. Even given controlled materials such as we have here, the actual writing of the essay itself remains as a real test of the student's ability to shape them into coherence. The importance of the instructor in accompanying him through the five chapters and helping him to read and think honestly, thoroughly, and scientifically is in no way minimized, but rather emphasized because of the unity of concentration and direction here possible.

In order to encourage students to familiarize themselves with the facilities of their library, several lists of topics are provided for more extensive research as time and preference permit. These topics are of two kinds: (1) for bibliographical exercises, and (2) for actual research on John Brown to supplement the documents used in this text.

To avoid any unnecessary confusion due to inconsistencies in the original sources, proper names have been standardized in this volume according to their correct spellings.

I am indebted to David Levin's *What Happened in Salem?* (Twayne), the pioneer in the Controlled Materials method of teaching the Research Paper project. Francis E. Bowman of Duke University, John Ciardi of Rutgers University, and Alfred W. Goodyear of Prentice-Hall, Inc., both liked and encouraged my project; so did Henry W. Sams of the University of Chicago, certain of whose pages in *New Problems in Reading and Writing* were my starting point; and Milton C. Russell of the Virginia State Library always answered inquiries cheerfully. Most of the work on this book was done while I was with the University of Virginia, where John C. Wyllie, the staff of the Alderman Library, William E. Stokes, Jr., Walter Harding, Edward A. Stephenson and Bernard Mayo were very helpful in finding materials or ideas. Valuable suggestions for the shape the book finally took came from George F. Horner of the University of North Carolina; Glen Leggett of the University of Washington; Hans Gottschalk of the State University of New York Teachers College at Geneseo; and Colonel G. R. Stephens of the United States Military Academy. Finally, Donald R. Hammonds and David Vanderburgh of Prentice-Hall, Inc. guided it through from the start; and here as elsewhere during the past ten years I have been helped and heartened by that eminent authority on Southern life and letters—Jay B. Hubbell, Professor Emeritus of Duke University.

EDWARD STONE

CONTENTS

Chapter I

PRELUDE

No. 1   THE FUGITIVE SLAVE ACT [OF 1850]

Statutes at Large of the United States (Boston, 1863), vol. IX, p. 462

An Act to Amend, and Supplementary to, the Act entitled "An Act respecting Fugitives from Justice and Persons escaping from the Service of their Masters," approved February 12, 1793.

Be it enacted by the Senate and House of Representatives of the United States of America in Congress assembled. . . .

SEC. 6. That when a person held to service or labor in any State or Territory . . . has heretofore or shall hereafter escape into another State or Territory of the United States, the person or persons to whom such service or labor may be due, or his, or her, or their agent or attorney . . . may pursue and reclaim such fugitive person, either by procuring a warrant from some one of the courts, judges, or commissioners aforesaid . . . for the apprehension of such fugitive from service or labor, or by seizing and arresting such fugitive, where the same can be done without process, and by taking, or causing such person to be taken, forthwith before such court . . . , whose duty it shall be to hear and determine the case . . . in a summary manner. . . . In no trial or hearing, under this act, shall the testimony of such alleged fugitive be admitted in evidence; and the certificates in this and the first section mentioned shall be conclusive of the right of the person or persons in whose favor granted, to remove such fugitive to the State or Territory from which he escaped, and shall prevent all molestation of such person or persons, by any process issued by any court, judge, magistrate, or other person, whomsoever.

SEC. 7. That any person who shall knowingly and willingly obstruct, hinder, or prevent such claimant . . . from arresting such a fugitive . . . or shall rescue or attempt to rescue such fugitive . . . or shall aid, abet, or assist such person . . . to escape from such claimant . . . or shall harbor or conceal such fugitive . . . shall, for either of said offences be subject to a fine not exceeding one thousand dollars, and imprisonment not exceeding six months . . . and shall moreover forfeit and pay . . . to the party injured . . . one thousand dollars for each fugitive so lost. . . .

No. 2   SPEECH OF THE HON. J. R. GIDDINGS ON THE [MISSOURI] COMPROMISE MEASURES, HOUSE OF REPRESENTATIVES, MARCH 16, 1852

Speeches on Slavery, a collection of pamphlets in the University of Virginia Library

. . . I am aware that men in high official stations have announced . . . that the slave questions are settled—that all agitation has ceased [now that the Compromise has passed]. But what are the facts? We see and know that discussion has increased and extended more rapidly since the enactment of those laws than at any former period. . . .

To the maintenance of the Compromise measures as a *final settlement* of the slave question, the President, in his message, exhorts the people to adhere. The Whig and the Democratic parties are each striving to go beyond the other in their devotion to this plan for silencing all further agitation of the questions of liberty and slavery. . . .

Men, women, and children, are purchased in this District, and in the Northern slave States, and placed on board these slave ships and carried to the torture and premature deaths which . . . await them upon the cotton and sugar plantations. There they are murdered under a slow torture by the lash of inhuman overseers. . . . The blood of these victims rests upon the members of this body. We have the power to stop this flood of human gore. But while these victims toil in chains, and sigh and weep . . . , members here refuse to examine this subject, refuse to permit the introduction of a bill to repeal this law. . . .

Those portions of the law which authorize and require the appointment of officers to grant process for the arrest of slaves; that part which makes it the duty of judges to grant such process; that part which directs marshals and deputy marshals to arrest the slave; which authorizes them to call on the people to assist in that piratical work; which renders it penal for a man to feed a famishing or starving fugitive . . . —these provisions are each of them unconstitutional, unjust, abhorrent . . . , inhuman, and barbarous. . . .

I now repeat, that to the full extent to which the law of 1850 involves this Government, its officers, and the people of the free States, in the burden, the expense, and disgrace, of recapturing and returning fugitive slaves, it is *unconstitutional.*

. . . Mr. Chairman, the day of redemption for this people *must come.* . . . [The] stain of slavery shall be wiped from our national escutcheon. . . . [A] band of patriots, of philanthropists, are now laboring to bring about this "consummation so devoutly to be wished." Upon the broad basis of truth, of justice, of equal rights, of the brotherhood of man and of nations, we have taken our stand. Our numbers are increasing. The effects of our labors are becoming manifest. Our cause is advancing. Our moral and political influence is extending, and our final triumph is certain. . . .

No. 3   SPEECH OF HON. GERRIT SMITH IN CONGRESS ON THE REFERENCE OF THE PRESIDENT'S MESSAGE, DECEMBER 20, 1853

Speeches on Slavery

. . . . Alas, what a disgusting spectacle does the Administration present, in its deliberate corruption of the Bible, for the guilty purpose of sparing so abominable and vile a thing as slavery! Alas, what a pitiable spectacle of self-degradation does this nation present, in choosing such an Administration, and in remaining patient under it! And how rank . . . is the hypocrisy upon the brow of this nation, who, whilst her feet are planted on the millions she has doomed to the horrors, and agonies, and pollutions of slavery, holds, nevertheless, in one hand that precious, Heaven-sent volume, which declares that God "hath made of one blood all nations of men, for to dwell on all the face of the earth"; and in the other, that emphatically American paper, which declares that "all men are created equal"! And how greatly is the guilt of this nation in her matchless oppressions, aggravated by the fact that she owes infinitely more than ever, than any other nation, to Christianity and liberty and knowledge; and that she is, therefore, under infinitely greater obligation than was ever any other nation to set an example . . . both at home and abroad! . . . .

No. 4   SPEECH OF STEPHEN DOUGLAS IN THE SENATE ON THE NEBRASKA TERRITORY BILL, JANUARY 30, 1854

Henry M. Flint, *The Life of Stephen A. Douglas* (New York, 1860). Part II: "Speeches and Reports," pp. 89-91

. . . . They talk about the bill being a violation of the compromise measures of 1850. Who can show me a man in either house of Congress who was in favor of those compromise measures in 1850 and who is not now in favor of leaving the people of Nebraska and Kansas to do as they please upon the subject of slavery, according to the principle of my bill? . . . . This tornado has been raised by abolitionists, and abolitionists alone. They have made an impression upon the public mind . . . by a falsification of the law and the facts. . . .

Now, I ask the friends and the opponents of this measure to look at it as it is. Is not the question involved the simple one [of] whether the people of the Territories shall be allowed to do as they please upon the question of slavery, subject only to the limitations of the Constitution? . . . . Let all this quibbling about the Missouri compromise, about the territory acquired from France, about the act of 1820, be cast behind you; for the simple question is, will you allow the people to legislate for themselves upon the subject of slavery? Why should you not?

When you propose to give them a Territorial Government, do you not acknowledge that they ought to be erected into a political organization; and when you give them a legislature, do you not acknowledge that they are capable of self-government? Having made that acknowledgment, why should you not allow them to exercise the rights of legislation? Oh, these abolitionists say they are entirely willing to concede all this, with one exception. They say they are willing to trust the Territorial legislature, under the limitations of the Constitution, to legislate in regard to religion, education, and morals, to legislate in regard to the relations of husband and wife, of parent and child, of guardian and ward, upon everything pertaining to the dearest rights and interests of white men, but they are not willing to trust them to legislate in regard to a few miserable negroes. That is their single exception. . . .

No. 5   "THE CRIME AGAINST KANSAS"
SPEECH OF HON. CHARLES SUMNER
IN THE SENATE, MAY 19-20, 1856

Speeches on Slavery

. . . . Mr. President, . . . the Nebraska Bill, on its very face, openly cleared the way for slavery, and it is not wrong to presume that its originators intended the natural consequences of such an act, and sought in this way to extend slavery. Of course, they did. And this is the first stage in the Crime against Kansas.

But this was speedily followed by other developments. The bare-faced scheme was soon whispered, that Kansas must be a slave State. In conformity with this idea was the Government of this unhappy Territory organized in all its departments; and thus did the President, by whose complicity the prohibition of slavery had been overthrown, lend himself to a new complicity. . . . The Governor, Secretary, Chief Justice, Associate Justices, Attorney, and Marshall . . . , nominated by the President and confirmed by the Senate, were all commended as friendly to slavery. . . . With such auspices the conspiracy proceeded. Even in advance of the Nebraska Bill, secret societies were organized in Missouri, ostensibly to protect her institutions, and afterwards . . . these were multiplied throughout the western counties of that state, *before any counter-movement from the North*. It was confidently anticipated, that, by the activity of these societies, and the interest of slave-holders everywhere, with the advantage derived from the neighborhood of Missouri, and the influence of the Territorial Government, slavery might be introduced into Kansas, quietly but surely, without arousing a conflict—that the crocodile egg might be stealthily dropped in the sunburnt soil, there to be hatched unobserved until it sent forth its reptile monster.

But the conspiracy was unexpectedly balked. The debate, which convulsed Congress, had stirred Congress, had stirred the whole country. Attention from all sides was directed upon Kansas, which at once became the favorite goal of emigration. . . . Thus, while opening the Territory to slavery, the bill also opened it to emigrants from every quarter, who might by their votes redress the wrong. The populous North, stung by a sharp sense of outrage, and inspired by a noble cause, poured into the debatable land, and promised soon to establish a supremacy of numbers there, involving, of course, a just supremacy of Freedom.

Then was conceived the consummation of the Crime against Kansas. What could not be accomplished peaceably, was to be accomplished forcibly. . . . All efforts were now given to the dismal work of forcing slavery on Free Soil. In flagrant derogation of the very Popular Sovereignty whose name helped to impose this Bill upon the country, the atrocious object was now distinctly avowed. And the avowal has been followed by the act. Slavery has been forcibly introduced into Kansas, and placed under the formal safeguards of pretended law. . . . Slavery now stands erect, clanking its chains on the Territory of Kansas, surrounded by a code of death, and trampling upon all cherished liberties. . . . And, sir, all this has been done . . . for the sake of political power, in order to bring two new slave-holding Senators upon this floor. . . .

No. 6 SPEECH OF STEPHEN A. DOUGLAS IN REPLY TO MR. SEWARD AND MR. TRUMBULL IN THE SENATE, FEB. 29, 1860

Flint, *Douglas*, Part II, pp. 175-177

. . . I hold that the question of slavery is one of political economy, governed by the laws of climate, soil, productions, and self-interest, and not by merely statutory provision. I repudiate the doctrine that because free institutions may be best in one climate, they are necessarily the best everywhere; or that because slavery may be indispensable in one locality, therefore it is desirable everywhere. . . . Hence I answer the question of the Senator from Wisconsin, that I am willing that a Territory settled by white men shall have negroes, free or slave, just as the white men shall determine, but not as the negroes shall prescribe. . . .

I was speaking of the scarcity of labor growing up in our northern manufacturing towns, as a legitimate and natural consequence of the diminution of the demand for the manufactured article; and then the question is, what cause has reduced this demand, except the "irrepressible conflict" that has turned the southern trade away from northern cities into southern towns and southern cities? Sir, the feeling among the masses of the South we find typified in the dress of the Senator from Virginia (MR. MASON); they are determined to wear the homespun of their own productions rather than trade with the North. That is the feeling which has produced this state of distress in our manufacturing towns.

The Senator from New York has also referred to the recent action of the people of New Mexico, in establishing a code for the protection of property in slaves, and he congratulates the country upon the final success of the advocates of free institutions in Kansas. He could not fail, however, to say, in order to preserve what he thought was a striking antithesis, that popular sovereignty in Kansas meant State sovereignty in Missouri. No, sir; popular sovereignty in Kansas was stricken down by unholy combination in New England to ship men to Kansas—rowdies and vagabonds—with the Bible in one hand and Sharps' rifle in the other, to shoot down the friends of self-government. Popular sovereignty in Kansas was stricken down by the combinations in the northern States to carry elections under pretence of emigrant aid societies. In retaliation, Missouri formed aid societies too; and she, following your example, sent men into Kansas and then occurred the conflict. Now, you throw the blame upon Missouri merely because she followed your example, and attempted to resist its consequences. I condemn both; but I condemn a thousand-fold more those that set the example and struck the first blow, than those who thought they would act upon the principle of fighting the devil with his own weapons, and resorted to the same means that you had employed. . . .

No. 7   DRED SCOTT v. JOHN F. A. SANDFORD, 19 HOW. 393 (1856)

United States Supreme Court Reports (Newark N.Y., 1884), vols. 58-60 [in one], pp. 691-720

Mr. Chief Justice Taney delivered the opinion of the court:
. . . The only matter in issue before the court . . . is, whether the descendants of . . . slaves, when they shall be emancipated, or who are born of parents who had become free before their birth, are citizens of a State, in the sense in which the word "citizen" is used in the Constitution of the United States. . . . We think they are not, and that they are not included, and were not intended to be included, under the word "citizens" in the Constitution, and can, therefore, claim none of the rights and privileges which that instrument provides for and secures to citizens of the United States. On the contrary, they were at that time considered as a subordinate and inferior class of beings, who had been subjugated by the dominant race, and, whether emancipated or not, yet remained subject to their authority, and had no right or privi-

leges but such as those who held the power and the Government might choose to grant them. . . .

In discussing this question, we must not confound the rights of citizenship which a State may confer within its own limits, and the rights of citizenship as a member of the Union. . . . Each State may . . . confer them upon an alien, or any one it thinks proper . . . ; yet he would not be a citizen in the sense in which that word is used in the Constitution of the United States, nor entitled to sue as such in one of its courts, nor to the privileges and immunities of a citizen in the other States. The rights which he would acquire would be restricted to the State which gave them. . . .

It is very clear, therefore, that no State can, by any act or law of its own, passed since the adoption of the Constitution, introduce a new member into the political community created by the Constitution of the United States. . . . It is true, every person, and every class . . . of persons, who were at the time of the adoption of the Constitution recognized as citizens in the several States, became also citizens of this new political body; but none other; it was formed by them, and for them and their posterity, but for no one else. . . .

In the opinion of the court, the legislation and histories of the times, and the language used in the Declaration of Independence, show, that neither the class of persons who had been imported as slaves, nor their descendants, whether they had become free or not, were then acknowledged as a part of the people, nor intended to be included in the general words used in that memorable instrument. . . . But there are two clauses in the Constitution which point directly and specifically to the negro race as a separate class of persons, and show clearly that they were not regarded as a portion of the people or citizens of the Government then formed.

One of these clauses reserves to each of the thirteen States the right to import slaves until the year 1808, if he thinks it proper. . . . And by the other provision [the Fugitive Slave Act] the States pledge themselves to each other to maintain the right of property of the master, by delivering up to him any slave who may have escaped from his service, and be found within their respective territories. . . . And these two provisions show, conclusively, that neither the description of persons therein referred to, nor their descendants, were embraced in any of the other provisions of the Constitution. . . .

It seems . . . to be supposed that there is a difference between property in a slave and other property, and that different rules may be applied to it in expounding the Constitution of the United States. . . .

[If] the Constitution recognizes the right or property of the master in a slave, and makes no distinction between that description of property and other property . . . , no tribunal . . . , whether it be legislative, executive, or judicial, has a right to draw such a distinction. . . . Now . . . the right of property in a slave is distinctly and expressly affirmed in the Constitution. The right to traffic in it, like an ordinary article of merchandise . . . , was guaranteed . . . for twenty years. And the Government in express terms is pledged to protect it in all future time, if the slave escapes from his owner. . . . And no word can be found in the Constitution which gives Congress a greater power over slave property . . . than property of any other description. . . .

Upon these considerations, it is the opinion of the court that the act of Congress which prohibited a citizen from holding and owning property of this kind in the territory of the United States north of the line therein mentioned, is not warranted by the Constitution, and is therefore void; and that neither Dred Scott himself, nor any of his family, were made free by being carried into this territory; even if they had been carried there by the owner, with the intention of becoming a permanent resident. . . .

So . . . as Scott was a slave when taken into the State of Illinois by his owner, and was there held as such, and brought back in that character, his *status,* as free or slave, depended on the laws of Missouri, and not of Illinois. . . .

No. 8   JOURNAL OF THE PROVISIONAL CONSTITUTIONAL CONVENTION [MAY 8-10, 1858, CHATHAM, CANADA WEST]

Select Committee on the Harper's Ferry Invasion, U.S. Senate, *Rep. Com. No. 278* (June 15, 1860), Appendix, pp. 44-59 [This source is hereafter referred to as *The Mason Report.*]

SAT., MAY 8: 10 a.m.—Convention met in pursuance to call of John Brown and others . . . On the motion of Mr. Brown, Mr. J. H. Kagi was elected secretary. . . . Mr. Brown then presented a plan of organization, entitled "Provisional Constitution and Ordinances . . . ," and moved the reading of the same. . . . The articles 1-45 inclusive, were then read and adopted. On the reading of the 46th, Mr. Reynolds moved to strike out the same. . . . The question was . . . lost. . . . The 47th and 48th articles . . . were then adopted. . . .

6 p.m.— . . . On the motion of Mr. Bell, the convention then went

into the election of officers . . . : Mr. Whipple nominated John Brown for Commander-in-Chief, who was . . . elected by acclamation. Mr. Realf nominated J. H. Kagi for Secretary of War, who was elected in the same manner. . . .

MON., MAY 10: 9 a.m.— . . . The convention . . . went into the election of members of congress. Messrs. Alfred M. Ellsworth and Osborn Anderson were elected. After which the convention went into the election of secretary of state, to which office Richard Realf was chosen. . . .

2½ p.m.— . . . The following resolution was then introduced by Mr. Brown, and unanimously passed: *Resolved,* that John Brown, J. H. Kagi, Richard Realf, L. F. Parsons, C. P. Tidd, E. Whipple, C. W. Moffett, John E. Cook, Richard Richardson, W. H. Leeman, and John Lawrence, be . . . appointed a committee, to whom is delegated the power of the convention to fill by election all the offices specially named in the provisional constitution which may be vacant after the adjournment of this convention. The convention then adjourned *sine die.* J. H. KAGI, *Secretary of the Convention.*

PROVISIONAL CONSTITUTION AND ORDINANCES FOR THE PEOPLE OF THE UNITED STATES

Preamble

Whereas slavery . . . is . . . a most barbarous, unprovoked, and unjustifiable war of one portion of its citizens upon another portion . . . in utter disregard and violation of those eternal and self-evident truths set forth in our Declaration of Independence:

Therefore, we, citizens of the United States, and the oppressed people who, by a recent decision of the Supreme Court, are declared to have no rights which the white man is bound to respect, together with all other people degraded by the laws thereof, do, for the time being, ordain and establish for ourselves the following Provisional Constitution and Ordinances, the better to protect our persons, property, lives, and liberties, and to govern our actions:

ARTICLE I: . . . All persons of mature age, whether proscribed, oppressed, and enslaved citizens, or of the proscribed and oppressed races of the United States, who shall agree to sustain and enforce the Provisional Constitution . . . shall be held to be fully entitled to protection under the same. ARTICLE II: The provisional government . . . shall consist of three branches, viz: legislative, executive, and judicial. III: The legislative branch shall be a Congress . . . composed of not less than five nor more than ten members, who shall be elected by all citizens of mature age and sound mind connected with this organization. . . . IV: The executive branch . . . shall consist of a President and Vice-President, who shall be chosen by the citizens. . . . V: The judicial branch . . . shall consist of one Chief Justice of the Supreme Court and four associate judges . . . , each constituting a circuit court. . . . VIII: A Commander-in-Chief of the army shall be chosen by the President, Vice-President, a majority of the Provisional Congress, and of the Supreme Court. . . . VIII: A Treasurer, Secretary of State, Secretary of War, and Secretary of the Treasury, shall each be chosen. . . . XVI: The President, with the Secretary of State, shall . . . give special attention to secure from amongst their own people men of integrity . . . to act as civil officers . . . as well as teachers, chaplains, . . . agents. . . . They shall make special efforts to induce . . . persons and families of that description to locate themselves within the limits secured by this organization. . . . XXII: The punishment of crimes not capital . . . shall be . . . by hard labor on the public works, roads, etc. . . . XXIV: Courts-martial for companies . . . shall be called by the chief officer of each. . . . XXVIII: All captured or confiscated property and all property the product of the labor of [our members] shall be held as the property of the whole, equally. . . . XXIX: All money, plate, watches, or jewelry captured by honorable warfare . . . shall be held sacred to constitute a liberal safety or intelligence fund. . . . XXXIV: The persons and property of all non-slaveholders who shall remain absolutely neutral shall be respected so far as the circumstances can allow. . . . XXXVI: The entire personal and real property of all persons known to be acting . . . with or for the enemy . . . or found willfully holding slaves shall be confiscated. . . . XLVI: The foregoing articles shall not be construed so as in any way to encourage the overthrow of any State government, or of the general government of the United States, and look to no dissolution of the Union, but simply to amendment and repeal. And our flag shall be the same that our fathers fought under in the Revolution.

No. 9   "THE IRREPRESSIBLE CONFLICT": A SPEECH BY WILLIAM H. SEWARD AT ROCHESTER ON OCT. 25, 1858

Campaign Documents, 1860, a collection of pamphlets in the University of Virginia Library

. . . Our country is a theatre which exhibits in full operation two radically different political systems: the one resting on the basis of servile labor, the other on the basis of voluntary labor of free men. . . . Hitherto the two systems have existed in different States, but side by side within the American Union. This has happened because the Union is a confederation of States. But in another aspect the United States constitute only one nation. Increase of population, which is filling the States out to their very borders, together with a new and extended network of railroads and other avenues, and an internal commerce which daily becomes more intimate, is rapidly bringing the States into a higher and more perfect social unity or consolidation. Thus, these antagonistic systems are continually coming into closer contact, and collision results.

Shall I tell you what this collision means? They who think that it is accidental, unnecessary, the work of interested or fanatical agitators, and therefore ephemeral, mistake the case altogether. It is an irrepressible conflict between opposing and enduring forces, and it means that the United States must and will sooner or later become either entirely a slave-holding nation or entirely a free-labor nation. . . .

It remains to say on this point only one word, to guard against misapprehension. If these States are to again become universally slave-holding, I do not pretend to say with what violations of the Constitution that end shall be accomplished. On the other hand, while I do confidently believe and hope that my country will yet become a land of universal Freedom, I do not expect that it will be made so otherwise than through the action of the several States cooperating with the Federal Government, and all acting in strict conformity with their respective Constitutions. . . .

TOPICS FOR ESSAYS

INSTRUCTIONS: *You have read a dozen or so varied documents relating to the slavery question from 1850 to 1858 both nationally and in Kansas. Compare them as to thoroughness and reliability, and, synthesizing their contents, construct from them a brief essay. Document it as your instructor prescribes.*

SUGGESTED LENGTH (*words*):

(1) *The Road to Chatham*   200
(The Convention met and drafted its constitution as a result of a chain of actions and attitudes. What were they? How were they related?)

(2) *Why Kansas Bled*   300
(Apparently the answers disagree violently. What are the points of view? Are they reconcilable? Incidentally, by the time you finish Chapter II you will have an opportunity to discuss this topic more fully.)

TOPICS FOR LIBRARY RESEARCH

BIBLIOGRAPHY. Instructions: *In the list below, as in those in the following chapters, are names and events ranging from famous to obscure. About some there will be little or no material in the library, particularly those whose reputation was merely regional or even local. But inasmuch as so many regions or even localities figure in the Incident, getting up a bibliography of any one of the obscure topics can prove a test of your persistence, the library's holdings, or both. As for the famous topics, a bibliography of any one may be limited as follows: (A) Two books; (B) Two magazine articles or essays; (C) Two newspaper articles; and (D) Two public or private documents.*

Stephen A. Douglas	William H. Seward
J. R. Giddings	The Missouri Compromise
The Nebraska Territory Bill	Gerrit Smith
Dred Scott	Charles Sumner

Chapter II

THE RAID

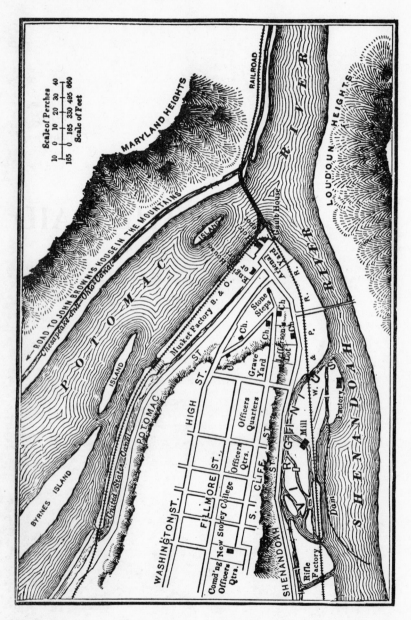

Map of Harper's Ferry, from the *Century Magazine*, July 1883

THE TOWN

No. 10

Thomas Jefferson, *Notes on the State of Virginia,* 8th Am.
ed. (Boston, 1801), pp. 27-28

. . . The passage of the Patowmac through the Blue ridge is
perhaps one of the most stupendous scenes in nature. You stand on a
very high point of land. On your right comes up the Shenandoah,
having ranged along the foot of the mountain an hundred miles to
seek a vent. On your left approaches the Patowmac, in quest of a
passage also. In the moment of their junction they rush together
against the mountain, rend it asunder, and pass off to the sea. The first
glance of this scene hurries our senses into the opinion that this earth
has been created in time, that the mountains were formed first, that
the rivers began to flow afterwards, that in this place particularly they
have been dammed up by the Blue ridge of mountains, and have formed
an ocean which filled the whole valley; that continuing to rise they
have at length broken over at this spot, and have torn the mountain
down from its summit to its base. The piles of rock on each hand,
but particularly on the Shenandoah, the evident marks of their dis-
rupture and avulsion from their beds by the most powerful agents of
nature, corroborate the impression. But the distant finishing which
nature has given to the picture is of a very different character. It is
a true contrast to the foreground. It is as placid and delightful, as
that is wild and tremendous. For the mountain being cloven asunder,
she presents to your eye, through the cleft, a small catch of smooth
blue horizon, at an infinite distance in the plain country, inviting you,
as it were, from the riot and tumult roaring around to pass through
the breach and participate of the calm below. Here the eye ultimately
composes itself; and that way too the road happens actually to lead.
You cross the Patowmac above the junction, pass along its side through
the base of the mountain for three miles, its terrible precipices hanging
in fragments over you, and within about 20 miles reach Fredericktown,
and the fine country round that. This scene is worth a voyage across the
Atlantic. . . .

No. 11   HARPER'S FERRY

Samuel Kercheval, *A History of the Valley of Virginia*
2d ed. (Woodstock, Va., 1850), pp. 318-319

. . . This is the location of the U.S. Armory, and in the
several shops are generally employed about three hundred first-rate
mechanics, engaged in the manufactory of arms for the purposes of
war. There are annually made about six or seven thousand muskets,
two or three thousand rifles, beside an immense number of swords,
pistols, and other side arms. The government employs at this establishment a superintendent general, a paymaster and a number of clerks.
The quantity of iron, steel, brass and other materials annually wrought
up is immense. A vast number of strangers annually visit this place
to gratify their curiosity in seeing and inspecting the public works and
great mechanical operations, so extensively carried on.—The machinery
of the musket factory is wrought by the waters of the Potomac, and
that of the rifle factory by the waters of the Shenandoah.

This site for the public works it is said was first marked out or
recommended by the immortal Washington, and is certainly evidence
of his superior skill and judgment in all military matters.

A railroad from Winchester to Harper's Ferry has been lately con-
structed, which has rendered Winchester a place of deposit for the
vast products of our valley but little inferior to some of our seaport
towns. A turnpike road from Winchester to Parkersburg on the Ohio
River, a distance of about two hundred and eighty miles, has lately
been finished; and another McAdamized turnpike road from Winchester to Staunton has just been put in operation, and it is almost inconceivable what vast quantities of produce now find a ready way to
Baltimore from the increased facilities of our improved roads to that
market.

. . . . several turnpikes are passable at all seasons of the year, and
greatly expedite the passenger's journey from east to west. These several
turnpikes have been made at vast expense to the State and stockholders,
notwithstanding which, improvements are still going on. A few years
more and Western Virginia will vie with our northern and sister States
with her vast improvements. Our valley is making great improvement
in every agricultural pursuit. Copying after our great and good country-
man, Washington, immense improvements have already been made,

and are still making, in the rearing of fine animals of every variety.
Stage coaches travel all our turnpike roads, drawn by the most splendid
horses; and most of our substantial farmers rear the finest cattle, sheep,
and hogs, and are greatly improving the fertility of their lands. Our
valley furnishes the several markets with vast quantities of superior
beef, pork, mutton, butter, and the finest of bread-stuffs. The quantities
of oats annually raised for market are incalculable. Immense crops of
the finest timothy, clover, and orchard grass hay, and corn fodder are
annually consumed by our farmers' stock; . . .

No. 12

D. H. Strother, in *Harper's Weekly,* Nov. 5, 1859, p. 712

FROM OUR OWN ARTIST-CORRESPONDENT

Harper's Ferry is situated in Jefferson County, Virginia, at
the confluence of the Potomac and Shenandoah rivers, on a point just
opposite the gap through which the united streams pass the Blue Ridge
on their way toward the ocean. The Ridge here is about 1200 feet
in height, showing bare, precipitous cliffs on either side of the river,
and exhibiting some of the most beautiful and imposing natural scenery
to be found in the country. The town was originally built on two
streets stretching along a narrow shelf between the base of the bluff
and the rivers, meeting at the point at nearly a right angle, and named
respectively Potomac and Shenandoah streets. To accommodate its
increasing population the town has struggled up the steep bluff, and
in detached villages and scattered residences, occupies the level ground
above—about 400 feet above the streams.

It has altogether a population of 5000; is distant from Richmond 173
miles; from Washington City, 57 miles by turnpike road; and from
Baltimore, 80 miles by rail. Here the Baltimore and Ohio Railroad
crosses the Potomac by a magnificent covered bridge, 900 feet long,
and passes along Potomac Street westward, its track lying 40 feet
above the river. The Winchester and Harper's Ferry Railroad, lying
along Shenandoah Street, connects with the Baltimore and Ohio at
the bridge. Potomac Street is entirely occupied by the workshops and
offices of the National Armory, and its entrance is inclosed by a handsome gate and iron railing. Nearly at the angle of junction are the
old arsenal buildings, where usually from 100, to 200,000 stand of arms

are stored. The other buildings on the point, and nearer the bridge, are railroad offices, hotels, eating-houses, stores, shops, etc. Shenandoah Street contains stores and dwelling-houses for half a mile or more, when we come to Hall's rifle-works, situated on a small island in the Shenandoah River. . . .

THE REPORTERS

No. 13

The National Intelligencer, Washington, D.C., Tues., Oct. 18, 1859

REPORTED INSURRECTION AND CAPTURE OF THE ARSENAL AT HARPER'S FERRY

BALTIMORE, OCT. 17—The following despatch has just been received from Frederick, but, as it seems very improbable, it should be received with great caution until confirmed:

FREDERICK, OCT. 17, A.M.—There is an insurrection at Harper's Ferry. A band of armed Abolitionists have full possession of the United States Arsenal. The express train was fired into twice, and one of the railroad hands—a negro—killed while trying to get the train through the town. The insurgents arrested two men who came into town with a load of wheat, took the wagon, loaded it with rifles, and sent them into Maryland. The band is composed of a gang of about two hundred and fifty whites, followed by a band of negroes, who are now fighting.

Second Despatch

BALTIMORE, OCT. 17, 10 A.M.—A despatch received at the railroad office says that the affair is greatly exaggerated, and has its foundation in a difficulty at the armory; also, that the negroes have nothing to do with it.

Third Despatch

BALTIMORE, 12:30.—It is apprehended that the affair at Harper's Ferry is more serious than people here are willing to believe. The telegraph wires are cut from Harper's Ferry; consequently we have no communication beyond Monocacy. The reported stampede of negroes is from Maryland. The train due here early this morning has not yet arrived. There are many wild rumors here, but nothing authentic yet.

Fourth Despatch

BALTIMORE, 2 P.M.—The mail agent on the westward-bound train has returned to Monocacy and reports that the train was unable to get through. He states that the town of Harper's Ferry is in possession of the negroes, who arrest every one they can catch and imprison them.

21

The train due here at three this afternoon could not get through the town, and the agent came down on an empty engine.

Another account by train says that the bridge across the Potomac was filled with insurgents, all armed, and that every light in the town last night was extinguished. The hotels were all closed, and all the streets were in possession of the mob, and every road and lane leading into the town were barricaded and guarded. Men were seen in every quarter with muskets and bayonets, who arrested every citizen and pressed them into their service, including many negroes. This being done, the United States Arsenal and Government Pay Office, in which was said to be a large amount of money, together with all the public works, were seized by the mob. Some persons were of the opinion that the object of the insurgents is to plunder and rob the Government of the funds deposited there on Saturday. During the night a demand was made on the Wager Hotel for provisions, and the demand enforced by a body of armed men. The citizens are in a terrible state of alarm, the insurgents having threatened to burn the town.

The following despatch has just been received from Monocacy— the nearest telegraph station to Harper's Ferry:

The Western train has just arrived, and the officers confirm the statement first received. They say that the bridge-keeper last night discovered that the light had been extinguished, and on going to ascertain the cause was pursued and fired upon by a gang of whites and blacks. The colored assistant baggage-master was shot and mortally wounded, and Conductor Phelps was threatened that the train should not proceed. Being uncertain as to the condition of the bridge, he thought it prudent to wait until daylight, which detained the train six hours. The insurgents numbered two hundred whites and blacks, and had full possession of the armory. They are commanded, or rather led, by a man named Anderson, who lately arrived at Harper's Ferry. The rioters seized a wagon which was filled with wheat, loaded it with a quantity of muskets, and sent it up into Virginia. The military of Frederick have been ordered out.

The above is the substance of what has been received, but how far it is reliable is a matter of doubt. It is generally believed here to be an exaggeration.

Later Despatches

BALTIMORE, 8 P.M.—There is great excitement here. Our military are moving, and several companies are in readiness. It is stated that the President has ordered out the troops, and a special train is now getting ready to take them from this city; that he has also accepted the company at Frederick, and has ordered some of the artillery companies from Old Point. It is now considered there is something serious ahead.

Still Later. The mail train for the West got as far as Sandy Hook. The baggage-master and another party started on foot for the bridge, which they crossed and were taken and imprisoned. They went before the captain of the insurgents, who refused to let anything pass. All of the eastward-bound trains are lying west of Harper's Ferry.

The insurgents have been taking persons from this side of the river, tying them, and carrying them off for slaves. The mail train bound West has returned to Monocacy. There are now from five to seven hundred whites and blacks engaged.

Another account from Frederick says a letter has been received from a merchant at Harper's Ferry, sent by some boys who had to cross the mountain and swim the river. The writer says all the principal citizens have been imprisoned and many of them killed. The agent at the depot was shot twice and the watchman at the depot shot dead.

BALTIMORE, 4:30 P.M.—The train is filling with military, including the Law Grays, City Guards, and Shields Guards; and it is believed that other companies left here in the 4 o'clock train for Harper's Ferry. Reporters for the press accompany them.

BALTIMORE, 10 P.M.—The *American*'s special reporter at eight o'clock telegraphs from Plane Number 4, thirty-one miles this side of Harper's Ferry, that the train consists of seventeen cars, containing four hundred troops from Baltimore, under Major Reynolds, a corps of laborers, under the road master, to repair the track, and several telegraphers to repair the wires. The latter are prepared with instruments and batteries to open a way station near the bridge if necessary.

Three companies from Frederick are in an advance train, and Col. Harris, with his command of marines, follows in a special train. The whole combined force is under command of Col. Lee, of the army, who is invested with full powers to order the Maryland troops to cross into Virginia if necessary.

BALTIMORE, 11 P.M.—The following despatch is from the special Reporter of the *American:*

MONOCACY BRIDGE, 9 P.M.—Luther Simpson, the baggage-master of the Express mail train, gives the following particulars: "I walked up the bridge, but was stopped. I was afterwards permitted to go up and see the captain of the insurgents. I was taken to the armory and saw the captain, who is named 'Bill Smith,' and was kept a prisoner for more than an hour. I saw from five to six hundred negroes, all having arms, and two or three hundred white men with them. All the houses were closed, but I went to a tavern kept by one Chambers. About thirty inhabitants were collected with arms. They said most of the inhabitants had left, but that they had declined to go. It was reported there that five or six persons had been shot." Mr. Simpson was escorted back over the bridge by six negroes.

The train from Frederick is lying at the Point of Rocks, and a train with the Directors of the Pennsylvania Railroad on board is on the other side of Harper's Ferry. It was believed that the insurrectionists intended to leave as soon as it became dark. Orders have been received here that the train is to stop at Sandy Hook until Col. Lee, who is following in the special train, arrives. There are any number of rumors circulating in regard to the object, numbers, and probable action of the insurgents. . . .

BALTIMORE, OCT. 18—1 O'CLOCK A.M.—The special train with Col. Lee's command passed Monocacy at 11:30. It is supposed the delay is now caused by a difficulty in adjusting the break in the telegraph line this side of Harper's Ferry. . . .

RICHMOND, OCT. 17, P.M.—It is reported here . . . that Gov. Wise has ordered volunteer troops to Harper's Ferry. . . .

Still later—The Richmond Greys and Company F have left their armories with full ranks, expecting to take a special train to-night for Harper's Ferry.

No. 14

The National Intelligencer, Thurs., Oct. 20, 1859

. . . The arrival [at Baltimore] of the train that brought the intelligence to Frederick was . . . looked for with great interest, and at half-past 12 o'clock, when it reached the depot, the following corroboration of the rumors by telegraph was obtained from the officers of the train . . . : They state that their train (the regular passenger train from the West) reached a point near the bridge at Harper's Ferry at 20 minutes to one o'clock this morning, when it was stopped.

Conductor Phelps received the following statement from a Mr. Phillips, one of the watchmen at the bridge: "I started to take my post on the bridge, as watchman, about 12 o'clock; I had not heard from the man (named Williamson) who was watching the bridge up to that time.

We usually hear from him every half-hour. When I arrived on the other side of the bridge I was suddenly challenged, and commanded to stand or die. Four or five white men raised their rifles and pointed them at me. One of them tried to get my lantern. I turned and ran, and they fired upon me. I escaped without injury."

The other watchman shortly made his appearance and stated to Conductor Phelps that he had been seized about 9½ o'clock and locked up in the guard house at the other end of the bridge, and that he had just made his escape.

Conductor Phelps and the baggage-master, Cromwell, then entered the bridge and had hardly got half-way through when they were commanded to stand, and three white men levelled rifles at them. They then retreated back, and were fired upon, but were not injured.

A colored man named Shephard Hayward, who is employed by the Railroad Company to attend to the baggage at Harper's Ferry, took off his shoes and made the attempt to get through the bridge to see what was going on at the armories, but he was discovered about the time that Phelps and Cromwell were fired upon and they also fired upon the negro. One of the balls took effect in his back, going through his body and coming out of the nipple of his left breast.

At first Conductor Phelps was at a loss how to act, and concluded to send over a person to the vicinity of the Ferry to ascertain the cause of the proceedings, when the leader of the party—a man of rather prepossessing appearance and supposed to be nearly sixty years of age—appeared, and stated that he preferred holding communication with the conductor. Mr. Phelps went over alone, and was told by the same man that he and his party had determined not to allow another train to pass over the road, but that they would give him five to ten minutes to get his train through.

In the meantime other persons from the train ventured across the bridge above the Ferry, and soon coming into contact with the rioters (who were reputed as about two hundred in number, half of whom seemed to be black), one of the party, a passenger, was captured.

The train was delayed by the proceedings until half-past six o'clock, when steam was raised and they reached the Camden station at noon today. Upon the train leaving, Mr. Phelps was particularly requested by the leader of the gang to state to the superintendent of the road that under no circumstances would another train be permitted to pass Harper's Ferry. During the night a large two-horse wagon, laden with wheat, came in from one of the neighboring counties of the State. The rioters immediately seized the driver, took possession of the wheat, and loading the vehicle with weapons from the armory sent it back up the country.

The engineer states that he took particular notice of the crowd, which he thinks numbered at least three hundred persons; that amongst them were several strapping negroes, who occasionally shouted out that they longed for liberty, as they had been in bondage long enough.

The ringleader, who is said to be named Anderson, made his appearance at Harper's Ferry five or six days ago, and since that time has been driving around the place in an elegant barouche drawn by two horses.

These officers report that the United States Armory and the neighboring country have been taken possession of by the rioters, all of whom are well armed with short rifles and other United States arms. When the workmen of the armory repaired there for the purpose of resuming work they were seized by the parties, forcibly dragged within the gates, and imprisoned.

A number of the party proceeded to the proprietors of the hotel near the armory and . . . ordered breakfast for fifty . . . persons, adding that they were determined to keep possession of the place. . . .

From a gentleman well known in this city, who came passenger in the western train, reaching Baltimore about noon on Monday, we have the following account: The express train . . . reached Harper's Ferry about one o'clock this morning (17th). On arriving, the clerk of the Wager House informed Capt. Phelps, conductor . . . , that serious trouble was existing in the town. . . . The captain of the outlaw band . . . was a middle-aged man with gray hair, beard, and moustache. His name was signed to a paper or note as Andreas, or something similar thereto. He assumed to be the chief . . . and was heard to say, in addressing the conductor, that "if you knew me and understood my motives as well as I and others understand them, you would not blame me so much." This person also announced, in a bold, determined manner, that if he was interfered with or resisted, his party would instantly set fire to the town and destroy it with everything therein. He likewise threatened to burn down the railroad bridge and cut off all communication. The citizens were in a terrible state of consternation, most of them being shut up in their houses, and not a light to be seen in the streets. . . . The belligerents seemed to evince no actual antipathy against the railroad. What Government employees they could find were captured by them and pressed into their service, being forced. . . . In another speech the marauder chief was heard to exclaim: "If you knew

my heart and history you would not blame me." . . . . When our informant left, the whole town . . . [was] in the hands of the insurgents,
who seemed to be gradually receiving reinforcements . . . of negroes
and white men, from the surrounding country. One man was killed
instantly; another was found . . . shot through the body. . . . A good
deal of firing was heard. . . . No passenger belonging to the railroad
was injured, nor did there appear to be any disposition . . . to molest
them beyond detaining the cars. There were but few ladies on
board. . . .

MONOCACY, OCT. 17—The following are all the particulars that
can be gathered at this point . . . : The mail train bound west got as
far as Sandy Hook when Walter Simpson, the baggage master, and
Mr. Trasher started on foot to the bridge . . . but were taken and
put in prison. They went before the captain of the insurrectionists, and
he refused to let anything pass. All the eastward-bound trains are lying
west of the Ferry. The insurrectionists have been taking persons from
this side of the river, tying them up, and taking off all their slaves.
The mail train bound west has returned to this station. There is said
to be from 500 to 700 whites and blacks in the outbreak.

FREDERICK, OCT. 17— . . . Your correspondent has just seen a
letter from a merchant of Harper's Ferry, which was sent by two boys
over the mountain, and who had to swim the river. . . . The letter
states that most all the leading people of Harper's Ferry are in jail,
and that several have been killed. The robbers have taken all the works
in their possession, and have taken the money from the vaults. The
powder house is in their possession, and they will not permit any
one to leave the town. F. Beckham, the railroad agent, was shot twice
by the gang. . . .

WASHINGTON, OCT. 17—On the receipt of intelligence from
Harper's Ferry this morning, orders were issued for three companies of
artillery at Old Point and the Corps of Marines at the Washington
barracks to proceed thither without delay. The Marines, about 93 in
number, with two twelve-pound howitzers and a full supply of ammunition, left . . . this afternoon . . . under orders to force the bridge
tonight at all hazards. Col. Faulkner accompanied them.

It is reported on good authority that some weeks ago Secretary Floyd
received an anonymous epistle stating that about the 15th of October
the abolitionists and negroes, with other disaffected persons, would make
an attempt to seize the arsenal and hold the place. This statement . . .
appeared so . . . ridiculous as to be regarded as not worthy of any attention. . . .

At the Relay House the Baltimore troops met the detachment of
. . . marines from Washington, under Lieut. Israel Green, having with
them two pieces of artillery, under the command of Col. Harris. The
cars carrying the marines were switched off and connected with the
Baltimore military train, and about five o'clock the whole train of
fifteen cars started for Harper's Ferry. At 6½ o'clock in the evening a
special express train reached the Relay House from Washington bearing
Col. R. E. Lee, of . . . the United States Army, and his aid, Lieut.
J. E. B. Stewart, the former under instructions from the Secretary of
War to assume command of the United States troops ordered to Harper's Ferry. He immediately telegraphed to the stations ahead of his
train bearing the troops, ordering a halt, and followed in a special
train. . . .

MONOCACY, OCT. 17, half-past 11.—The special train with Col.
Lee has just passed here on its way to the Ferry. The train with the
Baltimore military is probably at Sandy Hook now, which is one mile
on this side of Harper's Ferry. The Frederick military, finding they
were not sufficiently strong to make an attack . . . , stopped at the Point
of Rocks, ten miles this side of the seat of war. They have probably
gone on with the Baltimore forces. . . .

HARPER'S FERRY, OCT. 18, 1 A.M.—Train arrived and halted below town, where runners communicated the state of affairs. The Jefferson County regiment had entered the town from the Virginia side, and
the Frederick troops crossed the bridge. There had been a good deal
of firing and some nine persons were killed. Mr. Beckham, agent of the
railroad company, was shot through, and his murderer fell almost at
the same instant. . . . The troops have landed and are in the town. The
insurgents are willing to surrender, but on terms of safe conduct out
of difficulty; otherwise they threaten to sacrifice the lives of Lewis
Washington and Col. Daingerfield, whom they now hold as prisoners.
Capt. Aaron Stevens, of Norwich, Connecticut, is now dying of his
wounds, and makes the following statement: the plan has been con-
cocting for a year or more; the parties rendezvoused at a farm a few
miles from here, rented for the purpose of Capt. Brown, of Kansas
notoriety, under the name of Smith.

Among the insurgents are Kagg [sic], of Ohio; Todd [sic], of Maine;
Wm. Seaman [sic] and Brown, of Ohio. . . .

HARPER'S FERRY, OCT. 18, 2 A.M.—There has been serious work
at the bridge, and a number of lives lost on both sides. The Virginia
volunteers opened with their cannon upon the insurgents on the bridge,
and the first gun was just fired when a musket ball pierced the heart

of the marine who fired it. Nine or ten lives were lost in taking the bridge, but after that the taking of the town was quick work.

The insurgents, at least all of them who are alive, are barricaded in the engine-house within the Armory enclosure. They have a number of citizens with them whom they refuse to release.

Several companies of Virginia troops are on the ground, and now guard the village. The marines are posted at the Armory. Several of the citizens have been killed, and they have killed several of the insurgents.

HARPER'S FERRY, 2½ A.M.—The town has been taken possession of by the military from Charlestown, Shepherdstown, Virginia, and Frederick, Maryland.

The rioters are entrenched in the Armory, and hold Mr. Washington and Mr. Daingerfield as prisoners.

The insurrectionists were commanded by Capt. Brown, of Kansas notoriety, who gave his name as Anderson to conductor Phelps. They numbered originally seventeen white men and five negroes, but were reinforced during the day.

Several of the military have been shot, including two of the Martinsburg companies, who were shot dead whilst charging on the Armory.

A portion of the insurgents have left under the command of Capt. Bill Cook, with a large party of slaves, all supposed to be moving towards Pennsylvania.

Allen Evans, one of the insurgents, a white man, is lying here dying, with a ball through his breast. He is from Connecticut, but has been in Kansas. He says the whole scheme was got up by Capt. Brown, who represented that the negroes would rise by thousands, and Maryland and Virginia would be made free states.

Col. Shriver, of Frederick, has just had an interview with Capt. Brown in the Armory. He asked to be allowed to march out with his men, and avowed his intention to defend himself to the last. They are very strongly posted in the engine-house, and cannon cannot be used against them for fear of injuring the prisoners, whom they still hold.

Some sixteen persons are known to be killed. Fontaine Beckham, the railroad agent, was shot dead from the Armory windows. Three rioters are lying dead under the bridge, shot by the Shepherdstown troops in the charge on the bridge.

Captain Cook, who is second in command of the rioters, is said to be posted in the school-house, four miles distant, with a large body of runaway slaves.

The Armory was taken possession of by the rioters about nine o'clock on Sunday night last, and was so quietly done that the citizens knew nothing of it until the train was stopped.

Colonel Lee has arrived, and thinks that there are abundant troops here to capture the rioters.

It seems perfectly certain that the original number consisted of not more than twenty white men and five free negroes.

Captain Brown had been about here and rented a farm four miles off, which was the rendezvous of the rioters. Captain Cook had also lived in the vicinity, and at one time taught school here. All the other white men are unknown, but are supposed to be men who have been connected with Captain Brown in Kansas.

It is reported, but not certain, that the rioters have carried off a considerable amount of Government funds. No attempt was made to pillage the town or to insult females.

Captain Brown, who is barricaded in the Armory with his men, claims easy terms on account of his moderation.

HARPER'S FERRY, OCT. 18, 3:10 A.M.—The battle was mainly fought by the railroad tonnage men from Martinsburg, who came down in great force, led by Capt. Alburtis. They attacked the rioters single-handed, and fought most valiantly. One of the freight conductors, named Evan Dorsey, was killed in the fight, and two other conductors, named Bowman and Holbert, were seriously wounded.

No damage has been done to the railroad or to the bridge, and little or none to the property in the town. The purpose of the insurrectionists seems to have been to hold the town until several thousand slaves could be collected, and then make a stampede through Maryland and cross the Pennsylvania line. The parties that have started will be immediately pursued.

The general intention appears to be to hang all the prisoners as soon as those in the Armory are captured in the morning. We will conse-quently have an exciting time here to-morrow. . . .

HARPER'S FERRY, 6 A.M.—Preparations are making for an attack on the Arsenal, where the insurgents are in full force. The soldiers have surrounded the entire grounds, and for the last hour every thing has been quiet.

The rioters still have the following persons prisoners: Armistead Ball, chief draughtsman of the Armory, Benjamin J. Mills, master armorer, John P. Daingerfield, paymaster's clerk, Lewis Washington, farmer and a prominent citizen, John Allstadt, farmer, and son, the latter sixteen years old. The three last named were seized on farms several miles from this place.

George W. Turner, a graduate of West Point, and one of the most distinguished citizens in this vicinity, was shot yesterday while coming into town, and died during the night.

Three rioters are lying dead in the streets; three are lying dead in the river, and several more are said to be lying within the Armory enclosure.

The killed among the citizens, as far as ascertained, are Fountain Beckham, Mr. Hayward, a negro porter at the railroad station, Joseph Burnley, of Harper's Ferry, Evan Dorsey, and George Richardson, of Martinsburg.

Another rioter (negro), named Lewis Leary, has just died. He confessed to the particulars of the plot, which he says was concocted by Brown at a fair held in Ohio some two months ago.

The rioters have just sent out a flag of truce; but if not protected by the soldiers the bearers will be captured and hung. . . .

HARPER'S FERRY, 8 A.M.—The arsenal has been stormed and taken, after a desperate resistance. Col. Shutt approached with a flag of truce and demanded an immediate and unconditional surrender. After some expostulation the insurgents refused the demand.

The marines advanced to the charge, and endeavored to break down the door with sledge-hammers, but it resisted all efforts. A large ladder was then used as a battering ram, and the door gave way. The rioters fired briskly through the door and shot three marines. The marines returned their fire through the partly broken door, and then forced through the break at the point of the bayonet. After a few moments' conflict inside the resistance was at an end. The insurgents were brought out one after another amidst the most intense excitement, and many of the armed militia endeavored to shoot them as they passed but the marines covered them with their persons.

Capt. "Osawatomie" Brown and his son were both shot. The latter is dead and the former is dying. He lies in the arsenal enclosure, talking freely. He acknowledged that he is the old *Osawatomie* Brown whose deeds in Kansas have stamped his memory with infamy. . . .

Colonel Lee has received a despatch from the Secretary of War, stating that District Attorney Robert Ould, of Washington, will proceed to Harper's Ferry to take charge of legal proceedings against the prisoners and bring them to trial. (Mr. Ould left Washington for Harper's Ferry this evening. . . .)

. . . During [Monday] afternoon a sharp little affair took place on the Shenandoah side of the town. The insurrectionists had also seized Hall's rifle works, and a party of their assailants found their way in through the mill-race and dislodged them. In this rencontre it was said that three of the insurrectionists were killed, but we found but one dead body, that of a negro, on that side of the city. Night had by this time come on, and active operations ceased. . . .

Besides Captain Brown the prisoners taken are his son, who is seriously wounded in the abdomen . . . ; Edwin Coppoc, who belongs to Iowa, and a negro named Shields Green, who came from Pittsburg [*sic*] to John Brown. The stories of all these men are precisely the same; they agree as to the object they proposed to accomplish and the number of parties in the movement. Young Brown, in answer to a question, said that there were parties in the North connected with the movement—thus differing with his father on this point. Coppoc, the other white prisoner, is quite young, and seems less shrewd than the others. He said he did not wish to join the expedition, and when asked, gave a reply which showed the influence Brown had over him. He said: "Ah! you gentlemen don't know Captain Brown; when he calls for us we never think of refusing to come." . . . .

No. 15
The Baltimore Weekly Sun, Sat., Oct. 22, 1859

. . . . A gentleman who returned from the scene in the 6:30 train, describes the storming of the bridge. A smart firing occurred, and the rioters were driven from the bridge. One man was killed here and another arrested.

A man ran out of the building and tried to escape by swimming the river. A dozen shots were fired after him, and he partially fell, but rose again, threw his gun away and drew his pistols. Both snapped, and he drew a bowie knife, cut his heavy accoutrements off, and plunged into the river. One of the soldiers was about ten feet behind, the man turned round, threw up his hands, and said "don't shoot." The soldier fired, and the man fell into the water with his face blown away. His coat skirts were cut from his person, and in the pockets was found a Captain's commission to Captain E. H. Leeman, from the Provisional Government. The commission was dated October 15, 1850, and signed by A. W. [*sic*] Brown, Commander in Chief of the Army of the Provincial Government of the United States.

A party of five of the insurgents armed with Minnie rifles, and posted in [Hall's] rifle armory, were expelled by the Guards and others. They all ran for the river, and one who was unable to swim, was drowned.

The other four swam out to the rocks in the middle of the Shenandoah and fired upon the citizens and troops upon both banks. This drew upon them the muskets of between 200 and 300 men, and not less than 400 shots were fired at them from Harper's Ferry, about 200 yards distant. One was finally shot dead.

The second, a negro, attempted to jump over the dam, but fell shot, and was not seen afterwards. The third was badly wounded, and the remaining one was taken unharmed.

The white insurgent, wounded and captured, died a few moments after in the arms of our informant. He was shot through the breast, arm and stomach. He declared there were only nineteen whites engaged in the insurrection.

For nearly an hour a running and random firing was kept up by the troops and the rioters. Several were shot down, and many managed to limp away wounded. During the firing the women and children ran shrieking in every direction, but when they learned that the soldiers were their protectors they took courage, and did good service in the way of preparing refreshments and attending the wounded.

Our informant, who was on the hill when the firing was going on, says all the terrible scenes of a battle passed in reality beneath his eyes. Soldiers could be seen pursuing singly and in couples, and the crack of the musket and rifle was generally followed by one or more of the insurgents biting the dust. The dead lay in the streets where they fell. The wounded were cared for.

Aaron D. Stevens, a captain of the rioters, shot at the bridge, was taken into the Carroll Hotel, where his dreadful wounds were dressed by Dr. McGarrity. Heavy bullets passed through his breast, head and one arm. He said to those around him that as he expected to die before morning, he wanted somebody to telegraph to his father, at Norwich, Conn., to say to him that his son died at Harper's Ferry, in an attempt at high treason against the State of Virginia. He was alive at four o'clock yesterday morning.

He is represented as a remarkably fine looking man, six feet six inches high, and possessed of great nerve. While lying in bed a number of the outraged citizens crowded into the room and attempted to dispatch him, pointing cocked muskets at his head, but Stevens, as he lay helpless, folded his arms, and looked them calmly in the eye, without uttering a word.

Our special reporter sent to the scene of action . . . had a conversation with the dying man Anderson. He said that the elder Brown had been their leader, and he had always looked up to him as a great man. A

letter was found in his pocket from his brother, J. J. Anderson, of
Chilicothe, stating that the contents of his last letter upon the question
of slavery were "devoured with eagerness." Upon the body of Hazlett
was found a lock of his wife's hair and a piece of her dress.

Upon the person of the leader, the notorious "Osawatomie Brown,"
of Kansas, was found by one of the volunteer surgeons . . . the sum of
$305 in gold, which was handed by him over to Major Russell, of the
marine corps. In a conversation with the writer as he lay weltering in
his blood, he stated that he had figured in Kansas, and was known as
"Osawatomie Brown" or "Old Brown." He had had a son killed in
Kansas (as well as two here). He hated slavery, and he desired to avenge
his son's death. His confederates desired to surrender when they were
summoned by Colonel Lee; but he refused because he did not believe
that the general government would slaughter his companions for the
sake of killing him. He had always treated his prisoners with courtesy.
He hoped that his interrogators would not put words in his mouth, but
permit him to make his own declarations. He hoped Major Russell
would permit him to die in peace, and would treat him humanely. . . .
It has been stated subsequently that his wounds are not mortal, unfortunately perhaps for himself.

The prisoner Edwin Coppoc, upon being asked what he expected
would be his fate, said that he only asked his country to give him a fair
trial and he would abide the consequences. He manifested no concern
or apprehension with respect to his punishment. The prisoner Brown,
son of the leader, was too debilitated from his wounds to realize his
situation.

The wounded have been removed to the hospital of the arsenal, including the rioter A. D. Stevens. Such was the excitement on Monday
night that Stevens would have been shot in his bed, had it not been for
the restraint exercised by others upon those who permitted their passions
to become ungovernable. . . . He is reported to be fatally wounded, but
it is thought by some that his four wounds are not fatal. During the
deep suspense pending the attack of the marines upon the insurgents in
the engine-house a party of Baltimore "Roughs," recognized as members
of the clubs, numbering twenty or more, were seen right up at the gate
of the public buildings, each with a musket or rifle in hand, "eager for
the fray." Their anxiety to participate in the engagement was so manifest
that Colonel Shutt called out to them not to fire, because there were
citizens held in the building whose lives they might endanger. Finally
they were ordered away from their close proximity to the scene of the
contest. When the crisis of the engagement arrived even the outside

military and citizens could hardly restrain themselves from rushing forward, and discharging their arms. Loud calls of order arrested their impulses. When the prisoners came out there were vociferous cries of "hang them" constantly repeated. The companies and citizens were afterwards admitted to the government grounds, and all had an opportunity to view the corpses of the deluded fanatics who had so foolishly forfeited their lives. . . .

About the middle of the stream of the broad Potomac lies the body of one of the insurgents named Wm. H. Leeman, who was shot on Monday, while attempting to make his escape from the town. His black hair may just be seen floating upon the surface of the water and waving with every ripple. The visitors, upon discovering the body today, saluted it with a shower of balls, but the action was one of very questionable taste and propriety. . . . The following [is] a true copy of the document found in his pocket:/ HEAD-QUARTERS WAR DEPARTMENT,/ Near Harper's Ferry, Md./ Whereas, W. H. Leeman has been nominated a captain in the army established under the *Provisional Constitution;* now, therefore, in pursuance of the authority vested in me by said constitution, we do hereby appoint and commission the said Wm. H. Leeman captain./ Given at the office of the Secretary of War, this day, 15th of October, 1859./ JOHN BROWN,/ Commander in Chief./ H. [KAGI], Secretary War.

There was taken from the person of Stevens a printed pamphlet of twenty-five pages, containing the constitution, &c. of Mr. Brown's provisional government. The work is in the possession of Col. Lee, and would be treasonable were it not too ridiculous.

An anonymous letter, not thought worthy of attention, had been received by Gov. Floyd, the Secretary of War, while at Old Point, lately. It stated that insurrections would occur simultaneously at Wheeling, Harper's Ferry, and Washington, for the purpose of freeing slaves. It is understood that many slaves have lately escaped from Virginia and Maryland under the agency of the emissaries. . . .

. . . It appears that for months Capt. Brown resided about eight miles from Harper's Ferry, on the Maryland side of the Potomac, and was generally esteemed as an intelligent man. His visits to Harper's Ferry were frequent, and he was in the habit of calling at the office of the United States Armory where he spent many hours in social conversation, nor was once suspected of entertaining any design against the people or property of the neighborhood.

Possessed of a cunning necessary for the prosecution of such a scheme as he would have carried out, had it been possible, he was careful to let but few of the arms which he received be landed at Harper's Ferry, lest suspicion might be excited against him. He ordered them to be dropped at Hagerstown and Sandy Hook, whence they were removed to his house in wagons. The people of the neighborhood in which Capt. Brown resided visited his house, and when the large boxes containing the arms were seen, he remarked to them that they were tools for mining, consisting of pickaxes, shovels and spades. Though they accumulated for a period of eight months he was not suspected, and to complete the delusion of his neighbors he frequently took home with him parcels of earth which he pretended to analyze, in search of minerals. Often his neighbors would visit him when he was making his chemical experiments, and so well did he act his part that he was looked upon as one of profound learning, and calculated to be a most useful man to the neighborhood. There was but little communication between him and Captain Cook, so far as the people knew, though it became plain that they held frequent interviews. . . .

On Tuesday the Independent Grays . . . made a scout on the Maryland side, and marched directly for the school house where it was thought Capt. Cook had fortified himself. The march was along the base of the mountain, and the most intense anxiety was manifested for the success of the expedition. When they reached the school house, two miles distant from Harper's Ferry, they found that it was the storehouse for the arms. They recovered 200 Sharps rifles, several boxes of revolvers, and about 1000 pikes. All of them are formidable weapons. The revolvers are six-shooters with ten-inch barrels, and fire with the fulminated powder instead of percussion caps. The pikes are two-edged, blade about eight inches long, and protected where it enters the staff by a strong guard and heavy iron ferule. The staff is of hickory and about six feet long. . . .

There was no person near the school house at the time, and after a guard was placed over it, the remainder of the company passed on for the house of Capt. Brown, four miles further on the road. Shortly before they reached it they were met by two females, who . . . informed Lieut. Simpson that [Cook] had only a few minutes before gone off at a gallop. . . . They passed to the house but found it had just been deserted. There was a fire on the hearth, and on a table nearby a piece of pork which someone had begun to slice. . . . Two wagons were in the yard, and the horses were already harnessed. Cook, it was thought, had been engaged in hauling arms from the house . . . to the school house. Here, too, were found a large parcel of papers. . . .

After the train left on Tuesday afternoon, a detachment of marines, with a number of volunteers, were sent to the farm house . . . to search it. They returned about six o'clock . . . with a wagon loaded with several hundred pikes or spears, two boxes of Sharps rifles, tents, blankets, boots, and shoes, clothing, &c. . . .

The most valuable article brought in by the marines, however, was a carpet bag filled with documents and letters connected with the expedition. They were taken possession of by Governor Wise and many of them read in public at night. Among the most important are:

A letter from Gerrit Smith, the Abolition Presidential candidate, containing some financial statements, and enclosing a draft for $200, endorsed by the cashier of a New York bank;

A letter from Frederick Douglass, enclosing a $10 note contributed by a lady for the good of the cause;

Several letters from Henry Smith and John Smith, prominent northern abolitionists;

A number of letters from different parts of Connecticut;

Printed pamphlets of the constitution of the provisional government to be established by Capt. Brown. It was said these letters would implicate a number of prominent abolitionists at the North and West, as being cognizant of and favoring the project.

There were letters of introduction to Captain Brown presented to him by Aaron Stevens, one of the insurgents, in which he was commended to him as worth a dozen ordinary men in a fight. The writers of these letters stated that they had engaged him to join the expedition, which he had agreed to do on condition that they would give his wife, who lives in Missouri, $100 to support his family during the winter, pay some small debts for him and pay his traveling expenses to Harper's Ferry. . . .

LETTER FROM GERRIT SMITH TO CAPT. JOHN BROWN

"*Peterboro,* June 4, '59. Capt. John Brown—My dear friend:—I wrote you a week ago. . . . I have done what I could thus far for Kansas, and what I could to keep you at your Kansas work. . . . I send you herewith my draft for $200. Let me hear from you. . . . You live in our hearts, and our prayer to God is that you may . . . continue in your Kansas work. . . ./ GERRIT SMITH."

LETTER FROM CHARLES BLAIR

"Collinsville, Conn., June 10, 1859. Friend Brown: Your favor of the 7th instant was duly received, with the draft on New York for $300. I have made arrangements to have the goods finished up as soon as possible. The only man I could think of in this vicinity who is in a situation to do it I have agreed with. But he would not agree to get them all out in less time than eight weeks. . . . I find that some of the handles have come up missing, and I shall not be able to make out more than about 950. . . . I could have furnished them when I had them under way for much less than I can now. Wishing you peace and prosperity, I remain yours, truly, CHARLES BLAIR."

There was also found the following receipt: "Received, Collinsville, June 4th, 1850 [sic], of John Brown, on contract of 1859, $150./ CHARLES BLAIR."

LETTER FROM FRED DOUGLASS

"My dear Captain Brown—I am very busy at home. Will you please come up with my son Fred, and take a mouthful with me? In haste . . . , FRED DOUGLASS. . . ."

Besides the above were several letter sheets of manuscript . . . and several papers which were taken by Gov. Wise. . . . A manual of guerilla warfare, with instructions to use the lance, so many of which were found, was carefully preserved. . . .

The following is a copy of an anonymous letter sent to the Hon. Secretary of War from Cincinnati some two months since . . . : "Sir, I have lately received information of a movement of so great importance that I feel it to be my duty to impart it to you without delay. I have discovered the existence of a great secret organization, having for its object the liberation of the slaves of the South by a general insurrection. The leader of the movement is "Old John Brown," late of Kansas. He has been in Canada during the winter, drilling the negroes there, and they are only waiting his word to start for the South to assist the slaves. They have one of their leading men (a white man) in an armory in Maryland; where it is situated, I am not enabled to learn.

"As soon as everything is ready, those of their number who are in the Northern States and Canada are to come in small companies to their rendezvous, which is in the mountains of Virginia. They will pass down through Pennsylvania and Maryland, and enter Virginia at Harper's Ferry. Brown left the North about three or four weeks ago, and will arm the negroes and strike a blow in a few weeks, so that whatever is done must be done at once. They have a large quantity of arms at their rendezvous; and are probably distributing them already. I am not fully

in their confidence. This is all the information I can give you. I dare
not sign my name to this, but trust that you will not disregard this
warning on this account."

HARPER'S FERRY, OCT. 19, 9 P.M.—The insurgent prisoners have
all been taken to Charlestown jail, under guard of the Marines. Governor
Wise accompanied the party. The Marines have since returned. . . . The
sending of the prisoners to Charlestown is believed to be a concession to
the views of Gov. Wise, who claims to try them by the laws of Virginia. . . .

About 8 o'clock there was a general alarm. A man crossed the bridge
on horseback, stating that murder was being committed at Sandy Hook;
that the abolitionists had possession of the place. . . . The report is that
Cook's party is murdering slaveholders. . . . It is undoubtedly a false
alarm. . . .

Gov. Wise has offered $1,000 for the arrest of Capt. Cook, who is
supposed to be in the mountains with a number of negroes. . . . The
rumor that a large amount of government money had been stolen . . .
is untrue. It is all safe. Dr. Murphy, the paymaster, has in his possession
between $200 and $300 of the money of old John Brown, of Kansas
notoriety, who is among the wounded.

HARPER'S FERRY, Oct. 20— . . . Governor Wise arrived here today
in the train from Charlestown. . . .

The Governor expressed his mortification at the disgrace which had
been brought upon the State. He would rather have lost both legs and
both arms from his shoulders and hips than such a disgrace should have
been cast upon it, that fourteen white men and five negroes should have
captured the government works and all Harper's Ferry, and have been
able to retain them for one hour. Col. Lee, with twelve marines, settled
the matter in ten minutes. That nineteen men should capture one hundred prisoners was something like the policeman who captured ten
men, and said, "Faith, I surrounded them." They should read Shake-
speare and study Falstaff's oaths. A prisoner remarked that there were
ten of them (*laughter*) prisoners, and nine insurgents, but that the
latter were each armed with three Sharps rifles and two Colt's revolvers.
"We were . . . huddled in like a flock of sheep." "Yes," said the
Governor, "you were in a corner, and you were very much like sheep.
They certainly cornered all Harper's Ferry. . . ."

Andrew Hunter, Esq., former attorney of the Baltimore and Ohio
Railroad, has been employed by the county authorities to assist the
commonwealth attorney to prosecute the cases in the State courts. The
best legal counsel in the neighborhood will be assigned the prisoners. . . .

No. 16

D. H. Strother, in *Harper's Weekly*, Sat., Nov. 5, 1859, p. 714

FROM OUR OWN ARTIST-CORRESPONDENT

. . . And all about this good-humored, good-for-nothing, half-monkey race—the negroes. Let us walk through the streets of Harper's Ferry and see what part they have played in the drama. . . . [There] is not the remotest suspicion that a single individual among them had any foreknowledge of Brown's movement, . . . that neither threats, promises, nor persuasion could induce one of them to join the movement when it was proposed. . . . Hayward was shot dead while heroically expressing his horror of their nefarious designs. Brown discovered early that he could make no use of such as he had captured, and on Monday morning sent Cook and two other white men, with eleven negro prisoners over to the Maryland side, where they were employed in removing the arms and munitions of war from the Kennedy farm to the log school-house in the mountain opposite the town. This was done that they might be more convenient for those imaginary recruits which the insane brigands still seemed confidently to expect. As Cook and his companions went at times to the river to fire across at the Virginians, these negroes escaped, dodging through the woods, swimming the river, and, running every hazard, returned to their respective homes. I conversed with several of them. . . . One fellow said that, when he was taken, a pike was put into his hands by Brown, who told him to take it and strike for Liberty.

"Good lord, Massa," cried Cuffee, in a tremor, "I don't know nuffin 'bout handlin' dem tings."

"Take it instantly," cried the philanthropist, "and strike home. This is a day that will long be remembered in the history of your race—a glorious anniversary."

"Please God, Massa, I'se got a sore finger," and Cuffee exhibited a stump, the first joint of which he had lost in a wheat-machine some years before.

Finding that he had no mind to be a hero, Brown took him to the Armory, and during the siege, sent him out for water. As soon as he got out of range of their guns he broke the pitcher and fled for his life. I narrate the story faithfully as it was told to me. Many similar anecdotes

I gleaned from the darkeys themselves, but have not space to relate them. In the town they were passing to and fro with entire freedom, jubilating over their own escapes and jeering at the dead carcasses of the Liberators. Several told me that Brown, in urging them to arm, said, repeatedly, "Don't you know me? Did you never hear of John Brown of Kansas— old Osawatomie Brown?" This only frightened the negroes more. They dropped the pikes, like the devil's gifts, and took to their heels, hiding every where under straw ricks, barns, and stables. On the other hand, there is sufficient and full evidence to show that, had their masters been present in any instance, the slaves would, in their defense, have very cheerfully thrust the pikes into the bodies of the pseudo-philanthropists, proving that they were not so ignorant of the pitch-fork exercise as they pretended.

As for the non-slaveholding inhabitants, on whom Brown calculated so confidently for assistance, it is estimated that at least four out of five of those who volunteered so promptly were non-slaveholders and of non-slaveholding families. They were the fighting men of the occasion, the stormers, who went to work with a remorseless ferocity equaling that of the outlaws themselves. . . .

No. 17

D. H. Strother, in *Harper's Weekly*, Sat., Nov. 12, 1859, p. 729

The more I see of Brown, the more I am convinced that, in addition to his abolition monomania, he is under the influence of a ferocious vanity. Influenced by the infuriate babblings of persons better educated but no wiser than himself, he goes to Kansas, where he earns a reputation as a partisan leader, and at the same time gets a taste of human blood. "Ira brevis furor est." That miserable contest, fomented by unprincipled politicians for party and personal purposes, at length ceased. The belligerent parties shook hands, took a drink, and peacefully turned their energies to cheating one another and the rest of the world. Not so John Brown. The demon which those border forays had awakened is destined never again to sleep. Old Brown—Osawatomie Brown, Brown of Kansas, the Topeka Governor, the dread of Border Ruffians, the Moses of the higher law—can not descend into the vulgar stagnation of common life.

Aesop tells us of a certain harper who, having pleased the sots in an ale-house with his music, was so conceited as to go upon the stage and play for the great public. Here he failed ignominiously, and was hissed.

In his grand scheme to overthrow the Government of the United States and the Anglo-Saxon men in the South, with twenty-two men, Brown has failed as signally as the poor musicians. . . . Yet . . . to give the devil his dues, he bears himself stiffly under his misfortunes. Fierce as a gun-lock, cool as a sword, he makes no apologies, and yields no triumph to his enemies. In his bearing there is neither weakness nor bravado. Defiant only when stirred; otherwise civil and straightforward; communicative when questioned; and thankful for small favors.

In person, Brown is gaunt and tall—over six feet, I should think. He walks like a man accustomed to the woods. His face indicates unflinching resolution, evil passions, and narrow mind. . . .

THE RAIDERS—*JOHN BROWN*

No. 18

The Mason Report, Appendix, pp. 65-66

WEST ANDOVER, ASHTABULA COUNTY, OHIO
Thursday morning, September 8, 1859.

FRIEND HENRIE [KAGI]: . . . . *I am devoting my whole time to our company business;* shall immediately go out organizing, and raising funds. From what *I,* even, had understood, I had supposed you would not think it best to commence opening the coal banks before spring, unless circumstances should make it imperative. However, I suppose the reasons are satisfactory to you, and, if so, those who own smaller shares ought not to object. I hope we shall be able to get on in season some of those old miners of whom I wrote you; shall strain every nerve to accomplish this.

You may be assured that what you say to me will reach those who may be benefited thereby, and those who would take stock, in the shortest possible time . . .

Did the last shipment of boxes and one chest of household goods safely arrive? How did the mining *prospect* seem to strike our R——r friend; in short, was his faith increased in the practicability and profit in the work . . . ? . . . .

I feel that it is *all important* you should have that wire from the East, and hope you will not have to make any fence without it. . . .

. . . By the way, I notice, through the "Cleveland Leader," that "Old Brown" is again figuring in Kansas. Well, every dog must have his day, and he will no doubt find the end of his tether. Did you ever know of such a high-handed piece of business? However, it is just like him. The Black Republicans, some of them, may wink at such things, but I tell you, . . . he is too salt a dose for many of them to swallow, and I can already see symptoms of division in their ranks. We are bound to roll up a good, stiff majority for our side this fall. . . .

JOHN [BROWN]

No. 19   THE GOVERNOR'S INTERVIEW
          WITH OLD BROWN
          The Baltimore Weekly Sun, Sat., Oct. 22, 1859

On Wednesday morning Governor Wise, accompanied by District Attorney Ould and several others, visited this remarkable man in his bedroom. Brown was propped up in bed, evidently suffering pain from his numerous wounds, but with his mind collected, and looking calmly about him, now and then giving vent to a groan . . . and he voluntarily made the following important disclosures:

"I rented the 'Kennedy Farm' from Dr. Kennedy, of Sharpsburg, . . . Md., and named it after him. Here I ordered to be sent from the East all things required for my undertaking. The boxes were double, so no one could suspect the contents of them, even the carters engaged in hauling them up from the wharf. All boxes and packages were directed to J. Smith & Son. I never had more than 22 men about the place, but I had it so arranged that I could arm, at any time, 1500 men with . . . 200 Sharps rifles, 200 Maynard's revolvers, 1000 spears and tomahawks. I would have armed the whites with the rifles and pistols, and the blacks with the spears, they not being sufficiently familiar with the other arms. I had plenty of fixed ammunition and enough provisions, and had a good right to expect the aid of from 2000 to 5000 men at any time I wanted. Help was promised me from Maryland, Kentucky, North and South Carolina, Virginia and Canada. The blow was struck a little too soon. The passing of the train . . . did the work against us—that killed us. I should not have let it pass. But I only regret I have failed. . . . I have no apologies to make or concessions to ask now. Had we succeeded, when our arms and funds were exhausted by an increasing army, contributions would have been levied on the slave-holders and their property appropriated to defray expenses, and carry on the war of freedom. Had I known government money was in the safe here I would have appropriated it."

. . . Gov. Wise told him he had better be preparing for death. . . . Brown responded that [the Governor] . . . would have a good deal to answer for at last, and had better be preparing now too.

No. 20   CONVERSATION WITH CAPT. BROWN

The National Intelligencer, Tues., Oct. 25, 1859

Several of the reporters who visited Harper's Ferry last week availed themselves of an opportunity to be present at an interview which Mr. Senator MASON, of Virginia, the Hon. Mr. FAULKNER, also of Virginia, and Mr. VALLANDIGHAM, of Ohio, had with Capt. Brown and Capt. Stevens, two of the conspirators who were wounded and taken prisoners. The conversation is thus reported:

. . . MR. VALLANDIGHAM: Did you get up the expedition yourself?

MR. BROWN: I did.

MR. VALLANDIGHAM: Did you get up this document that is called a constitution?

MR. BROWN: I did. They are a constitution and ordinance of my own contriving and getting up.

MR. VALLANDIGHAM: How long have you been engaged in this business?

MR. BROWN: From the breaking out of the difficulties in Kansas. Four of my sons had gone there to settle, and they induced me to go. I did not go there to settle, but because of the difficulties. . . .

MR. VALLANDIGHAM: Where did your men come from? Did some of them come from Ohio?

MR. BROWN: Some of them.

MR. V: From the Western Reserve? Of course none came from Southern Ohio?

BROWN: Oh yes! I believe one came from Steubenville, down not far from Wheeling. . . .

MR. V: Have you lived long in Ohio?

BROWN: I went there in 1805. I lived in Summit County, which was then Trumbull County. My native place is New York State. . . .

MR. V: When in Cleveland did you attend the Fugitive Slave Law Convention there?

BROWN: No! I was there about the time of the sitting of the court to try the Oberlin rescuers. I spoke there publicly on that subject. I spoke on the fugitive slave law and of my own rescue. Of course so far as I had any preference at all I was disposed to justify the Oberlin people for rescuing the slave, because I have myself forcibly taken slaves from bondage. I was concerned in taking eleven slaves from Missouri to Canada last winter. I think that I spoke in Cleveland before the Convention. I do not know that I had any conversation with any of the Oberlin rescuers. . . . I was part of the time in Ashtabula County.

MR. V: Did you see anything of Joshua R. Giddings there? . . . .

BROWN: I did . . . , I certainly met with him and had a conversation with him. . . .

BYSTANDER: Did you go out to Kansas under the auspices of the Emigrant Aid Society?

BROWN: No, sir. I went under the auspices of Old John Brown. . . .

MR. V: Did you talk with Giddings about your expedition here?

BROWN: . . . I won't answer that. . . .

MR. V: Have you had any correspondence with parties at the North on the subject of this movement?

BROWN: I have had correspondence.

BYSTANDER: Do you consider this a religious movement?

BROWN: It is in my opinion the greatest service a man can render to his God.

BYSTANDER: Upon what principle do you justify your act?

BROWN: By the golden rule. I pity the poor in bondage; that is why I am here; it is not to gratify any personal animosity or feeling of revenge or vindictive spirit. It is my sympathy with the oppressed and wronged, that are as good as you, and as precious in the sight of God.

BYSTANDER: Certainly; but why take the slaves against their will?

BROWN: (Warmly) I never did.

BYSTANDER: You did in one instance at least.

STEVENS: . . . You are right, sir; in one case I know the negro wanted to go back. (To Brown): Captain, the gentleman is right.

BYSTANDER (to Stevens): Where did you come from?

STEVENS: I lived in Ashtabula County, Ohio. . . .

MR. V: Who were your advisers in this movement?

BROWN: I have numerous sympathizers throughout the entire North.

MR. V: In Northern Ohio?

BROWN: No more than anywhere else. . . .

MR. V: But you are not personally acquainted in Southern Ohio?

BROWN: Not very much. . . . We expected no reward. . . . The cry of distress and of the distressed is . . . the only [reason] that impelled me.

BYSTANDER: Why did you do it secretly?

BROWN: Because I thought it necessary for success. . . .

BYSTANDER: You think that honorable, do you? Have you read

Gerrit Smith's last letter, in which he says "that it is folly to attempt to strike the shackles off the slave by the force of moral suasion or legal agitation," and predicts that the next movement made in the direction of negro emancipation will be an insurrection in the South?

BROWN: I have not; but . . . I should concur with it. I agree with Mr. Smith that moral suasion is hopeless. . . .

DR. B: Who lanced that woman's neck on the hill?

BROWN: I did. I have sometimes practised in surgery when I thought it a matter of humanity or of necessity . . . but I have not studied surgery.

DR. B (to the persons around): It was done very well. . . . These men have been very clever to the neighbors, I have been told, and we had no reason to suspect them, except that we could not understand their movements. . . .

Q: Was your only object to free the negro?

BROWN: Absolutely. . . .

BYSTANDER: But you went and took Col. Washington's silver and watch.

BROWN: Oh! yes, we intended freely to have appropriated the property of slaveholders to carry out our object. It was for that, only that; we had no design to enrich ourselves with any plunder whatever.

No. 21
Harper's Weekly, Sat., Oct. 29, 1859, pp. 694-695

Brown has had a conversation with Senator Mason, which is reported in the New York *Herald*. The following is a verbatim report . . . :

MR. MASON: Can you tell us at least who furnished money for your expedition?

MR. BROWN: I furnished most of it myself. I cannot implicate others. It is by my own folly that I have been taken. I could easily have saved myself from it had I exercised my own better judgment, rather than yielded to my feelings.

MR. MASON: You mean if you had escaped immediately?

MR. BROWN: No. I had the means to make myself secure without any escape, but I allowed myself to be surrounded by a force by being too tardy. . . .

MR. MASON: How do you justify your acts?

MR. BROWN: I think, my friend, you are guilty of a great wrong

against God and humanity . . . and it would be perfectly right for anyone to interfere with you so far as to free those you willfully and
wickedly hold in bondage. . . . I think I did right, and that others
will do right who interfere with you at any time. . . . I hold that the
golden rule . . . applies to all who would help others to gain their
liberty. . . .

MR. MASON: What wages did you offer [your men]?

MR. BROWN: None.

LIEUT. STUART: "The wages of sin is death."

MR. BROWN: I would not have made such a remark to you, if you
had been a prisoner and wounded in my hands.

BYSTANDER: Did you not promise a negro in Gettysburg twenty
dollars a month?

MR. BROWN: I did not.

BYSTANDER: He says you did.

MR. VALLANDIGHAM: Did you expect a general rising of the
slaves in case of your success?

MR. BROWN: No, Sir; nor did I wish it. I expected to gather them
up from time to time and set them free.

MR. VALLANDIGHAM: Did you expect to hold possession here
till then?

MR. BROWN: Well, probably I had quite a different idea. I do not
know that I ought to reveal my plans. I am here a prisoner and wounded,
because I foolishly allowed myself to be so. You overrate your strength
in supposing I could have been taken if I had not allowed it. I was too
tardy after commencing the open attack—in delaying my movements
through Monday night, and up to the time I was attacked by the
Government troops. It was all occasioned by my desire to spare the
feelings of my prisoners and their families and the community at large.
I had no knowledge of the shooting of the negro [Hayward].

MR. VALLANDIGHAM: What time did you commence your organization in Canada?

MR. BROWN: . . . [A]bout two years ago. . . . It was, I think, in
1858. . . .

REPORTER OF THE *HERALD:* I do not wish to annoy you; but
if you have anything further you would like to say, I will report it.

MR. BROWN: . . . I claim to be here in carrying out a measure I
believe perfectly justifiable, and not to act the part of an incendiary or
ruffian, but to aid those suffering great wrong. I wish to say, furthermore,
that you had better—all you people at the South—prepare yourselves for
a settlement of that question that must come up for settlement sooner

than you are prepared for it. The sooner you are prepared the better. You may dispose of me very easily. . . . These wounds were inflicted upon me . . . some minutes after I had . . . consented to a surrender, for the benefit of others, not for my own. (*This statement was vehemently denied by all around.*). . . . I could have killed [Lt. J. E. B. Stuart] just as easy as a mosquito when he came in, but I supposed he came in only to receive our surrender. There had been loud and long calls of surrender from us—as loud as men could yell—but in the confusion and excitement I suppose we were not heard. I do not think . . . anyone meant to butcher us after we had surrendered.

THE RAIDERS—*THE OTHERS*

No. 22   [OSBORN P. ANDERSON]

Osborn P. Anderson, *A Voice from Harper's Ferry* (Boston, 1861), Chapters 10-15

. . . The town being taken [Sunday night], Brown, Stevens, and the men who had no post in charge, returned to the engine-house, where council was held, after which Captain Stevens, Tidd, Cook, Shields Green, Leary and myself went to the country. On the road, we met some colored men, to whom we made known our purpose, when they immediately agreed to join us. They said they had been long waiting for an opportunity of the kind. Stevens then asked them to go around among the colored people and circulate the news, when each started off in a different direction. The result was that many colored men gathered to the scene of action. The first prisoner taken by us was Colonel Lewis Washington. . . . We . . . knocked, . . . entered . . . , and commenced a search for the proprietor. Col. Washington opened his room door, and begged us not to kill him. Capt. Stevens replied, "You are our prisoner," when he stood as if speechless or petrified. Stevens told him . . . that he *must* go along. The Colonel replied: "You can have my slaves, if you will let me remain." . . . Stevens left the house for a time, and with Green, Leary, and Tidd, proceeded to the "Quarters," giving the prisoner in charge of Cook and myself. . . .

During this time, Washington was . . . apparently much excited. When the Captain came in, he went to the sideboard, took out his whiskey, and offered us something to drink, but he was refused. His fire-arms were next demanded, when he brought forth one double-barrelled gun, one small rifle, two horse-pistols and a sword. Nothing else was asked of him. The Colonel cried heartily when he found he must submit, and appeared taken aback when, on delivering up the famous sword . . . , Capt. Stevens told me to step forward and take it. . . . [The] party drove forward to Mr. Allstadt's. . . . [He] went into as great a fever of excitement as Washington. . . . We could have his slaves, also, if we would only leave him. . . .

One old colored lady . . . a little way from the town had a good time over the message we took her. This liberating the slaves was the very thing she had longed for, prayed for, and dreamed about . . . ; and her heart was full of rejoicing. . . .

[On Monday] Capt. Brown was all activity, though I could not help thinking that at times he appeared somewhat puzzled. He ordered

Sherrard Lewis Leary, and four slaves, and a free man . . . to join John Henry Kagi and John Copeland at the rifle factory, which they immediately did. . . .

Among the arms taken from Col. Washington was one double-barrel gun. This weapon was loaded by Leeman with buckshot, and placed in the hands of an elderly slave man, early in the morning. After the cowardly charge upon Coppoc, this old man was ordered by Capt. Stevens to arrest a citizen. The old man ordered him to halt, which he refused to do, when instantly the terrible load was discharged into him. . . .

After these incidents, time passed away . . . without any further attack upon us. The cowardly Virginians submitted like sheep, without resistance, from that time until the marines came down. Meanwhile, Capt. Brown, who was considering a proposition for release from his prisoners, passed back and forth from the Armory to the bridge, speaking words of comfort . . . to his men. "Hold on a little longer, boys, . . . until I get matters arranged. . . ." This tardiness . . . was sensibly felt to be an omen of evil by some of us. . . . It was not part of the original plan to hold on to the Ferry, or to parley with prisoners. . . .

At eleven o'clock, Capt. Brown despatched William Thompson from the Ferry up to the Kennedy farm, with the news that we had peaceful possession of the town, and with directions to the men to continue on moving the things. He went; but before he could get back, troops had begun to pour in. . . .

It was about twelve o'clock [Monday] when we were first attacked by the troops. . . . When the Captain received the news that the troops had entered the bridge from the Maryland side, he . . . sent a message to the Arsenal for us to come forth also. . . . The troops soon came out of the bridge and up the street facing us. . . . When they got within sixty or seventy yards, Capt. Brown said, "Let go upon them!" which we did. . . . Again and again the dose was repeated. There was now consternation among the troops. . . . The consequence of their unexpected reception was, after leaving several of their dead . . . , they beat a confused retreat to the bridge, and there stayed under cover until reinforcements came. . . . On the retreat of the troops, we were ordered back to our former post. While going, Daingerfield Newby, one of our colored men, was shot through the head. . . . Newby was a brave fellow . . . and his death was promptly avenged by Shields Green, the Zouave of the band. . . . Green raised his rifle in an instant, and brought down the cowardly murderer, before the latter could get his gun back through the sash. . . . Of the four prisoners taken at the engine-house,

Shields Green, the most inexorable of all our party, a very Turco in his hatred against the stealers of men, was under Captain Hazlett, and consequently of our little band at the Arsenal; but when we were ordered by Captain Brown to return to our positions, after having driven the troops into the bridge, he mistook the order, and went to the engine-house instead of with his own party. Had he remained with us, he might have [escaped]. As it was, he was doomed, . . . and became a free-will offering for freedom, with his comrade, John Copeland. Wiser and better men no doubt there were, but a braver man never lived than Shields Green. . . .

Of the six men assigned a position in the Arsenal by Captain Brown, four were either slain or captured; and Hazlett and myself . . . never left our position until we saw, with . . . tense sadness, that we could be of no further avail to our commander, he being a prisoner [after the marines took the engine-house]. We therefore . . . concluded it was better to retreat while it was possible, as our work for the day was clearly finished. . . . John Brown's men at Harper's Ferry were and are a unit in their devotion to John Brown and the cause he espoused. To have deserted him would have been to belie every manly characteristic for which Albert Hazlett, at least, was known by the party to be distinguished, at the same time that it would have endangered the future safety of such deserter or deserters. John Brown gave orders; those orders must be obeyed. . . . [They] having captured our commander, we . . . went out at the back part of the building, climbed up the wall, and went upon the railway. Behind us, in the Arsenal, were thousands of dollars, we knew full well, but that wealth had no charms for us, and we hastened to communicate with the men sent to the Kennedy Farm; . . . [We] crawled or climbed up among the rocks in the mountains . . . and hid ourselves. . . . A few minutes before dark, the troops came. . . . They . . . marched and counter-marched, but' never attempted to search the mountains; we supposed . . . that they feared a host of armed enemies in concealment. Their air was so defiant . . . that . . . having a few cartridges on hand, we poured from our excellent position in the rocky wilds some well-directed shots. . . . [We] could see one bite the dust now and then. . . . Interchanging of shots continued . . . with much spirit, when it became quite dark, and they went down into the town. . . . Hazlett and I remained in our position three hours before we dared venture down.

As stated [before], the command of the rifle factory was given to Captain Kagi. Under him were John Copeland, Sherrard Lewis Leary, and three colored men from the neighborhood. At an early hour, Kagi saw from his position the danger in remaining, with our small company, until assistance could come to the inhabitants. Hence his suggestion to Captain Brown, through Jeremiah Anderson, to leave. His position being more isolated than the others, was the first to invite an organized attack with success; the Virginians first investing the factory with their hordes, before the final success at the engine-house. From [a prisoner taken and released after our escape from the Arsenal] we received the sad details. . . . Seven times during the day they were fired upon, while they occupied the interior part of the building, the insurgents . . . killing and wounding with fatal precision. At last, overwhelming numbers . . . battered the doors down. . . . The insurgents were then forced to retreat . . . to the river, and . . . they waded out to a rock . . . and there made a stand, being completely hemmed in. . . . They . . . kept on fighting until everyone was killed except John Copeland. . . . There fell poor Kagi, . . . the cleverest man in the party; and . . . Leary, . . . brave to desperation, . . . all . . . noble. . . .

No. 23   STATEMENT OF Annie Brown Adams

Statement made to the author, Oswald Garrison Villard, in *John Brown: A Biography Fifty Years After* [1910] (New York: Alfred H. Knopf, 1943), pp. 419-420. Reprinted with the kind permission of the publisher

. . . At Kennedy Farm my father wore a short beard. . . . He had made this change . . . on his return from Kansas, thinking it more likely to disguise him than a clean face or than the long beard.

Hazlett and Leeman were the hardest ones to keep caged of "my invisibles". . . . They would . . . even go down to Harper's Ferry, going to Cook's home and back in the daylight. We were so self-conscious that we feared danger when no man pursued. . . . Watson [Brown], Oliver [Brown], Leeman and Kagi were all a little more than six feet in height. . . . Daingerfield Newby was I think above medium size, spare and showed the Scotch blood plainly. . . . His father was a Scotchman, who took his family of mulatto children into Ohio and gave them their freedom. Newby was quiet, sensible and very unobtrusive. Stevens and Stewart Taylor were the only ones who believed in "spiritualism". . . . The latter . . . believed in dreams and all sorts of "isms." . . . He was all the time studying and "improving his mind". . . . He had learned to write shorthand. O. P. Anderson was accustomed to being confined in the house, being a printer . . . , so that he was not so restive as some of the others. William Thompson was an easygoing, good-

natured person. . . . Dauphin Thompson was the youngest one of a
family of eighteen children. He was a quiet person, read a good deal,
said little. He was a perfect blond, with yellow, curly hair, and blue
eyes . . . , a handsome young man. I heard Hazlett and Leeman . . .
saying that "Barclay Coppoc and Dauphin Thompson were too nearly
like good girls to make soldiers"; that they ought to have gone to
Kansas and "roughed it" . . . before coming down here. To while
away the time the men read magazines, sang, told stories, argued
questions, played cards and checkers, studied military tactics, and drilled
under Stevens. When there was a thunderstorm, they would jump about
and play, making all kinds of noise to rest themselves, as they thought
no one could hear them then.

No. 24   OWEN BROWN'S ESCAPE FROM HARPER'S FERRY

Ralph Keeler, in *The Atlantic Monthly*, XXXIII (March, 1874), pp. 344-347

. . . The last time I saw my father [Owen Brown told
me] was on the Sunday night of the attack, the 16th of October, 1859.
It was about eleven o'clock that night when he and his little company
started from what we called our boarding-house, on the Kennedy farm,
five miles north of Harper's Ferry. He left Barclay Coppoc, Frank J.
Meriam, and myself to guard the arms and ammunition stored on
the premises, until it should be time to move them, either to the
school-house, a mile from Harper's Ferry, or to the Ferry itself. Barclay Coppoc was a brother to Edwin. . . . The mother of the Coppocs
was a Quakeress. . . . Frank J. Meriam was of the wealthy Massachusetts Meriams. He was twenty-eight or thirty years old . . . He had
easy, unassuming manners. The only thing very positive about him
was his hatred of slavery. . . . .
    Neither of them had been with us in Kansas, and so I thought best
to stand guard all night myself, letting them sleep. No echo of the
events which were happening reached me in my long watch. But
towards six o'clock in the morning, we all heard firing in the direction
of Harper's Ferry. The rain, which continued at intervals all that day
and the next night, had already set in. About eleven o'clock that forenoon a slave of Col. Lewis Washington, whom with others my father
then held a prisoner, came up with a four-horse wagon after a load of
arms. One of my father's men came with him; I forget . . . who. . . .

They knew little more about the details of the fight than we did. While they put their team under shelter and fed it, I got dinner for them. . . . Then we loaded the wagon as quickly as we could with powder and boxes of revolvers and Sharps rifles, which father had managed to have shipped to him under the name of John Smith and Sons. The wagon drove away to the school-house . . . where the arms were to be stored. Between two and three that afternoon, we heard a great deal of firing. . . . Later . . . a black man came up on horseback, and asked us to go over to the Ferry and help in the fight. I don't know that he had any authority but his fears; for I think he must have come from the school-house where Washington's and Allstadt's slaves were congregated. At any rate I put things in order, feeling somehow as if we were never going to get back there again. I told some of the neighbors where they could help themselves to the provisions and things, if they wanted them, and I tied to the rude stairway . . . the pup. . . . Then, arming ourselves well . . . we started toward the Ferry through the rain, Coppoc, Meriam, and myself on foot, the negro riding his horse. . . . Shortly after we saw coming towards us in the dusk . . . one of my father's men—Charles Plummer Tidd, a large, strong, determined fellow . . . once a lumberman in his native . . . Maine. He had been with us in Kansas, and was a great friend of Stevens. . . . Tidd had been on duty at the school-house. He told us that our men were all hemmed in at Harper's Ferry, that many of them were killed, and that there was no chance for any of them to escape. "The fact is, boys," concluded Tidd, "we are used up; the best thing we can do is to get away from here as quick as we can." "We mustn't desert our friends," I said; and proposed to go on to the school-house, collect the slaves left there, and then cross the ravine up through the forest on to the point of rocks upon the mountain opposite Harper's Ferry, where with our long-range guns we might divert or frighten away the enemy, and let our people escape. Tidd thought the case hopeless, but consented to go with us to the school-house.

We had not gone on together over a mile . . . when we saw another armed man approaching us out of the dark. We ordered him to halt, and he replied by pluckily ordering us to halt ourselves. We recognized the voice of Cook,—John E. Cook. . . . "Our men are all killed but seven," said Cook. "Your father was killed at four o'clock this afternoon." He did not know whether my two brothers—Oliver and Watson —were . . . dead. . . . Then he told us particulars. . . . The best and only thing to do, in Cook's opinion, was to make good our escape. I was opposed to deserting any friends who might want to escape with us, and we argued. . . . I prevailed on Cook to go reluctantly as far as the school-house, for provisions, and to see what had become of the liberated slaves. . . . When finally we came near it, Tidd and I left the others concealed in a thicket. . . . Tidd . . . followed me . . . , revolver in hand, and I lit a candle and found the school-house—deserted.

There was in a corner nearly a barrelful of a kind of sweet biscuit which I had made myself, and I hurriedly thrust as many of them as I could into a bag. I took about twenty pounds of sugar in another bag. . . . That's all the provisions we took. Knew that we dared not build fires in our flight. Coming out of the school-house and joined by Cook, Meriam, Coppoc, and the negro, we lingered in the neighborhood perhaps an hour, calling the black men. The only answer that came to us out of the rain and darkness was the firing at Harper's Ferry, but a mile away. We saw no more of the liberated slaves. . . . It was plain now that we could not get to the top of the mountain opposite the Ferry before morning. Then our retreat would be cut off. I hated to give up the idea of helping our friends to escape, but I had to. . . . We finally decided to go back to . . . the Kennedy farm, and get our India-rubber blankets and other necessary things. I put the bags of biscuits and sugar across the negro's horse, and on the way made up my plan of escape. . . . I told the boys . . . I felt pretty sure I could get them safely through to the North, and to Canada, if necessary.

The firing by this time had spread gradually over the country. . . . We took a hasty supper at the boarding-house, and hurriedly seized what things we could. . . . We resolved to camp on the mountain, as near to the farm-house as we dared, so as to aid in the escape of any other stragglers who might find their way there. In point of fact, as I afterwards heard from one of them, two of our men who had escaped from the Ferry did reach the house the next day after we had gone. They were Hazlett and Anderson, the mulatto. Hazlett . . . was afterwards . . . hanged. . . . Osborn Anderson made his way into Canada. I saw him the next July. . . . Anderson, it is said, has since gone to Liberia, and if he is living—which . . . I . . . doubt—he is the only other survivor of all my father's company at Harper's Ferry. . . .

No. 25   JOHN E. COOK, "CONFESSION"

Charlestown, Va., Nov., 1859

I became acquainted with Capt. Jno. Brown in his camp on Middle Creek, Kansas Territory, just after the battle of Black Jack. . . . I next saw him at the Convention at Topeka, which was on the 4th of July, 1856. I next met him some days afterwards, in Lawrence. Did not see him again until the fall of 1857. . . . I was told that he intended to organize a company for the purpose of putting a stop to the aggressions of the pro-slavery men. I agreed to join him, and was asked if I knew of any other young men, who were perfectly reliable. . . . I recommended Rich. Realf, L. F. Parsons and R. J. Hinton. I received a note on the next Sunday morning . . . from Capt. Brown, requesting me to come up that day, and to bring [them] with me. Realf and Hinton were not in town. . . . Parsons and myself went and had a long talk with Capt. Brown.

A few days afterwards I received another note from Capt. Brown, which read, as near as I can recollect . . . : *"Dear Sir,*—You will please get everything ready to join me at Topeka by Monday night next. Come to Mrs. Sheridan's, two miles south of Topeka, and bring your arms, ammunition, clothing, and other articles you may require. Bring Parsons with you if he can get ready in time. Please keep very quiet about the matter./Yours, &c./JOHN BROWN."

I made all my arrangements for starting at the time appointed. Parsons, Realf and Hinton could not get ready. I left them at Lawrence, and started in a carriage for Topeka. Stopped at the hotel over night, and left early next morning for Mrs. Sheridan's, to meet Capt. Brown. Stayed a day and a half at Mrs. S's—then left for Topeka, at which place we were joined by Stevens, Moffett and Kagi. Left Topeka for Nebraska City, and camped at night on the prairie north-east of Topeka. Here, for the first time, I learned that we were to leave Kansas to attend a military school during the winter. It was the intention of the party to go to Ashtabula County, Ohio. Next morning I was sent back to Lawrence to get a draft of $80 cashed, and to get Parsons, Realf and Hinton to go back with me. I got the draft cashed. Capt. B. had given me orders to take boat to St. Joseph, Mo., and stage from there to Tabor, Iowa, where he would remain for a few days. I had to wait for Realf for three or four days; Hinton could not leave at that time. I started with Realf and Parsons, in a stage for Leaven-

worth. . . . I found C. P. Tidd and Leeman at Tabor. Our party now
consisted of Capt. John Brown, Owen Brown, A. D. Stevens, Chas.
Moffett, C. P. Tidd, Rich. Robertson, col., Rich. Realf, L. F. Parsons,
Wm. Leeman and myself. We stopped some days at Tabor, making
preparations to start. *Here we found that Capt. Brown's ultimate desti-
nation was the State of Virginia.* Some warm words passed between
him and myself in regard to the plan, which I had supposed was to be
entirely confined to Kansas and Missouri. Realf and Parsons were of
the same opinion with me. After a good deal of wrangling, we consented to go on, as we had not the means to return, and the rest of
the party were so anxious that we should go with them. At Tabor we
procured teams for the transportation of about 200 Sharps rifles, which
had been taken on as far as Tabor, one year before, at which place
they had been left, awaiting the order of Capt. Brown. There were,
also, other stores, consisting of blankets, clothing, boots, ammunition,
and about 200 revolvers of the Massachusetts Arms patent, all of which
we transported across the State of Iowa to Springdale, and from there
to Liberty, at which place they were shipped for Ashtabula County,
Ohio, where they remained till brought to Chambersburg, Penn., and
from there transported to a house in Washington county, Md., which
Capt. Brown had rented for six months, and which was situated about
five miles from H. Ferry. It was the intention of Capt. B. to sell his
teams in Springdale, and with the proceeds to go on with the rest of
the company to some place in Ashtabula County, Ohio, where we
were to have a good military instructor during the winter but he was
disappointed in the sale. As he could not get cash for the teams, it
was decided we should remain in the neighborhood of Springdale, and
that our instructor, Col. H. Forbes, should be sent on. We stopped in
Pedee, Iowa, over winter, at Mr. Maxsons's, where we pursued a course
of military studies. Col. H. Forbes and Capt. Brown had some words,
and he (Col. F.) did not come on; consequently, A. D. Stevens was our
drill master. The people of the neighborhood did not know of our
purpose. We remained at Pedee till about the middle of April, when we
left for Chatham, Canada, via Chicago and Detroit. We staid about two
weeks in Chatham—some of the party staid six or seven weeks. We
left Chatham for Cleveland, and remained there until late in June. In
the meantime, Capt. Brown went East on business, but previous to his
departure he had learned that Col. Forbes had betrayed his plans to
some extent. This, together with the scantiness of his funds, induced
him to delay the commencement of his work, and as the means, for
the time being, of disbanding the party. He had also received some

information which called for his immediate attention in Kansas. I wished to go with him, but he said I was too well known there, and requested me and some others to go to Harper's Ferry, Va., to see how things were there, and to gain information. While we were in Chatham he called a convention . . . to make a complete and thorough organization. He issued a written circular, which he sent to various persons in the United States and Canada. . . . I do not know to whom they were sent, though I wrote several of them. I learned, however, that one was sent to Frederick Douglass, and I think Gerrit Smith also received one. . . . Neither Douglass nor Smith attended the convention. I suppose some 25 or 30 of these circulars were sent. . . . [They] were directed by Capt. Brown or J. H. Kagi, . . . to none save those whom Capt. Brown knew to be radical abolitionists. . . . The place of meeting was in one of the negro churches in Chatham. . . . Its object was then stated— which was to complete a thorough organization and the formation of a constitution. . . . Elder Monroe, a colored minister, was elected President, and J. H. Kagi, Secretary. The next business was to form a constitution. Capt. Brown had already drawn up one, which, on motion, was read by the Secretary. . . . Most of the delegates . . . were from Canada. After the constitution was adopted the members took their oaths to support it. It was then signed by all present. . . . There were no white men at the convention, save the members of our company. Men and money had both been promised from Chatham and other parts of Canada. When the convention broke up, news was received that Col. H. Forbes, who had joined in the movement, had given information to the government. This, of course, delayed the time of attack. A day or two afterwards, most of our party took the boat to Cleveland. Jno. H. Kagi, Richard Realf, Wm. H. Leeman, Richard Robertson and Capt. Brown remaining. Capt. B., however, started in a day or two for the East. Kagi, I think, went to some other town in Canada, to set up the type and to get the constitution printed, which he completed before he returned to Cleveland. We remained in Cleveland for some weeks, at which place, for the time being, the company disbanded. Capt. Brown had had the *plan* of the insurrection in contemplation for several years—in fact, told me that it had been the chief aim of his life to carry out and accomplish the abolition of slavery.

In his trip East he did not realize the amount of money that he expected. The money had been promised *bona fide,* but owing to the tightness of the money market, they failed to comply with his demands. The funds were necessary to the accomplishment of his plans. I afterwards learned that there was a lack of confidence in the success of his scheme. It was therefore necessary that a movement should be made in another direction, to demonstrate the practicability of his plan. This he made about a year ago by his invasion of Missouri, and the taking of about a dozen slaves, together with horses, cattle, &c. into Kansas, in defiance of the U.S. Marshal and his posse. From Kansas he took them to Canada, via Iowa City and Cleveland. At the latter place he remained some days, and I think disposed of his horses there. It seems that the U.S. Marshal was afraid to arrest him, and this was all that was wanting to give confidence to the wavering in the practicability of his plan and its ultimate success. He came to Harper's Ferry about the last of June, though I did not see him till late in July, or the early part of August, when we met on Shenandoah Street, Harper's Ferry, opposite of Tearney's store. I do not know who were his aiders or abettors, but have heard him mention in connection with it the names of Gerrit Smith, of New York, Howe, of Boston, and Sanborn and Thaddeus Hyatt, of New York City. What connection, and how far connected with his plan I do not know; but I know he wrote a letter, a few weeks previous to his attack, to some gentlemen in Boston, which read, as near as I can recollect, as follows:

DATE ———— ————.

Gentlemen:—I have got nearly all my *machines* on, and shall be ready to start them in a few days, unless prevented by a special Providence. Every thing is working well. I shall want *all the funds* you promised me in a few days.

Yours, truly,

"CALM & STILL."

In the meantime the men who had engaged to go with him had most of them arrived at Chambersburg, Pa., had been sent to the place which he had rented in Washington co., Md., about 5 miles from H. Ferry. *The greater part of the men kept out of sight during the day, for fear of attracting attention.* The arms, munitions, &c., were carted from Chambersburg to his rendezvous. The spear-heads and guards came in strong boxes, and the shafts passed for fork handles. They were put together by our own men, at the house where most of them were found. Letters of importance came to the Chambersburg post office, and were sent by some of our own party to head-quarters. The letters of minor importance came to the Ferry to J. Smith & Sons. All allusions to our business were made in such a blind way that they would not have been understood by any outside parties, even should they have miscarried. The attack was made sooner than it was intended, owing to some friends in Boston writing a letter, finding fault with the management of Capt. B., and what to them seemed his unnecessary delay and expense. I do not know who those persons were, or how far they were cognizant of his (Capt. B's) plans. But I do know that Doctor Howe gave Capt. Brown a breech-loading carbine and a pair of muzzle-loading pistols, all of government manufacture. They were left either at the house of Capt. Brown, or at the school-house, where most of the arms were conveyed. At what time, and for what purpose they were given to Captain Brown, I do not know. It was supposed that Col. Hugh Forbes was dead. I was told by Capt. B. that when on East he had been told by Thaddeus Hyatt, of New York, that some of the negroes at that place had informed him (Hyatt) that Forbes had "gone up" — . . . that he had been killed. I do not think that Forbes had any cognizance of our plans from the time of our leaving Pedee, a year ago last April. Previous to his quarrel with Capt. Brown, we considered that he would hold a place next to Brown in command. I do not know the present whereabouts of Luke F. Parsons or Charles Moffett. . . . A short time before the attack on Harper's Ferry, Capt. Brown requested me to find out in some way, without creating suspicion, the number of male slaves on or near the roads leading from the Ferry, for a distance of 8 or 10 miles. . . . He gave me two dollars to pay my expenses with. I took the road from Harper's Ferry to Charlestown under the plea of gaining statistics for a work to be published by John Henri, and to decide a wager between him and Mr. Smith. I did not go on any other road. A few days after this Capt. Brown sent his wagon over by his son Oliver and Jeremiah Anderson, to bring my wife and myself to his house . . . in Washington Co., Md. The next day after dinner Capt. B. and his son Watson together with my wife and child started for Chambersburg. . . .

There were some six or seven in our party who did not know anything of our constitution and, as I have since understood, were also ignorant of the plan of operations until the Sunday morning [of] the attack. Among this number were Edwin Coppoc, Barclay Coppoc, Francis J. Meriam, Shields Green, John Copeland, and Leary. The constitution was read to them by A. D. Stevens and the oath afterwards administered by Capt. Brown. Sunday evening [before] our departure, Capt. Brown . . . gave his men their orders. In closing, he said, "and now gentlemen let me press this one thing on your minds, you all know how dear life is to you, and how dear your lives are to your friends; and in remembering that consider that the lives of others are as dear to them . . . ; do not, therefore, take the life of any one if you can possibly avoid it; but if it is necessary to take life in order to save your own, then make sure work of it."

After taking the town I was placed under Capt. Stevens, who received orders to proceed to the house of Col. Lewis Washington and to take him prisoner and to bring his slaves, horses and arms, and as we came back to take Mr. Allstadt and his slaves and to bring them all to Capt. Brown at the Armory.—When we returned I stayed a short time in the engine-house to get warm, as I was chilled through. After I got warm Capt. Brown ordered me to go with C. P. Tidd, who was to take William H. Leeman and I think four slaves with him in Col. Washington's large wagon across the river, and to take Terrence Burns and his brother and their slaves prisoners. My orders were to hold Burns and brother as prisoners at their own house while Tidd and the slaves who accompanied him were to go to Capt. Brown's house and to load in the arms and bring them down to the school house, stopping for the Burns' and their guard. —William H. Leeman remained with me to guard the prisoners. On return of the wagon, in compliance with orders, we all started for the school house. When we got there I was to remain, by Capt. Brown's orders, with one of the slaves to guard the arms, while C. P. Tidd, with the other negroes, was to go back for the rest of the arms, and Burns was to be sent with William H. Leeman to Capt. Brown at the Armory. It was at this time that William Thompson came up from the Ferry and reported that every thing was all right, and then hurried on to overtake William H. Leeman. A short time after the departure of Tidd I heard a good deal of firing and became anxious to know the cause, but my orders were strict to remain at the school house and guard the arms, and I obeyed the orders to the letter. About 4 o'clock in the evening C. P. Tidd came with the second load; I then took one of the negroes with me and started for the Ferry. . . . I came to the Lock kept by George Hardy, about a mile above the bridge, where I saw his wife and Mrs. Elizabeth Read, who told me that our men were hemmed in and that several of them had been shot. I expressed my intention to try to get to them, when Mrs. Hardy asked me to try and get her husband released from the engine-house. I told her I would. Mrs. Read begged of me not to go down to the Ferry. She said I would be shot. I told her I must make an attempt to save my comrades, and passed on down the road. A short distance below the Lock I met two boys whom I knew, and they told me that our men were all hemmed in by troops from Charlestown, Martinsburg, Hagerstown and Shepherdstown. The negro who was with me had been very much frightened at the first report we received, and as the boys told me the troops were coming up the road after us soon, I sent him (the negro) back to inform Tidd while I hastened down the road. After going down opposite of the Ferry, I ascended the mountain in order to get a better view of the position of our opponents.

I saw that our party were completely surrounded, and as I saw a body of men on High Street firing down upon them, they were about a half mile distant from me, I thought I would draw their fire upon myself; I therefore raised my rifle and took the best aim I could and fired. It had the desired effect, for the very instant the party returned it. Several shots were exchanged. The last one they fired at me cut a small limb I had hold of just below my hand, and gave me a fall of about fifteen feet, by which I was severely bruised and my flesh somewhat lacerated. I descended from the mountain. . . . I then passed down to the lock house and went down the steps to the lock, where I saw William McGreg, and questioned him in regard to the troops on the other side. He told me that the bridge was filled by our opponents and that all of our party were dead but seven—that two of them were shot while trying to escape across the river. He begged me to leave immediately. After questioning him in regard to the position and number of the troops, and from what sources he received his information, I bid him good night and started up the road at a rapid walk. I stopped at the house of an Irish family at the foot of the hill and got a cup of coffee and some eatables. I was informed by them that Capt. Brown was dead, that he had been shot about 4 o'clock in the afternoon. At the time I believed this report to be true. I went on up to the school house and found the shutters and door closed—called to Tidd and the boys, but received no answer; cocked my rifle and then opened the door. It was dark at this time.—Some of the goods had been placed in the middle of the floor, and in the dark looked like men crouching. I uncocked my rifle and drew my revolver, and then struck a match— saw that there was no one in the school house; went into the bushes back of the school house and called for the boys. Receiving no answer I went across the road into some pines and again called, but could find no one. I then started up the road towards Capt. Brown's house; I saw a party of men coming down the road; when within about fifty yards I ordered them to halt; they recognized my voice and called me. I found them to be Charles P. Tidd, Owen Brown, Barclay Coppoc, F. J. Meriam and a negro, who belonged to Washington or Allstadt. They asked me the news, and I gave the information that I received at the canal lock and on the road. It seemed that they thought it would be sheer madness in them to attempt a rescue of our comrades, and it was finally determined to return to the house of Capt. Brown. I found that Tidd, before leaving the school house to go for Brown, Coppoc and Meriam, had stationed the negroes in a good position in the timber back of the school house. On his return, however, they could not be found. We therefore left for Capt. Brown's house. Here we got a few articles which would be necessary and then went over into the timber on the side of the mountain, a few yards beyond the house, where the spears were kept. Here we laid down and went to sleep. About 3 o'clock in the morning one of our party awakened and found that the negro had left us. He immediately aroused the rest of the party, and we concluded to go to the top of the mountain before light. Here we remained for a few hours and then passed over to the other side of the mountain, where we waited till dark and then crossed the valley to the other range beyond.

I have forgotten to state previously, that before I left Capt. Brown in Cleveland, Ohio, *he gave me orders to trust no one with our secret,* and to hold no conversation with the slaves, which orders I obeyed with but a single exception, which I here mention. The exception to which I allude, is simply this—I met a party of four negroes—two free and two slaves—near Bolivar, Jefferson County, Virginia. I asked them if they had ever thought about their freedom. They replied "they thought they ought to be free," but expressed doubts that they ever would be. I told them that time might come before many years, but for the present to keep dark and look for the good time coming, and left them.

I see from some of the newspapers, that I have been represented as Capt. Brown's chief aid. This is incorrect. Kagi was second in command, Stevens third, Hazlett fourth. Further than this, I do not know that Capt. Brown had made known any preference as to superiority or rank. Edward Coppoc and Dauphin Thomas were the only lieutenants he commissioned. Owen Brown, Barclay Coppoc and F. J. Meriam were not at the Ferry during the time the attack was made, but remained by order of Capt. B. to take charge of the premises, and to guard the arms left at Brown's house in case of an attack. I do not know of any persons in the Ferry or its neighborhood, who knew of our plan, save our own party, and they were pledged to keep it secret. . . .

I was commissioned as captain on the Sunday of the insurrection, at the same time the others were, and with them took the oath prescribed in Article 48 in the constitution. George G. Gill joined us before leaving Iowa, in the spring, as did Stewart Taylor.

No. 26
The National Intelligencer, Sat., Dec. 17, 1859

. . . Another private letter from JOHN E. COOK, written before his conviction, has just been published. It is addressed to his wife and child. . . . The following are extracts . . . :
"You know that in the scheme which has resulted in the death of most of my companions, and which has made me a prisoner, that I was actuated only by the tenderest feelings of sympathy and humanity. I had been led to believe, as had my comrades, that . . . the masses of the slaves . . . were groaning beneath the yoke of oppression. . . . It had been represented to me and my comrades that when once the banner of freedom should be raised they would flock to it by thousands. . . . I gave heart and hand to a work which I deemed a noble and holy cause. The result has proved *that we were deceived;* that the masses of the slaves did not wish for freedom. There was no *rallying beneath our banner.* We were left to meet the conflict all alone. . . . Twelve of my comrades are sleeping now with the damp mould over them, and five are inmates of these prison walls. We have been deceived, but found out our error when too late. . . ."

No. 27
The Shepherdstown [Va.] Register, Sat., Oct. 22, 1859

. . . This same Capt. Cook was in our town last Spring, selling the Life of Washington, and married a Miss Kennedy, of Harper's Ferry, a few months since. He passed here as a literary character, and contributed several poetical effusions to the columns of the *Register,* a part of which proved not to be original. . . .

No. 28   [JOHN COPELAND]
The National Intelligencer, Sat., Nov. 5, 1859

It has been stated heretofore that John Copeland, one of the negro conspirators . . . , had made a confession to Mr. Johnson, marshal of the northern district of Ohio. We find a copy of it in the Cleveland *Herald* . . . :
. . . Have you any knowledge of an attempt to raise an insurrection

in any other States or region of our country? —I understood that there was an intention to attempt a movement of that kind in Kentucky about the same time.

Did you know from Brown or any other person that help was expected from the slaves . . . ? —I did from Brown, that help would come from the slaves; but I did not understand at any time until Monday morning after the fight had commenced, that anything else than running off slaves was intended, I being at the Rifle Works, half a mile from the engine-house.

Did you learn from Brown or any of the company that persons at Harper's Ferry sympathized with them, or were in any way connected with the movement? —From Brown I understood that there were laboring men at Harper's Ferry who wished to get rid of the slaves, and would aid in running them off.

No. 29   [EDWIN COPPOC]

The National Intelligencer, Tues., Dec. 13, 1859

The Iowa papers give publicity to an extract of a letter from EDWIN COPPOC, . . . now under sentence of death at Charlestown. . . . The letter is addressed to his mother and father . . . :

". . . I hope you will not reflect on me for what has been done, for I am not at fault; at least, my conscience tells me so, and there are others who feel as I do. We were led into it by those who ought to have known better, but who did not anticipate any danger. After stopping at Harper's Ferry we were surrounded and compelled to fight to save our lives, for . . . our leader would not surrender. . . . I am happy to say that no one fell by my hand, and I am sorry to say that I was induced to raise a gun. I was not looking for such a thing . . . [as] that my hand would be guilty of raising a weapon against my fellow man. . . .

No. 30 [JOHN H. KAGI] LETTER TO JOHN BROWN, JR.

From the copy by John Brown, Jr., in the Boston Public Library, as it appears in Oswald Garrison Villard, *John Brown: A Biography Fifty Years After* [1910] (New York: Knopf, 1943), pp. 422-423. Reprinted with the kind permission of the publisher and the Boston Public Library.

[Chambersburg, Penna.
October 10, 1859]

Your father was here yesterday but had not time to write before returning. I shall leave here this afternoon "for good." This is the last of our stay here, for we have not $5 left, and the men must be given work or they will find it themselves. We shall not be able to receive *any thing* from you after to-day. It will not do for any one to try to find us now. You must by all means keep back the men you talked of sending and furnish them work to live upon until you receive further instructions. Any one arriving here after to-day and trying to join us would be trying a very hazardous and foolish experiment. They must keep off the border until we open the way clear up to the line (M. & D's) from the South. Until then, it will be just as dangerous here as on the other side, in fact more so: for, *there* there will be protection also, but not here. It will not do to write to Harper's Ferry. It will never get there—would do no good if it did. *You* can communicate with us thus——————— (This must be a profound secret) Be sure no one gets into trouble in trying to get to us. We will try to communicate with you as soon as possible after we strike, but it may not be possible for us to do so soon. If we succeed in getting news from the outside our own district it will be quite satisfactory, but we have not the most distant hope that it will be possible for us to receive *recruits* for *weeks,* or quite likely *months* to come. We must first make a complete and undisputably open road to the free states. That will require both labor and time.

This is just the right time. The year's crops have been good, and they are now perfectly housed, and in the best condition for use. The moon is just right. Slaves are discontented at this season more than at any other, the reasons for which reflection will show you. We can't live longer without money—we couldn't get along much longer without being exposed. A great religious revival is going on, and has its advantages. Under its influence, people who are commonly barely *unfavorable* to slavery under religious excitement in meetings speak boldly against it. In addition to this and as a stimulant to the religious feeling, a fine slave man near our headquarters, hung himself a few days ago because his master sold his wife away from him. This also arouses the slaves. There are more reasons which I could give, but I have not time.

. . . John E. Cook's wife & children are here (at Mrs. R's) and will board here probably until *the end*. She came on Friday, has lived at the "Ferry." Her board is paid until the 1st of November, but after that we shall expect to see you or some one under your direction, have it paid monthly in advance, from $10 to $15 besides the necessary etceteras, clothing &c. —This must be our last for a time.

Yours   J. H. [KAGI]

No. 31   [CHARLES P. TIDD]

Thomas Wentworth Higginson, *Cheerful Yesterdays* (Boston, 1898), pp. 228-229

. . . Another and far abler refugee from Harper's Ferry was Charles Plummer Tidd, one of our Worcester emigrants [to Kansas],—afterwards well known as Sergeant Charles Plummer of the Twenty-first Massachusetts,—who told me, in an interview on February 10, 1860, of which I still preserve the written record, "All the boys opposed Harper's Ferry, the younger Browns most of all. In September it nearly broke up the camp. He himself [Tidd] left, almost quarreling with Brown. Finally, when they consented, it was with the agreement that men should be sent in each direction to burn bridges"; which was not done, however. Tidd pronounced the Harper's Ferry attack "the only mistake Brown ever made," and attributed it, as it is now generally assigned, to a final loss of mental balance from overbrooding on one idea. Brown's general project he still heartily indorsed; saying that the Virginia mountains were "the best guerilla country in the world,"— all crags and dense laurel thickets; that "twenty-five men there could paralyze the whole business of the South," and that "nobody could take them." The negroes, he said, had proved ready enough to follow Brown, but naturally slipped back to their masters when they saw that the enterprise was to fail. . . .

TOPICS FOR ESSAYS

SUGGESTED LENGTH (*words*):
(1) *Osborn Anderson's Memoir as History*   300
(2) *Owen Brown*   100-300
(3) *Brown's Raiders*   500
(4) *The Raid through Journalists' Eyes*   500

TOPICS FOR LIBRARY RESEARCH

BIBLIOGRAPHY:

Osborn P. Anderson   Aaron D. Stevens
John E. Cook   D. H. Strother
R. J. Hinton   Charles P. Tidd
Thaddeus Hyatt   Mr. Vallandigham of Ohio
John H. Kagi   Governor Henry A. Wise
Senator Mason

SUPPLEMENTARY RESEARCH:

(1) John Brown relished being called "Osawatomie Brown." Why? Look up this episode in Kansas history and write a documented essay on it.
500-1000

(2) What was the "Oberlin Rescuers" episode that Brown referred to during interrogation? Write a documented essay on this incident in Ohio history as a result of your own investigation.
500-1000

SOME PRISONERS

No. 32   [JOHN THOMAS ALLSTADT]

This statement was made at the Courthouse, Charlestown, April 15, 1909, to an unidentified person. The following is taken from a copy in the possession of Mrs. T. G. Henkle of Halltown, W. Va., who writes: "My copy ... is one which my late husband [a relative of Mr. Allstadt] had made at the time Mr. Allstadt told the story. ... I am sure that my copy is accurate as my husband was working at the courthouse at the time."

I had gone to the "protracted meeting" that night and had not been more than an hour at home and abed when the raiders reached our house. This was, I think, between one and two o'clock. I slept upstairs; my mother and father below. The crash of the fence rail against the door woke me with a jump. My sister, Lutie Allstadt, and my second cousin, whom we always called Aunt, Miss Hannah Hall, both of whom also slept above, sprang to their windows and leaned out, "Murder!"

"Take in your heads, or I'll blow your brains out!" shouted a colored man below, leveling his gun at them as he spoke.

I was a lad of eighteen at the time; having hustled on my clothes, seized my old country gun and ran for the stairs. Aunt Hannah, clinging to me, stooped and peered down the stairway under my arm. "The men all have guns; leave that behind, or they will surely kill you!" she begged. So I dropped the gun and ran down unarmed. My mother lay in bed. The room was full of armed men. "What are you going to do?" I asked.

"Carry your father and mother to Harper's Ferry. John Brown has taken possession of the government works."

"Taken possession of the government works! That isn't much," said I. "There's only one watchman there!"

"You shut your damned mouth, or I'll blow your brains out!" Stevens exclaimed; and ordered a Negro to keep me quiet with a revolver at my breast. The Negro, collaring me, obeyed. . . .

We arrived at the Armory just about daybreak. We were not taken inside the building until several men had fallen. In the interval we were permitted to walk up and down before the engine-house east and west; but not on the east side on which were the gates.

The citizens began shooting—first at the Hall Rifle Works about nine or ten o'clock. . . . Then, the fire having become hot, Brown's men

70

began to gather in the yard. . . . And not for protection the prisoners were herded into the watch-house which was in the western division of the engine-house building. The watch-house door stood open and Coppoc sat down in the doorway; about the door and overhead was much glass. . . .

Our open watch-house door commanded a view of the trestle. Fontaine Beckham walked back and forth on the trestle, twice, or several times; but as he was unarmed no one fired on him. Now he went behind the water tank and began peering around the corner as it might be to take aim. "If he keeps on peeking I am going to shoot" said Coppoc, from his seat in the doorway. I stood close by him. Mr. Beckham peeked again and Coppoc fired, but missed. "Don't fire, man, for God's sake! They'll shoot in here and kill us all!" shrieked the prisoners behind. Some were laughing; others overwhelmed with fear. But Coppoc was already firing again. . . . This shot killed Beckham. Undoubtedly, he would not have been fired upon but for his equivocal appearance. Coppoc fired no more from the watch-house; in fact, no one remained in sight. . . .

A very few moments after this, they selected fifteen or twenty of us from the prisoners in the watch-house and brought us into the engine-house—and an uneasy little trip we thought it, in the open between door and door. John Brown now ordered one of my father's old negroes, Phil Lucker, to pick some opening in the engine-house walls to use as port holes; but no sooner was it done than the fact became evident that the citzens outside only awaited the fall of brick to fire in. So the port holes, after all, were but little used.

Shortly after our transference it began to grow dark—too dark to see to shoot accurately; but the citizens' fire continued very heavy. Darkness fell. Then they shut fast the engine-house door. We had not light. Everything grew still, except the citizens outside shouted and whooped all night long. Captain Rowan's Company, it was said, lay at the gate. In the quiet of the night young Brown died. He had begged, again and again, in the agony of his wound, to be shot; but his father replied to him: "Oh, you will get over it" and, "If you must die, die like a man."

Now, John Brown talked, from time to time, with my father and Col. Washington, but I did not hear what was said. Young Brown lay quietly in a corner. His father called to him after a time. No answer. "I guess he is dead," said Brown.

In the morning, after the colloquy of surrender and refusal, came the breaking of the door by the Marines. It is absolutely untrue that Brown had, at any time, proposed to put his prisoners to the fore in case of attack. . . . Brown himself, at the moment of the breaking of the door, was just back of the engine. I could not tell who shot Quinn, but I did see that Coppoc fired, as Green knocked the gun up and it went off in the air. Green instantly slashed at Brown—at his head—with his sword, and the same sweeping stroke that cut Brown's head nicked my father's hat-band. I well remember Green's apology to my father, as we got outside, and asking to be allowed to get my father a new hat. Brown fell as Green struck him, and did not rise again.

The Marines had bayonets, but did not use them. Of course, in such an excitement, no one person was likely to see all that happened. . . . As the Marines swarmed in, and the call for surrender came, Coppoc and the rest threw down their guns; but while the parley for surrender had been going on earlier, at the door, no one of Brown's men spoke of surrender. After we were taken outside they asked me to go over to the Wager House to see if I could identify the prisoner. It was Stevens. A heavy guard stood at his door to prevent a repeating of the Thompson affair, which was disapproved. Mrs. Fouke had come out with her servant and carried Stevens into the Wager House, from the street. She was the most kind-hearted person alive. The dog in the engine-house, that belonged to Brown's party, was a big, black, mongrel fellow, with white feet and a white stripe down his back; he was not cross. The men of Brown's party did not fire from the hip, but dropped to one knee, aimed and shot. . . . When the breakfast came in from the Wager House, my father and Col. Washington remarked that it might be poisoned, and refused it; but I and a good many others ate. Fontaine Beckham had no slaves. I heard nothing of the Baylor matter, but it is indisputably true that the militia were afraid to storm the engine-house. A very few minutes after we chosen prisoners were removed from the watchhouse, the Martinsburg Company came and kicked open the window and let the other prisoners out. "Are there any of Brown's men in here?" they called (I heard them). "No; they are all in the other part," the prisoners called back. When we were taken away, no guard was left over the remainder, and there was no door between engine-house and watch-house. Therefore, they could have walked out, or climbed out themselves; but they did not know what might be outside. And Brown's men did not come around in front where there was any chance for the engine-house garrison to get a shot at them.

Be careful not to mix the terms "Arsenal" and "Armory." The engine-house was in the Armory enclosure—the Arsenal across the street.

They did not close the engine-house door until dark. The window of the watch-house was on the west side.

No. 33   [LIND F. CURRIE]

The Mason Report, Appendix, pp. 54-59

[Jan. 11, 1860]

LIND F. CURRIE sworn and examined.

. . . I live about 3½ miles from Charlestown . . . ; I am a farmer there. In connection with my farming operations I have been also teaching school. . . . On Monday the 17th of October last . . . an armed party appeared at the school-house . . . There were . . . Cook and Tidd, and . . . Leeman . . . [and some negroes]. They were all fully armed. . . . Cook . . . demanded possession of the school-house [half-way between the Kennedy farm and the Ferry]. . . . Cook said their intention was to free the negroes; that they intended to adopt such measures as would effectually free them, though he said nothing about running them off or anything of that kind. He said . . . that those slave-holders who would give up their slaves voluntarily would meet with protection, but those who refused . . . would be quartered upon and their property confiscated. . . . I asked Cook . . . "With how many men did you commence this foray down there?" He . . . said, "I do not know. . . . ; there may be 5,000 or . . . 10,000 for aught I know." . . . That Gerrit Smith knew of it, and was interested in it, and also Fred Douglass. . . . He said . . . that the efforts would be strong now . . . to extirpate the institution of slavery from the entire land. . . . He said, "We, as a little band, may perish in this attempt, but . . . there are thousands ready at all times to occupy our places, and to step into the breach." . . . It is our design to use every effort to disseminate our sentiments . . . among you in different ways; we will send our people among you as colporteurs and peddlers, and we will place them in your pulpits and schools . . . and by such means circulate our opinions and sentiments. . . .

No. 34   [TERENCE BYRNE]
The Mason Report, Appendix, pp. 13-21

[Jan. 6, 1860]
. . . . QUESTION. Did you have any conversation with
Brown while you were [a prisoner] in the engine-house, or did you hear
him conversing . . . on the subject of what brought him there, or what
he expected or intended to do?
ANSWER. Yes, sir; . . . a great deal. . . . I cannot recollect one
fifth part. . . . At one time I heard him remark: "Gentlemen, if you
knew my past history, you would not blame me for being here," or
something to that effect. He then went on to state that he had gone to
Kansas a peaceable man, and was hunted down like a wolf by the
pro-slavery men from Virginia and Kentucky, and he lost some members of his family; I think he said a son; "and now," said he, "I am
here." At that time he did not say for what purpose. . . .

No. 35   [DANIEL WHELAN]
The Mason Report, Appendix, pp. 21-23

[Jan. 6, 1860]
. . . I was a watchman at the Armory gate on Sunday
night. . . . [They] told me to be very quiet and still . . . or else they
would put me to eternity. . . . The head man of them, Brown, ordered
all the men to dispatch out of the yard, but he left a man at each side
of the big gate along with himself . . . and then he said, "I came here
from Kansas, and this is a Slave State; I want to free all the negroes in
this State; I have possession now of the United States Armory, and if
the citizens interfere with me, I must only burn the town and have
blood." . . .

No. 36   [COL. LEWIS W. WASHINGTON]
The Mason Report, Appendix, pp. 29-40

[Jan. 6, 1860]
. . . They appeared at my chamber door about half past
one o'clock in the morning. . . . I was in bed and asleep. As I opened
the door there were four armed men with their guns drawn. . . . The
person in command turned out to be Stevens. He asked me my name,
and then referred to a man of the name of Cook, who had been at

my house before, to know whether I was Colonel Washington. On being told that I was, he said, "You are our prisoner." I looked around, and the only thing that astonished me particularly was the presence of this man Cook, who had been at my house some three or four weeks before that. . . . When I asked for him at the Ferry [after that] they told me he had left, and I supposed . . . he had gone to Kansas, as he told me he intended to go in a few days. . . .

I only knew Cook's name at the time. I afterwards learned the others. The party consisted of Stevens, Cook, Tidd, Taylor, and the negro man Shields Green. There was a sixth man whom I did not see; but Cook afterwards told me his name was Meriam. He was engaged in hitching up the horses, as I understood. . . .

After looking around I observed that each man had two revolvers. . . . I remarked to them, "You are a very bold looking set of fellows, but I should doubt your courage; you have too many arms to take one man." I said to one of them, "I believe with a pop-gun I could take either of you in your shirt tail." At that time the fire began falling from the flambeau [the raiders carried], and I asked them to come in my room and light my candles. . . . After going in, and while dressing myself, I said, "Possibly you will have the courtesy to tell me what this means; it is really a myth to me." Stevens . . . said, "We have come here for the purpose of liberating all the slaves of the South. . . ." . . . I went on deliberately and dressed myself, and went into the dining room, and . . . Stevens said to me, "You have some fire-arms, have you not? . . . I want them." . . . They took them. Then Stevens said to me, "Have you a watch, sir?" . . . Said I, "You shall not have it." Said he, "Take care, sir. . . . Have you money?" . . . I then said to him, ". . . [You] told me your purpose was philanthropic, but you did not mention . . . that it was robbery and rascality. I do not choose to surrender my watch." He yielded the point. . . . After some little time they announced to me that my carriage was ready at the door.

. . . [the] carriage drove into the Armory yard nearly opposite the engine-house. . . . [Brown] said, "I presume you are Mr. Washington. . . . It is too dark to see to write at this time, but . . . I shall require you to write to some of your friends to send a stout, able-bodied negro; I think after a while, possibly, I shall . . . release you, but only on the condition of getting your friends to send in a negro man as a ransom. . . . I may get the worst of it in my first encounter, and if so, your life is worth as much as mine. . . . My particular reason for taking you first was that, as the aid to the governor of Virginia, I knew you

would endeavor to perform your duty, and perhaps you would have
been a troublesome customer to me; and, apart from that, I wanted
you particularly for the moral effect it would give our cause, having
one of your name as a prisoner." . . .

[My negroes] were brought in to the fire. The engine-house and the
watch-house are divided by a wall. I should suppose the engine-house
to be perhaps 22 or 24 feet square. The engine-house being partitioned
off, is of course about 22 or 24 feet, as the other may be, the one way,
by about 10 the other. The stove was in the small watch-house. The
engine-house and watch-house are divided. They are under the same
roof—a wall between them. There is no communication between them
through that wall. The servants were all taken into the engine-house,
and we into the watch-house, but they came in repeatedly to warm
themselves, each negro having a pike in his hand. . . . I went in there
about twelve o'clock on Monday, noon, and I was in there until Tuesday at seven. I was taken into the watch-house first, but he took us
out as hostages about eleven or twelve o'clock on Monday. . . .

There was only one negro of his party in the engine-house. There
were several slaves, but only one of his party, . . . Shields Green. . . .
[He was armed] like the rest, with a rifle and revolver, and a butcher
knife in his sheath. . . . [He fired] very rapidly and diligently. . . .
[His deportment] was rather impudent in the morning. . . . But when
the attack came on, he had thrown off his hat and all his equipments,
and was endeavoring to represent himself as one of the slaves. . . .

THE MILITARY

No. 37 [COLONEL R. E. LEE]

The Mason Report, Appendix, pp. 40-44

HEADQUARTERS HARPER'S FERRY
October 19, 1859.

COLONEL: . . . on arriving here on the night of the 17th instant, in obedience to Special Orders No. 194 of that date from your office, I learned that a party of insurgents, about 11 p.m. on the 16th, had seized the watchmen stationed at the armory, arsenal, rifle factory, and bridge across the Potomac, and taken possession of those points. They then dispatched six men, under . . . Captain Aaron C. Stevens, to arrest the principal citizens in the neighborhood and incite the negroes to join in the insurrection. The party took Colonel L. W. Washington from his bed about 1½ a.m. on the 17th, and brought him, with four of his servants, to this place. Mr. J. H. Allstadt and six of his servants were in the same manner seized about 3 a.m., and arms placed in the hands of the negroes. Upon their return here, John E. Cook, one of the party sent to Mr. Washington's, was dispatched to Maryland, with Mr. Washington's wagon, two of his servants, and three of Mr. Allstadt's, for arms and ammunition, &c. As day advanced, and the citizens . . . commenced their usual avocations, they were separately captured, to the number of forty, . . . and confined in one room of the fire-engine house of the armory, which seems early to have been selected as a point of defense. About 11 a.m. the volunteer companies from Virginia began to arrive, and the Jefferson Guards and volunteers from Charlestown . . . I understood, were first on the ground. The Hamtramck Guards, . . . ; the Shepherdstown troop, . . . ; and Captain Alburtis's company from Martinsburg arrived in the afternoon. These companies, under . . . Colonels R. W. Baylor and John T. Gibson, forced the insurgents to abandon their positions at the bridge and in the village, and to withdraw within the armory inclosure, where they fortified themselves in the fire-engine house, and carried ten of their prisoners for the purpose of insuring their safety and facilitating their escape, whom they termed hostages. . . . After sunset more troops arrived. . . . from Winchester and . . . from Fredericktown, Maryland, ... Later in the evening the companies from Baltimore . . . and a detachment of marines, commanded by Lieutenant J. Green accompanied by Major Russell, of that corps, reached Sandy Hook, about 1½ mile east

77

of Harper's Ferry. At this point I came up with these last-named troops, and leaving General Edgerton and his command on the Maryland side of the river for the night, caused the marines to proceed to Harper's Ferry, and placed them within the armory grounds to prevent the possibility of the escape of the insurgents. Having taken measures to halt, in Baltimore, the artillery companies ordered from Fort Monroe, I made preparations to attack the insurgents at daylight. But for fear of sacrificing the lives of some of the gentlemen held by them as prisoners in a midnight assault, I should have ordered the attack at once.

Their safety was the subject of painful consideration, and to prevent, if possible, jeopardizing their lives, I determined to summon the insurgents to surrender. As soon after daylight as the arrangements were made Lieutenant J. E. B. Stuart, 1st Cavalry, . . . was dispatched, under a flag, with a written summons. . . . Knowing the character of the leader of the insurgents, I did not expect it would be accepted. I had therefore directed that the volunteer troops, . . . should be paraded on the lines assigned them outside the armory, and had prepared a storming party of twelve marines, under their commander, Lieutenant Green, and had placed them close to the engine-house, and secure from its fire. Three marines were furnished with sledge-hammers to break in the doors, and the men were instructed how to distinguish our citizens from the insurgents; to attack with the bayonet, and not to injure the blacks detained in custody unless they resisted. Lieutenant Stuart was also directed not to receive from the insurgents any counter propositions. If they accepted the terms offered, they must immediately deliver up their arms and release their prisoners. If they did not, he must, on leaving the engine-house, give me the signal. My object was, with a view of saving our citizens, to have as short an interval as possible between the summons and attacks. The summons, as I had anticipated, was rejected. At the concerted signal the storming party moved quickly to the doors and commenced the attack. The fire-engines within the house had been placed by the besieged close to the doors. The doors were fastened by ropes, the spring of which prevented their being broken by the blows of the hammers. The men were therefore ordered to . . . use as a battering-ram a heavy ladder, with which they dashed in a part of the door and gave admittance to the storming party. The fire of the insurgents up to this time had been harmless. At the threshold one marine fell mortally wounded. The rest, led by Lieutenant Green and Major Russell, quickly ended the contest. The insurgents that resisted were bayoneted. Their leader John Brown, was cut down by the sword of Lieutenant Green, and our citizens were protected by both officers and men. The whole was over in a few minutes.

After our citizens were liberated and the wounded cared for, Lieutenant Mills, of . . . Maryland . . . with the Baltimore . . . Greys, . . . was sent on the Maryland side of the river to search for John E. Cook, and to bring in the arms, &c., belonging to the insurgent party, which were said to be deposited in a school-house 2½ miles distant. Subsequently, Lieutenant J. E. B. Stuart, with a party of marines, was dispatched to the Kennedy farm . . . in Maryland, about 4½ miles from Harper's Ferry, which had been rented by John Brown, and used as the depot. . . . Colonel Mills saw nothing of Cook, but found the boxes of arms (Sharps carbines and belt revolvers) and recovered Mr. Washington's wagon and horses. Lieutenant Stuart found also at the Kennedy farm a number of sword pikes, blankets, shoes, tents, and all the necessaries for a campaign. These articles have been deposited in the government storehouse at the armory.

. . . [It] appears that the party consisted of nineteen men—fourteen white and five black. That they were headed by John Brown, of some notoriety in Kansas, who in June last located himself in Maryland, at the Kennedy farm, where he has been engaged in preparing to capture the United States works at Harper's Ferry. He avows that his object was the liberation of the slaves of Virginia, and of the whole South; and acknowledges that he has been disappointed in his expectations of aid from the black as well as white population, both in the Southern and Northern States. . . .

I inclose a copy of the "Provisional Constitution and ordinances for the People of the United States," of which there were a large number prepared for issue by the insurgents. . . .

R. E. LEE, *Colonel Commanding.*

[To] Colonel S. Cooper,
Adjutant General, U.S. Army, Washington, D.C. . . .

No. 38   [COLONEL R. W. BAYLOR]

The Richmond [Va.] *Enquirer,* Fri., Oct. 28, 1859

CHARLESTOWN, Oct. 22d, 1859.

HON. HENRY A. WISE, Governor of Virginia: Sir—
. . . on the morning of the 17th instant . . . I immediately proceeded to the scene of action. In passing through Charlestown I met Colonel

Gibson, with the Jefferson Guards under arms. We proceeded to Hall Town . . . where the citizens . . . informed me [that] I could proceed no further with the train, as . . . the Winchester [and] also the Baltimore and Ohio Railroad track had been taken up. [That] they had taken 75 or 100 of our citizens prisoners, and had carried off many of our slaves. Thereupon I issued the following order to Col. L. T. Moore, of the 31st Regiment of Virginia Militia: "Sir—You are ordered to muster all the volunteer forces under your command, fully armed, and equipped, and report to me, forthwith, at Harper's Ferry." I placed the above order in charge of . . . the conductor on the Winchester road, and directed him to return with his train to Winchester, and deliver the order to Col. Moore. I proceeded on, with the few troops we had under arms, to Harper's Ferry, where we arrived about 12 o'clock. I found the citizens in very great excitement. By this time, the insurgents occupied all the lower part of the town, had their sentinels posted on all the different streets. . . . I here formed two companies of the citizens, and placed them under the command of Captain Lawson Botts and Captain John Avis. Their forces were variously estimated from 300 to 500 strong, armed with Sharps rifles and revolvers.

I detached the Jefferson Guards, under . . . Capt. Rowan, and ordered them to cross the Potomac River, in boats, about two miles above Harper's Ferry, and march down on the Maryland side, and take possession of the Bridge, and permit no one to pass. This order was strictly executed. The command under Capt. Botts was ordered to pass down the hill below Jefferson's Rock, and take possession of the Shenandoah Bridge—to leave a strong guard at that point, and to march down to the Galt House, in rear of the Arsenal building, in which we supposed their men were lodged. Capt. Avis's command was ordered to take possession of the houses directly in front of the Arsenal; both of the above commands were promptly executed. By this movement we prevented any escape. . . . About four o'clock we were reinforced by the arrival of the Hamtramck Guards, under the command of Capt. Butler, the Shepherdstown Troop, under the command of Capt. Reinhart, and some 30 citizens of Martinsburg, under the command of Capt. Alburtis. I ordered Capt. Alburtis to march down Potomac street through the Armory yard to the Arsenal. The Hamtramck Guards, and the Shepherdstown Troop (dismounted, and armed with muskets) under my command, proceeded down High Street to the centre of the town in front of the Arsenal. During this march, the insurgents having secreted themselves in the engine-house in the Armory yard,

opened a brisk fire on Captain Alburtis' company. The fire was quickly
returned by Capt. Alburtis' company, who behaved very bravely. The
different companies near at hand rallied to Capt. Alburtis' rescue.

The firing at this time was heavy, and the insurgents could not have
retained their position many minutes, when they presented at the
door a white flag. The firing thereupon ceased and I ordered the troops
to draw up in line in front of the Arsenal. During this engagement
and the previous skirmishes, we had ten men wounded, two I fear
mortally. The insurgents had eleven killed, one mortally wounded, and
two taken prisoners; leaving only five in the engine-house, and one
of them seriously wounded.

In this engagement we rescued about thirty of our citizens whom
they held as prisoners in the guard-house—they still held in the engine-
house ten citizens and five slaves.

Immediately after the troops were withdrawn, Capt. Brown sent to
me . . . a verbal communication stating that if I would permit him
to cross the bridge with his prisoners to some point beyond, he would
set them at liberty. I sent him the following reply . . . : ". . . Sir: The
terms you proposed I cannot accept. Under no consideration will I
consent to a removal of our citizens across the river. The only negotiations upon which I will consent to treat are those which have been
previously proposed to you. ROBERT W. BAYLOR, Col. Commandant
[3rd Regiment Cavalry]."

These terms he declined. Night by this time had set in, and the
weather being very inclement, I thought it best . . . to cease operations
for the night. Should I have ordered an attack at that hour and in
total darkness, our troops would have been as likely to have murdered
our own citizens as the insurgents, all being in the [engine-house].
Having concluded to postpone another attack until morning, guards
were posted . . . and every precaution taken to prevent escape. Our
troops by this time required some refreshment, having been on active
duty and exposed to a heavy fall of rain all day. A little after night we
were reinforced by Col. L. T. Moore . . . ; also three companies from
Frederick, Maryland, under the command of Col. Shiver. About 12
o'clock Col. Lee arrived, having under his command eighty-five Marines
from Washington. The Government troops took possession of the
Government property, and formed inside the Armory yard, . . . close
. . . to the engine-house. In this position Col. Lee thought it best to
remain until morning. The night passed with . . . intense excitement.
It was agreed between Col. Lee and myself that the volunteer forces

should form around on the outside of the Government property, and clear the streets . . . and to remain in that position whilst he would attack the engine-house with his Marines. . . .

I feel it my duty . . . to state that the arms in the possession of the volunteer companies . . . are almost worthless. I do not think we have 100 muskets in the county of Jefferson—a border county. . . . With such arms as we have, it is butchery to require our troops to face an enemy much better equipped. Col. Moore . . . informs me . . . that out of 135 men on duty, he had not thirty pieces that would fire with any effect. . . .

Knowing the general interest that will be felt throughout the State, and to vindicate the honor and valor of the troops under my command, I have been more than necessarily minute in this report. I am pleased to inform you that they obeyed every order with alacrity, and with . . . full determination. . . . /ROBERT W. BAYLOR/ Col. Commanding the Va. Troops at Harper's Ferry.

No. 39   [COLONEL J. T. GIBSON]

The Richmond [Va.] *Enquirer*, Fri., Oct. 28, 1859

HARPER'S FERRY, Oct. 18, 1859.

HENRY A. WISE, Governor of Virginia: Sir: Your order . . . dated . . . the 17th inst. . . . was not received till about 11 o'clock A.M. today, in consequence of the telegraphic posts round here having been cut. . . . On the morning of the 17th I received information at Charlestown that a band of abolitionists from the North had taken possession of the Arsenal and workshops . . . here. . . . I immediately ordered out the Jefferson Guard and the citizens of Charlestown, which order was quickly responded to, and by 10 o'clock A.M. they were armed and en route. . . . We left Charlestown with about 1000 men, and on reaching Hall Town . . . learned that the insurgents were in large numbers, and we at once dispatched orders to Col. L. F. Moore of Frederick County and to the "Hamtramck Guards" and Shepherdstown Troop to reinforce immediately. We reached Harper's Ferry about 11½ A.M. and took our position on Camp Hill. We immediately dispatched the Jefferson Guards, commanded to Capt. J. W. Rowan, . . . to cross the Potomac River, about a mile west of the Ferry, and march down on the Maryland side and take possession of the Potomac bridge; and a company of the citizens of Charlestown and vicinity, commanded by Capt. L. Botts, . . . to cross the Winchester and Potomac

Railroad, by way of Jefferson's Rock, to take possession of the Galt House, in the rear of the Arsenal, and commanding the entrance to the Armory yard. Capt. John Avis and R. B. Washington, Esq., with a handful of men, were ordered to take possession of the houses commanding the yard of the Arsenal. All these orders were promptly and successfully executed. The bridge across the Shenandoah River and that of the Baltimore and Ohio Railroad, at the west end of the trestle work, and the street leading from the rifle factory, were guarded by small attachments of men. Between three and four o'clock P.M. the Hamtramck Guards, Shepherdstown Troop, and a company from Martinsburg commanded by Capt. E. Alburtis arrived on the ground. The company from Winchester, commanded by Capt. B. B. Washington, did not arrive till late in the evening. [The] insurgents . . . retired with their prisoners into the guard house and engine room, just inside the gate of the Armory yard, which was firmly locked. About three o'clock P.M. the enemy, with the most prominent of their prisoners, concentrated in the engine room, leaving a large number of their prisoners fastened up in the guard-house. At this point, and after the arrival of the reinforcements from Shepherdstown and Martinsburg, Col. R. W. Baylor assumed command. . . . /JNO. THOS. GIBSON/ Com'dt 55th Regiment.

No. 40   [CAPTAIN ALBURTIS]

The Richmond Enquirer, Tues., Oct. 25, 1859

We received intelligence of this affair at Martinsburg, Va., at about one o'clock P.M. on Monday. A meeting was at once convened at the Court House, and volunteers were called for. . . . A great many immediately stepped out . . . and by a motion . . . they selected me to command them. We took the train . . . at two P.M. and arrived here . . . at three o'clock. We came along the upper ravine from the railroad, coming into Bolivar, where we were joined by a company from Shepherdstown. They preceded us . . . into the street. We came down and received orders from Lieut. Col. Baylor . . . that the company from Shepherdstown should take the street coming into Harper's Ferry, taking the gates. They to enter the gates and meet us along at the musket factory. We entered at the upper end of the shops, and after some consultation . . . I directed that 25 men should proceed down the main avenue; that a similar number should take the rear of the shops; and that the remainder should proceed through the shops or in any way that they could get. We came on down, the party a little in advance of myself. Upon our arrival between the first and second buildings on the right from the direction of the hotel, they were fired upon by the ruffians from between the engine-house in the Armory yard and the palings. The fire was immediately returned and the men retreated into the engine-house, keeping up a sharp fire by opening the door from three to five inches. The fire was briskly returned by our men, eight of whom were wounded; two, it is feared, mortally. . . .

During this fight there were confined in the building [guard room] adjoining the engine-house some thirty or forty prisoners. . . . The windows were broken open by this party, and they succeeded in making their escape. When this window was broken open the whole party was in the engine-house, and we could have ended the business, but we were not supported by the other companies. Immediately afterwards there was a flag of truce sent out by these men, and I think Stevens bore it, and was shot three times as he advanced between two armed men. . . . Having heard by this time, however, that the United States Marines and a number of troops from Baltimore were then on the way, we refused to accede to their proposition, and stationed guards round to prevent their escape. All this time we had a small piece of cannon in range, but were directed not to bring it to bear upon them because of there being seven men held by them. . . . In the morning the Marines took charge of the matter. What struck me as strange was that these men did not fire a single gun whilst they [the Marines] were getting into position. The Marines marched into the yard immediately in front of the engine-house door, through which they had fired the previous afternoon. . . .

No. 41   [LIEUTENANT J. E. B. STUART]

Letter by J. E. B. Stuart to his mother, Jan., 1860. H. B. McClellan, *The Life and Campaigns of Major General J. E. B. Stuart* (Boston and New York, 1885), pp. 29-30

Colonel Lee was sent to command the forces at Harper's Ferry. I volunteered as his aid. I had no command whatever. The United States Marines are a branch of the naval force—there was not an enlisted man of the army on hand. Lieutenant Green was sent in command. Major Russell had been requested by the Secretary of the Navy to accompany the marines, but being a paymaster, could exercise no command; yet it was his corps. For Colonel Lee to have put me in command of the storming party would have been an outrage to Lieutenant Green, which would have rung through the navy for twenty years. As well might they send him out here [Kansas] to command my company of cavalry. . . .

I, too, had a part to perform, which prevented me in a measure from participating in the very brief onset made so gallantly by Green and Russell, well backed by their men. I was deputed by Colonel Lee to read to the leader, then called *Smith,* a demand to surrender immediately; and I was instructed to leave the door after his refusal, which was expected, and wave my cap; at which signal the storming party was to advance, batter open the doors, and capture the insurgents at the point of the bayonet. Colonel Lee cautioned the stormers particularly to discriminate between the insurgents and their prisoners.

I approached the door in the presence of perhaps two thousand spectators, and told *Mr. Smith* that I had a communication for him from Colonel Lee. He opened the door about four inches and placed his body against the crack, with a cocked carbine in his hand: hence his remark after his capture that he could have wiped me out like a mosquito. The parley was a long one. He presented his propositions in every possible shape, and with admirable tact; but all amounted to this: that the only condition upon which he would surrender was that he and his party should be allowed to escape. Some of his prisoners begged me to ask Colonel Lee to come and see him. I told them he would never accede to any terms but those he had offered; and as soon as I could tear myself away from their importunities I left the door and waved my cap, and Colonel Lee's plan was carried out. . . .

When "Smith" first came to the door I recognized old *Osawatomie Brown,* who had given us so much trouble in Kansas. No one present but myself could have performed that service. I got his bowie-knife from his person, and have it yet. . . .

No. 42   [LIEUTENANT GREEN]

Israel Green, ''The Capture of John Brown,'' *The North American Review,* CXLI (Dec., 1885), pp. 564-569

. . . With a detachment of ninety marines, I started for Harper's Ferry that afternoon on the 3:30 train, taking with me two howitzers. It was a beautiful clear autumn day, and the men, exhilarated by the excitement of the occasion, which came after a long, dull season of confinement in the barracks, enjoyed the trip exceedingly.

At Frederick Junction I received a dispatch from Colonel Robert E.
Lee. . . . He directed me to proceed to Sandy Hook . . . and there
await his arrival. At ten o'clock in the evening he came up. . . . His
first order was to form the marines out of the car, and march from the
bridge to Harper's Ferry. This we did, entering the enclosure of the
arsenal grounds through a back gate. At eleven o'clock Colonel Lee
ordered the volunteers to march out of the grounds, and gave control
inside to the marines, with instructions to see that none of the insurgents
escaped. . . . Brown and his men kept quiet during the night. At half-
past six in the morning Colonel Lee gave me orders to select a detail
of twelve men for a storming party, and place them near the engine-
house. . . . The engine-house was a strong stone building . . . perhaps
thirty feet by thirty-five. In the front were two large double-doors, between which was a stone abutment. Within were two old-fashioned
heavy fire-engines, with a hose-cart and reel standing between them,
and just back of the abutment between the doors. They were double-
battened doors, very strongly made. . . . Lieutenant J. E. B. Stuart . . .
was ordered to go . . . to the front of the engine-house and demand
the surrender of the insurgent party. . . . On the way to the engine-
house, Stuart and myself agreed upon a signal for attack in the event
that Brown should refuse. . . . Stuart would wave his hat, which was
then, I believe, one very similar to the famous chapeau which he wore
throughout the war. I had my storming party ranged alongside of
the engine-house, and a number of men were provided with sledge-
hammers. . . . I stood in front of the abutment between the doors.
Stuart hailed Brown and called for his surrender, but Brown at once
began to make a [counter]-proposition . . . . Suddenly . . . Stuart waved
his hat, and I gave the order to my men to batter in the door. Very
little impression was made with the hammers . . . and in a few minutes
I gave the order to desist. Just then my eye caught sight of a ladder, lying
a few feet from the engine-house, in the yard, and I ordered my men
to catch it up and use it as a battering-ram. The reserve of twelve men
I employed as a supporting column for the assaulting party. The men
took hold bravely and made a tremendous assault upon the door. The
second blow broke it in. . . . I instantly stepped from my position . . .
and entered the opening made by the ladder. . . . [Upon] reflection I
should say that Brown had just emptied his carbine at the point broken
by the ladder, and so I passed in safely. . . . The first person I saw was
Colonel Lewis Washington, who was standing near the hose-cart, at
the front of the engine-house. On one knee, a few feet to the left, knelt
a man with a carbine in his hand, just pulling the lever to reload.

"Hello, Green," said Colonel Washington, and he reached out his hand to me. I grasped it with my left hand, having my saber uplifted in my right, and he said, pointing to the kneeling figure, "This is Osawatomie."

As he said this, Brown turned his head to see who it was. . . . Quicker than thought I brought my saber down with all my strength upon his head. He was moving as the blow fell, and I suppose I did not strike him where I intended, for he received a deep saber cut in the back of the neck. He fell senseless on his side, then rolled over on his back. He had in his hand a short Sharps-cavalry carbine. I think he had just fired as I reached Colonel Washington, for the marine who followed me into the aperture made by the ladder received a bullet in the abdomen, from which he died in a few minutes. The shot might have been fired by some one else . . . but I think it was from Brown. Instinctively as Brown fell I gave him a saber thrust in the left breast. The sword I carried was a light uniform weapon, and, either not having a point or striking something hard . . . , did not penetrate. The blade bent double.

By that time three or four of my men were inside. . . . They bayoneted one man skulking under the engine, and pinned another fellow up against the rear wall, both being instantly killed. I ordered the men to spill no more blood. The other insurgents were at once taken under arrest, and the contest ended. The whole fight had not lasted over three minutes. . . .

I saw very little of the situation within until the fight was over. Then I observed that the engine-house was thick with smoke, and it was with difficulty that a person could be seen across the room. In the rear, behind the left-hand engine, were huddled the prisoners. . . . Colonel Washington was one of these. . . . When I met him he was as cool as he would have been on his own veranda entertaining guests. . . . I remember that he would not come out . . . , begrimed and soiled as he was . . . , until he had put a pair of kid gloves upon his hands. . . .

Colonel Lee . . . stood on a slight elevation, about forty feet from the engine-house, during the assault. He was in civilian dress and . . . wore no beard, except a dark mustache, and his hair was slightly gray. He had no arms upon his person, and treated the affair as one of no very great consequence. . . . A part of the scene, giving color and life to the picture, was the bright blue uniform of the marines. They wore blue trousers then, as they do now, and a dark blue frock-coat. Their belts were white, and they wore French fatigue caps. . . . We had no use for the howitzers. . . .

I had little conversation with [Brown] and spent very little time with

him. . . . I can only recall the fleeting picture of an old man kneeling
with a carbine in his hand, with a long gray beard falling away from
his face, looking quickly and keenly toward the danger that he was
aware had come upon him. He was not a large man, being perhaps
five feet ten inches when he straightened up in full. His dress, even, I
do not remember distinctly. I should say that he had his trousers tucked
in his boots, and that he wore clothes of gray—probably no more than
trousers and shirt. I think he had no hat upon his head.

. . . Brown had . . . only five or six fighting men, and I think he
himself was the only one who showed fight, after I entered the engine-
house. There were no provisions in the building, and it would have
been only a question of time when Brown would have had to surrender. . . .

No. 43

The Shepherdstown [Va.] *Register*, Sat., Oct. 29, 1859

The following correspondence, between Capt. Butler and
Col. Baylor, we clip from *The Baltimore Sun:*

Jefferson Co. Oct. 26, 1859
To The Editors of *The Baltimore Sun:*

Having heard from various quarters, even from as far as Baltimore
city, reports that the Hamtramck Guards, which I command, had behaved in a cowardly manner at the late disturbance at Harper's Ferry,
I request that you will publish the following correspondence between
Col. Robt. W. Baylor, who was in command on that day, and myself. . . . I should state . . . that Lt. Lee had command of my second
platoon after I went up in the house with the first.

V. M. Butler,
Capt. Hamtramck Guards,

Shepherdstown, Oct. 22nd, 1859
Col. Robt. W. Baylor—Sir—As there have been circulated reports
prejudicial to the Hamtramck Guards, which I have the honor to
command, . . . will you please answer the following questions cate-
gorically?—

Did you give any order to me that I did not report to my company,
and was not said order promptly executed by the Hamtramck Guards?

Did you not order me to take possession of the house adjoining the engine-house, and to fire from the windows of the same upon the insurgents below?

Did I not promptly obey said orders?

Did you not peremptorily countermand the order of Lt. Lee to charge upon the insurgents?

Did you in a conversation with Gov. Wise state that much praise was due to the Charlestown and Martinsburg Companies, withholding any mention of my company . . . ?

By promptly answering the above questions you will very much oblige your ob't serv't.

> V. M. Butler
> Capt. Hamtramck Guards

Wood End, Oct. 22, 1859

Capt. V. M. Butler—Dear Sir—It affords me much pleasure to answer your questions. I did not give any order to my knowledge, which was not strictly obeyed, by your company. If my recollection serves me, I did direct you to send a portion of your men up stairs in the house adjoining the engine-house.

Having at that time pressed on myself to the gate I am not certain whether you went up stairs or not, but my impression is that you did for when I returned I found Lt. Lee standing in front of the engine-house with his company, and I recollected perfectly of having ordered him to withdraw further back. In answer to your last question, my official report will be the best answer. I reported to Governor Wise the following: During the march the insurgents opened a brisk fire on Capt. Alburtis' company, who behaved very bravely. The balance of the troops being near at hand, rallied to his rescue. The firing at this time was heavy, and the insurgents would not have retained their position many moments longer, when they presented at the door a white flag; the firing thereupon ceased. The above is copied from my official report to Gov. Wise, and in that I speak of all the companies alike, except the Martinsburg company. . . .

> Robt. W. Baylor
> Col. Third Regt. Cavalry

No. 44   [A LETTER TO THE EDITOR]

The Shepherdstown [Va.] *Register,* Sat., Oct. 29, 1859

Mr. Zittle—There seems to be considerable talk and gossip through some parts of this community about the conduct of the Hamtramck Guards, at Harper's Ferry during the insurrection there. Being an eye witness to the whole affair, after the arrival of the above company, I deem it but my duty to make a statement through the columns of your paper, of facts concerning the affair, which must exonerate the Guards, from the malicious accusations enviously heaped upon them.

The Hamtramck Guards, commanded by Capt. Butler, got to the Ferry about 4 o'clock on Monday, entering through Bolivar, by direction of Col. Baylor. While they were marching down the hill, entering Harper's Ferry, there were shouts ahead for them to "come on." Capt. Butler ordered the company to march by "double quick time," and at the command they marched forward until they were commanded to "halt" near the front of the Armory buildings, to wait for further orders from the Colonel.

The next order was for Capt. Butler to take his men into a building nearby, to fire down upon the insurgents, which he did, leaving a portion in the street. A few guns were fired from the house—when they were ordered to cease firing—fearing the safety of prisoners; by that fire, however, one of the insurgents was killed in the engine-house.

The company was again taken into the street, where Capt. Butler waited for further orders, but such was the state of excitement, that he could get none from the Officer in command.

All the commands given during the evening, were from a sett [*sic*] of drunken fellows, whooping and bellowing like a pack of maddened bulls, evidently too drunk, many of them, to hold their guns.

During this excitement, the Martinsburg party, drunken and maddened, made an attack upon a building, where there were many prisoners (but no insurgents), and released the prisoners, who could have done it themselves, had they not been too cowardly; and while this party were getting away from the building some of their own party opened fire upon them, and this accounts for the killed and wounded from Martinsburg.

Late in the evening, Col. Baylor called for twenty Volunteers to storm the engine-house (but wanted some other person to command them, however), but could not get a single man, from all the brave and bold from Martinsburg, Harper's Ferry, and Charlestown. During all this time Capt. Butler, of the Hamtramck Guards, was calm, collected and unmoved, as were all his men, who were at their posts, ready for any order from their Captain. . . .

And where were the Charlestown Guards all this time? Why, scattered in every direction. Their Capt. could not get them in ranks, and did not the whole evening; all that were kept together were held at their posts by their Officers; such was the bravery of that company. And for the Harper's Ferry men, they have not got a man who will stand his ground a moment, or they would not have permitted a negro to hold possession of their main street, some six hours; and at last a preacher had to shoot him. . . .

An Observer

No. 45   [GOVERNOR WISE]

Speech in Richmond, Fri., Oct. 21, 1859, from *The Richmond Enquirer,* Tues., Oct. 25, 1859

. . . The volunteers of Jefferson, with Cols. Baylor and Gibson, rushed to the scene, and soon came the men of Berkeley, unorganized, in working-day dress and without arms or munition, supposing they could get arms and fixed ammunition at the Arsenal. . . . But with what arms they had, they attacked them. . . . They could have stormed and taken them in an hour, but they were anxious for the lives and safety of their neighbors and friends who were under the muzzles and knives of the ruffians, and they were restrained by their apprehensions that they might be slaughtered by the desperadoes. By this hesitation they allowed the insurgents to hold the Arsenal all day Monday. On Monday night that gallant and noble Virginian, Colonel Robert Lee . . . arrived with his regular corps of marines. He waited only for light, then tendered the assault, in State pride, to the Virginia volunteers who were there. Their feelings for the prisoners made them decline the risk of slaying their own friends, and Lee could not delay a moment to retake the Arsenal. . . . His gallantry was mortified that the task was so easy. He saw a United States Arsenal in possession of bandits . . . and he felt the regular army and his native State were alike dishonored. With mortification and chagrin inexpressible, he picked 12 marines and took the engine house, in ten minutes, with the loss of one marine killed and one wounded, without hurting a hair of one of the prisoners. And now I say to you that I would have given my arm to its shoulder, for that feat to have been performed by the Volunteers

of Virginia on Monday before the marines arrived there. But there was
no cowardice or panic on the part of the inhabitants who were made
prisoners or on the part of the volunteers. . . . They loved Washington,
and Allstadt, and Mills . . . and would not risk *their* lives. This was
wrong, but natural and not cowardly. . . . I was ready to weep when I
found that the whole force overcome was only some 12 or 15 men and
the Virginia volunteers had not captured them before Colonel Lee
arrived! . . .

THE COLLABORATORS

No. 46 [JOHN BROWN, JR.]

Ralph Keeler, "Owen Brown's Escape from Harper's Ferry," *The Atlantic Monthly*, XXXIII (March, 1874), p. 343

. . . John [Brown, Jr.] told me enough [during my interview with him at his home on the eastern shore of Lake Erie] of his father's plans to give a dignity to the attempt at Harper's Ferry which I confess it had never before seemed to me, in my ignorance, to have. John Brown, Jr., was at home in Ashtabula County, Ohio, at the time of the attack. He had just returned from Canada, where he had been organizing the pluckiest and most trustworthy of the escaped slaves, at some of the border towns. He would have been at Harper's Ferry, if his father had not been driven to begin operations before the appointed time. The reason for striking the blow so soon was that he had been betrayed to the government. Moreover, the people in the neighborhood had begun to suspect him. John Brown's entire plan has never, I think, been published. His object, as his friends know, was to make slaveholding so unsafe and unstable as to render it unprofitable, and so lead to its abolition. He and his company had already in effect driven slavery out of Kansas, and lessened the value of slaves in Missouri and the Border States to the amount of at least a million dollars. This had been done by a handful of men, with the combined power and influence of the government against them. John Brown remembered that the Seminoles were never fairly conquered, and had, twenty years before, while surveying in the neighborhood of Harper's Ferry, resolved to make the Alleghany and Cumberland Mountains and the Dismal Swamp his everglades. The least he expected the government to send against him was an army of twenty thousand; and his plans were so laid that they could never capture over one hundred of his men at a time, and of these all but two or three should be fugitive slaves. The risings were planned to take place in a dozen different directions in a night, the companies to be kept separate. The slaves were not to be taken to the North, but drilled and taught to conquer their homes in the South. They were to be officered by men who had proved worthy, and who were to restrain them from acts of violence. The slave-holders were to be taken prisoners where they stood in the way, and injured personally only if they resisted. It was John Brown's desire to show the slaveholders from the first the humanity of his intentions, that caused him to delay his escape from the engine-house at Harper's Ferry until it was too late. Hundreds of men were sworn to be there, and if he could have waited till the time in the spring agreed upon for the attack, it would probably have been successful. . . .

No. 47   [FRED DOUGLASS]
Harper's Weekly, Nov. 12, 1859, p. 726

Fred Douglass has published a manifesto in which he says: "Wholly, grievously, and most unaccountably wrong is Mr. Cook, when he asserts that I promised to be present in person at the Harper's Ferry insurrection. . . . I have never made a promise so rash and wild as this. The taking of Harper's Ferry was a measure never encouraged by my word or by my vote, at any time or place. . . .

"I am ever ready to write, speak, publish . . . and even to conspire against slavery, when there is a reasonable hope for success. Men who live by robbing their fellow-men of their labor and liberty have forfeited their right to know any thing of the thoughts, feelings, or purposes of those whom they rob and plunder. . . .

"I may be asked, why I did not join John Brown—the noble old hero. . . . My answer to this has already been given. . . . 'The tools to those that can use them.' Let every man work for the abolition of slavery in his own way.

"I have no apology for keeping out of the way of those gentlemanly United States Marshals who are said to have paid Rochester a somewhat protracted visit lately, with a view to an interview with me. A government recognizing the validity of the *Dred Scott* decision at such a time as this is not likely to have any very charitable feelings toward me, and if I am to meet its representatives, I prefer to do so at least upon equal terms.

"Some reflections may be made upon my leaving on a tour to England, just at this time. I have only to say, that my going to that country has been rather delayed than hastened by the insurrection at Harper's Ferry. All knew that I had intended to leave here in the first week of November."

FREDERICK DOUGLASS.

No. 48   [JOSHUA R. GIDDINGS]

The Mason Report, Appendix, pp. 147-156

[Feb. 3, 1860]

JOSHUA R. GIDDINGS affirmed and examined.

. . . Jefferson, Ashtabula County, Ohio, is my residence. . . . I represented that district in the House of Representatives for twenty-one years. . . . I saw John Brown . . . in the spring or summer last. . . . I said at once, let him come and lecture. Mr. Brown was regarded as a man of some considerable distinction, or notoriety, if you please. He had lectured in the surrounding villages. . . .

QUESTION: What was the subject of his lecture in your village?

ANSWER: Slavery entirely. The duty of Christians in relation to the institution of slavery; the obligations which Christians were under to do to the slaves as they would have the slaves do to them under an exchange of circumstances. . . . He carried that to an extent that we were bound to aid the slaves in escaping, so far as we could, even in the slave States. That was the distinguishing feature in which he differed perhaps from our people. . . .

My [own] lectures were . . . mostly upon the principles of our government; the legitimate powers and constitutional duties of human governments. That is one of my lectures. The Higher Law constitutes another. . . . What I mean by The Higher Law is that power which for the last two centuries has been proclaimed by the philosophers and jurists and statesmen . . . the law of nature. . . . Wherever a human soul exists, that law applies . . . and wherever such soul exists, there is the right to live . . . to attain knowledge . . . to sustain life . . . and enjoy heaven or happiness. . . . The meanest slave who treads the footstool of God holds from his Creator the same right to live and attain knowledge and to liberty that you and I possess. . . . [Whenever], without going into any other State, we have the opportunity to sustain the right of a fellow being, it is our duty to do it. I have never felt myself called upon to advocate nor to encourage the entering into other States to speak thus to slaves; but wherever in my own State, where I can do it without violation of law, or enactments erroneously called *law,* I uniformly arm the slave; I uniformly tell him to defend his life and his liberty. . . . My lectures inculcate this: . . . that any acts violative of those eternal principles of right and liberty are void;

that they are the mandates of despots; . . . that right and wrong are established by Heaven's law. . . .

QUESTION: . . . At any period after you first became acquainted with John Brown, [were you] aware . . . of his purpose to attempt the liberation of slaves in the South?

ANSWER: . . . I had an impression that he would do as he had done in Missouri. . . . I suppose the history of the day has shown him to have taken off slaves from Missouri, as he himself stated in Virginia that he had done, and that that was his object in entering Virginia. He had taken away some twelve or fifteen slaves from Missouri. . . . That impression was an inference from what he had done, and from the fact that he was known as an outlaw; a price had been set upon his head, as he stated; that he had no fixed place of residence; that he was destitute of regular employment; that he was advocating the right of all men to liberty, and particularly that it was the duty of Christians to aid slaves in the slave States to escape. . . . I understood that there was no personal violence . . . [in the Missouri raid]. There were threats. He was surrounded by force, and the marshal of Kansas or the deputy marshal . . . and he, by display and address, came off without the shedding of blood. That was my impression. I did also get the impression . . . that he was very much opposed to shedding blood. . . .

No. 49   [T. W. HIGGINSON]

Thomas Wentworth Higginson, *Cheerful Yesterdays* (Boston, 1898), pp. 219-223

. . . I met [John Brown] at the American House [in Boston] in March, 1858.

Of grand tactics and strategy Brown knew as little as Garibaldi; but he had studied guerilla warfare for himself in books, as well as in Europe, and had for a preceptor Hugh Forbes, an Englishman who had been a Garibaldian soldier. Brown's plan was simply to penetrate Virginia with a few comrades, to keep utterly clear of all attempt to create slave insurrection, but to get together bands and families of fugitive slaves, and then be guided by events. If he could establish them permanently in those fastnesses, . . . so much the better; if not, he would make a break from time to time, and take parties to Canada, by paths already familiar to him. All this he explained to me and others, plainly and calmly, and there was nothing in it that we considered either objectionable or impracticable; so that his friends in Boston—

Theodore Parker, Howe, Stearns, Sanborn, and myself—were ready to cooperate in his plan as thus limited. Of the wider organization and membership afterwards formed by him in Canada we of course knew nothing, nor could we foresee the imprudence which finally perverted the attack into a defeat. We helped him in raising the money, and he seemed drawing toward the consummation of his plans, when letters began to come to his Massachusetts supporters from Hugh Forbes, already mentioned, threatening to make the whole matter public unless we could satisfy certain very unreasonable demands for money. On this point our committee was at once divided, not as to refusing the preposterous demands, but because the majority thought that this threat of disclosure made necessary an indefinite postponement of the whole affair; while Howe and myself, and Brown also, as it proved, thought otherwise.

He came again to Boston (May 31, 1858), when I talked with him alone, and he held, as I had done, that Forbes could do him no real harm; that if people believed Forbes they would underrate his (Brown's) strength, which was just the thing he wished; or if they overrated it, "the increased terror would perhaps counter-balance this." If he had the means, he would not lose a day. But as I could not, unaided, provide the means, I was obliged to yield, as he did. He consented to postpone the enterprise and return to Kansas, carrying with him $500 in gold, and an order for certain arms at Tabor, which had belonged originally to the [Massachusetts] State Kansas Committee, but had since been transferred, in consideration of a debt, to our friend Stearns, who gave them to Brown on his own responsibility. Nearly a year now passed, during which I rarely heard from Brown, and thought that perhaps his whole project had been abandoned. A new effort to raise money was made at Boston in the spring of 1859, but I took little part in it. It had all begun to seem to me rather chimerical. The amount of $2000 was, nevertheless, raised for him at Boston, in June, 1859, and I find that Sanborn wrote to me (June 4), "Brown has set out on his expedition"; and then on October 6, "The $300 desired has been made up and received. Four or five men will be on the ground next week from these regions and elsewhere." Brown's address was at this time at West Andover, Ohio, and the impression was that the foray would begin in that region, if at all. Nobody mentioned Harper's Ferry.

No. 50   [SAMUEL G. HOWE]

The Mason Report, Appendix, pp. 156-172

[Feb. 3, 1860]

SAMUEL G. HOWE sworn and examined.
. . . I reside in Boston. . . . I am . . . a physician; I do not practice. . . . I have charge of two charitable public institutions. . . . My
acquaintance [with John Brown] was first formed by correspondence in
. . . 1856 or 1857. . . . I became acquainted with him in 1857, as
[Brown was] the agent of the Kansas Aid Committee . . . and in one
sense I was the agent, inasmuch as I went to Kansas for . . . the Kansas
Aid Committee of Massachusetts. . . . The first business [of our com-
mittee] . . . was to transport [arms, provisions, clothing up the Missouri
River] and Mr. Brown, or Captain Brown . . . , was appointed the
agent. . . . [To] the best of my knowledge . . . 200 Sharps rifles were
committed to his care. . . . They were the property of [my] committee.
. . . They were purchased by . . . contributions . . . for the aid of
Kansas. . . . My impression is that [Brown] deposited them at Tabor,
in Iowa. . . . [In] what way John Brown afterwards got possession of
them, when he brought them to . . . Harper's Ferry . . . I have no
means of knowing. . . . In the year 1858, I received a communication
from a Mr. Forbes . . . that Captain Brown . . . would probably use
[these arms] for purposes not intended by the committee. A meeting
was called. The committee had then virtually dissolved; it had nothing
more to do; but the members were called together. A vote was passed,
instructing the chairman to write to Captain Brown and direct him, if
he held any property, arms, or otherwise, belonging to the committee,
to take them into Kansas, there to be used only for the defense of freedom in Kansas. Such a vote was passed, such a letter was written, and,
I have no doubt, received by him. I think that was the last record of
the committee which was made. . . . [The letter was written by] Mr.
George L. Stearns. . . . About the same time [I received from Mr.
Wilson, of the Senate, a letter stating] that he had reason to believe that
Captain Brown had in his possession arms belonging to the Massachusetts
Aid Committee, which he would be likely to use for purposes not contemplated by the committee . . . and [Mr. Wilson] advised by all means
that measures be taken to prevent this. It was a short letter . . . but I
recollect he distinctly expressed his disapprobation . . . of John Brown's
general career. . . .

Forbes's letter . . . was to this intent, that he had been engaged . . . by . . . the Northern Abolitionists to go to Kansas and drill men; that he never got any money for it; that he was in great distress; that he must have money; that . . . if Captain Brown was allowed to go on it would be disastrous; that he would denounce it. . . . It was a very long letter, full of vituperation and abuse. I had never seen Captain Forbes, nor heard of him before. . . . I have no distinct recollection of having [communicated Forbes's message to Brown]. It is possible I may have done so. . . .

I saw [Brown] in Boston in . . . 1858. . . . The impression I got from him was that he wished persons to render him . . . assistance . . . as a man having suffered in the cause of Kansas. . . . For what purpose those contributions were wanted by Brown . . . I have no definite knowledge. . . . He never gave me a definite statement of any plan or purpose. . . . Captain Brown was considered to have suffered a good deal in Kansas, and a subscription was raised to purchase him a homestead. . . . I contributed to his aid at various times . . . in the same way that I contribute to the aid of other anti-slavery men. . . .

QUESTION: Did you have any knowledge of where John Brown was, from the time you saw him in Boston, in 1859, until the outbreak at Harper's Ferry?

ANSWER: Not the slightest. . . .

No. 51   [THEODORE PARKER]

Letter to Francis Jackson, from James Redpath (ed.), *Echoes of Harper's Ferry* (Boston, 1860), pp. 73-92

Rome, Nov. 24, 1859

My Dear Friend:

. . . we must give up DEMOCRACY if we keep SLAVERY or give up SLAVERY if we keep DEMOCRACY. . . . [Though sick], I wish yet to set down a few thoughts . . . :

(1) A man held against his will as a slave has a natural right to kill every one who seeks to prevent his enjoyment of liberty. . . . (2) It may be a natural duty of the slave to develop this natural right in a practical manner, and actually kill all those who seek to prevent his enjoyment of liberty. . . . (3) The freeman has a natural right to help the slaves recover their liberty, and in that enterprise to do for them all which they have a right to do for themselves. . . . (4) It may be a natural duty for the freeman to help the slaves to the enjoyment of

their liberty, and, as means to that end, to aid them in killing all such as oppose their natural freedom. . . . (5) The performance of this duty is to be controlled by the freeman's power and opportunity to help the slaves. . . .

[It] is said in the Democratic newspapers that "Captain Brown had many friends at the North, who . . . furnished him with some $20,000. . . ." I think much more than that is true of us. . . .

A few years ago it did not seem difficult first to check Slavery, and then to end it without any bloodshed. I think this cannot be done now, nor ever in the future. . . . [John Brown] sought by violence what the Anti-Slavery Society works for with other weapons. The two . . . differ only in the means. . . .

No. 52   [RICHARD REALF]

John E. Cook, *Confession* (Charlestown, Va., 1859)

Richard Realf, one of our original party, and our Secretary of State, came from Chatham to Cleveland, a few days before Capt. Brown's arrival from the East. Soon after his arrival, he (Capt. B.) sent Realf to New York City, at which place he embarked for England for the purpose of carrying out the plans of Capt. Brown. Realf was born and raised in England. He is a peasant's son, but his native talents brought him into the notice of some of the nobility, who took charge of him, and made arrangements to give him a finished education. He was taken into the family of Lady Noel Byron, where he made his home whilst pursuing his studies. Falling in love with a young lady of noble birth, who was a relative of Lady Byron's, he was censured by Lady B. for his presumption. He became offended at her interference, and finally left Lady B. to work his own way in the world. About this time the Chartist movement was made, which Realf joined, and the result was, he was obliged to seek safety by emigrating to America. He made his home some years in New York city. A part of the time he was there, he was engaged as assistant superintendent of the Five Points Mission. He is well known as an author and a poet. He gave up his situation as assistant superintendent, and went to Kansas in the summer or fall of 1856. I first met him in Lawrence, Kansas T. No word was received from him, to my knowledge, after he left for England, to which place he went in his own capacity and that of our Secretary of State, to solicit funds for the support of our organization. He proposed to deliver a course of lectures in various parts of England, and the net proceeds of which were to be given to carry out Capt. Brown's plans. He is a man of rare talents, and a powerful and fluent speaker. He is about twenty-eight years of age. Mr. Kagi, I believe, got a letter from some one in England a few months ago, stating that Realf had sailed for this country, and that he had quite a sum of money with him, but further than that, we have been unable to find any trace of him. Capt. Brown and the rest of our company who knew him, think that he is dead. . . .

No. 53
Richard J. Hinton, memoir in *Poems by Richard Realf* (New York, 1898), p. xlii

. . . Of John Brown's personal influence he [Realf] once said: "He possessed that strange power which enables one man to impress many with his views, and he so psychologized his associates that, seeing only through his medium of vision, they consequently were unable to controvert his theories; therefore the movement went blindly on. For myself, too, it is certain that had I not been to New York, where, out of reach of his great mesmeric power, I could in some sort master the questions involved, I should have been with the enterprise to the bitter end. I should, indeed, have had no other choice. Had John Brown sent a man on an errand to Hades he must have started hither, for Brown was one of God's own commanders."

No. 54 [F. B. SANBORN]
F. B. Sanborn, "Comment by a Radical Abolitionist," *The Century Magazine,* XXVI (July, 1883), pp. 413-414

. . . Brown's plan of action in Virginia was wholly his own. . . . Beyond his own family and the armed followers who accompanied him, I have never supposed that his Virginia plan was known to fifty persons. Even to those few it was not fully communicated, though they knew that he meant to fortify himself somewhere in the mountains of Virginia or Tennessee, and from that fastness, with his band of soldiers, sally out and liberate slaves by force. His plan to this extent was known, early in 1858, by Frederick Douglass, Gerrit Smith (at whose house and in whose presence I first heard Brown declare it), Theodore Parker, Dr. S. G. Howe, George L. Stearns, T. W. Higginson, and myself, and we all raised money to aid Brown. . . . [Some] of the money and nearly all the correspondence . . . passed through my hands in 1858-9. . . . Brown's general purpose of attacking slavery by force, in Missouri or elsewhere, was known in 1857-8-9 to R. W. Emerson, A. Bronson Alcott, Henry Thoreau, Wendell Phillips, ... and others of the anti-slavery men of Massachusetts, none of whom discountenanced it, while most of them, in my hearing, distinctly approved it; generally, however, as a last resort or a measure of retaliation for the outrages of the slave-holders and their allies. Had these gentlemen known of the Virginia plan, most of them would have strongly disapproved it as premature or impracticable. Such, also, it seemed at first, and generally afterward, to those of us who contributed money to aid Brown in it. I speak particularly of Gerrit Smith, Theodore Parker, George L. Stearns, Dr. Howe, Col. Higginson, and myself. But we all felt, as Governor Andrew afterward said, that whatever the old worthy might plan or do, "John Brown himself was *right*," and upon that feeling we acted, in spite of doubts and many misgivings. The end has justified our instinctive sentiment; and it has . . . glorified Brown. . . .

No. 55   [GERRIT SMITH]

The National Intelligencer, Thurs., Nov. 24, 1859 [*Buffalo Gazette*]

UTICA, N.Y., Nov. 11, 1859

The Hon. Gerrit Smith, ex-Member of Congress, has been confined in the Lunatic Asylum here since Monday last. . . . It was only by strategem that his friends succeeded in getting him here. He has been, ever since the arrest of Brown . . . , haunted with the idea that he was culpably responsible for all the lives that have and will be sacrificed; and so much have this reflection and the fear of being called on to answer at the bar of justice preyed upon him, that his mind, never exempt from a tendency to be unhinged, gave way. . . . For some days . . . he manifested a most nervous anxiety to anticipate the requisition which he expected would be made upon him, and to proceed to Virginia and surrender himself. . . . When it was resolved to place him under restraint, this anxiety of his was taken advantage of. His friends pretended to chime in with his notion, and when he set out for Utica he was under the impression he was on his way to Richmond or Charlestown.

I am assured that, although he sympathized with and sustained John Brown in Kansas, he is in no way implicated in the recent movements of that individual. . . . That Gerrit Smith's case is one of decided lunacy is certain. Still his friends consider it far from hopeless.

No. 56   [GEORGE L. STEARNS]

The Mason Report, Appendix, pp. 225-245

[Feb. 24, 1860]

GEORGE L. STEARNS affirmed and examined.

. . . I made [Brown's] acquaintance early in January, 1857, in Boston. . . . [I was] president of the Massachusetts State Kansas Committee, [whose] object was to relieve the wants and sufferings of the men in Kansas. . . . I have given him money from time to time, . . . say, from $1,500 to $2,000. . . .

QUESTION: Did he ever sell those [200 Sharps] rifles, as he was thus empowered [by you]?

ANSWER: . . . I never knew. . . . He never gave me any intimation. . . .

QUESTION: Did he ever account with you for the proceeds?

ANSWER: No, sir. . . .

QUESTION: Did he draw [on you] for the $400 that you authorized . . . ?

ANSWER: Yes, sir. . . .

QUESTION: Have you any information . . . as to whether Brown asked for authority or permission in any way to bring those arms to Harper's Ferry—the carbines and the pistols?

ANSWER: . . . He did not.

QUESTION: Were you aware of where Brown was in the summer of 1859 . . . ?

ANSWER: No, sir. . . .

QUESTION: Was there any communication . . . between Brown and any member of your committee . . . which enabled him to claim those arms as his property?

ANSWER: . . . I think he would have reason to consider the revolvers as his property, because I paid for them . . . as something put into his hands for his use, expecting that they were to be used in Kansas. As to . . . the rifled carbines, . . . I see no reason why he should have claimed them, for they were . . . only entrusted to him. . . .

QUESTION: Did you at any time . . . in any way . . . understand that there was any purpose on the part of Brown to make any inroad . . . in any of the States?

ANSWER: . . . I did suppose that he would go into Virginia or some other State and relieve slaves . . . in any way he could give them liberty . . . , by force if necessary . . . [but] I never supposed that he contemplated anything like what occurred at Harper's Ferry. . . . I supposed that [he would do] what he did in Missouri. . . . I should have disapproved of [what he did at Harper's Ferry] if I had known of it; but I have since changed my opinion; I believe John Brown to be the representative man of this century, as Washington was of the last—the Harper's Ferry affair, and the capacity shown by the Italians for self-government, the great events of this age. One will free Europe and the other America. . . .

. . . In accordance with a request of Mr. Stearns, the following letter [to him is] appended to his testimony:

CHICAGO, March 19, 1860

There was only one meeting of the National Kansas Committee in the city of New York, and that was [on] the 24th [of January, 1857], when it commenced and continued in session for six days.

I wish to call your attention to . . . the application of John Brown for aid from that committee. It is this: when Mr. Brown was pressing his claim for the aid desired, I asked him . . . : "If you get the arms and money you desire, will you invade Missouri or any slave territory?" To which he replied: "I am no adventurer; you all know me; you are acquainted with history; you know what I have done in Kansas; I do not expose my plans; no one knows them but myself, except perhaps one; I do not wish to be interrogated; if you wish to give me anything, I want you to give it freely; I have no other purpose but to serve the cause of liberty." This is the substance of what he said. . . . [This] reply was not satisfactory to all, and the arms were voted back to your committee to be disposed of as you thought best. . . . Yours, &c., H. B. HURD.

TOPICS FOR ESSAYS

INSTRUCTIONS: *From now on it will often be necessary to refer to documents in earlier assignments.*

SUGGESTED LENGTH (*words*):

(1) *Lieut. Green's Memoir as History*	100
(2) *Governor Wise on the Virginia Militia*	300
(3) *John Cook*	300
(4) *Colonel Washington's Capture*	300
(5) *Brown's Motives at Harper's Ferry*	300
(6) *The Military Action, Oct. 16-Oct. 17, 1859*	500
(7) *The Taking of the Engine-House*	500
(8) *Were the Collaborators Responsible?*	500
(9) *"Bleeding" Kansas: A Supplementary View*	500

TOPICS FOR LIBRARY RESEARCH

BIBLIOGRAPHY:

Col. R. W. Baylor	T. W. Higginson	F. B. Sanborn
Frederick Douglass	Samuel G. Howe	Lieut. J. E. B. Stuart
Col. Hugh Forbes	Col. Robert E. Lee	George L. Stearns
Col. J. T. Gibson	Theodore Parker	Col. Lewis W. Washington
Lieut. Israel Green	Richard Realf	

SUPPLEMENTARY RESEARCH:

(1) John Brown's actions would not have been possible without the [Kansas] Emigrant Aid Society. Look up this Society and write a documented essay on it.   500-1000

(2) A number of Brown's collaborators were New Englanders who appear to have espoused Brown's cause as a matter of principle. Investigate New England Abolitionism and write a documented essay on it.   500-1000

Chapter III

THE LAW

THE TRIALS

No. 57

The Richmond Enquirer, Tues., Oct. 25, 1859

[Speech of Governor Wise in] RICHMOND, VA., Friday, Oct. 21, 1859.

I remained in Harper's Ferry and went to Charlestown to protect the prisoners . . . against lynch-law, determined as I am that the laws shall reign whilst I am Chief Magistrate of this Commonwealth. Our people were incensed beyond expression, but they felt as I do, that it would be disgraceful and cowardly to murder these prisoners, after failing to take them for twenty-four hours.—They were securely guarded and safely lodged in the Charlestown jail, to be tried in the Virginia court, under Virginia laws. The United States served warrants for two cases of murder and for treason against the United States, but there was no difficulty about jurisdiction. I told the officers of the United States that they might have the bodies of the prisoners after Virginia tribunals were done with them! I would not have delivered up these prisoners to any claim of priority of jurisdiction if the President of the United States had so ordered. But there was no issue of jurisdiction, and there was no occasion for any except as to the pardoning power. I will protect and guard the prisoners with the law and the mercy and the might of our own sovereignty.

No. 58   TRIAL OF THE INSURRECTIONISTS

The Richmond Enquirer, Tues., Oct. 25, 1859

CHARLESTOWN, Jefferson County, Va., Oct. 21—The Circuit Court of Jefferson County . . . which commenced its session today, was occupied to-day with the trial of the case of State *vs.* Dillard. . . . The examination trial of the insurrectionists, Brown and his associates, before eight justices of the peace, will take place on Tuesday [Oct. 25] in the court room, the Circuit Court adjourning for that purpose.

Judge Parker's charge to the grand jury was an able and appropriate effort. . . . The following is the commitment of the insurrectionists and the warrant to the sheriff to summon eight justices to examine the facts with which they stand charged:

"State of Virginia, Jefferson County, to wit: To the sheriff, court, and to the keeper of the jail of said county: These are to command you, in the name of the commonwealth of Virginia, forthwith to convey and deliver into the custody of the keeper of said jail, and to receive and safely keep the bodies of John Brown, Aaron C. Stevens and Edwin Coppoc, and Shields Green and John Copeland, negro, and charged before me, Roger Chew, a justice of the peace for the said county, on the oaths of Henry A. Wise, Andrew Hunter, and John W. McGinnis, and upon the free admission and confession of said parties, made in my presence and hearing, that they and each of them did feloniously conspire with each other, and with other parties unknown, to make an abolition insurrection and open war against the commonwealth of Virginia, by making an armed attack upon and murdering her citizens at a certain place called Harper's Ferry; and then and there to riot, on the 17th, 18th and 19th days of October, 1859; did feloniously, and of their malice, kill and murder with firearms, called Sharps rifles and revolver pistols, divers citizens of this commonwealth; and Fontaine Beckham, George W. Turner, and Thomas Boerly, free white persons, and Luke Quinn, a soldier of the United States government, also Hayward Shepherd, a free negro; and did there and then feloniously conspire with divers slaves belonging to citizens of this commonwealth, in the county aforesaid, to me unknown, to revel and make insurrection against the government and laws of this commonwealth, that they may be examined for the said offence before the proper examining court and otherwise dealt with according to law—given under my hand and seal this 20th day of Oct., 1859 ["Roger Chew."] The final trial will take place at the present term, which will commence in a few days. . . .

CHARLESTOWN, Va., Oct. 22—The Circuit Court of Jefferson county—Hon. Richard Parker, Judge; Charles D. Harding, Esq., Commonwealth's Attorney.

The cases of the State of Virginia vs. John Brown, Aaron C. Stevens and Edwin Coppoc, white persons, and Shields Green and John Copeland, negroes, will be taken up Tuesday for examination trial previous to the action of the grand jury, *ex parte,* thereon—a form peculiar to Virginia. It is understood that the Court will assign Robert Y. Conrad, Esq., a talented lawyer of Winchester, as the counsel of the prisoners. . . .

No. 59   EXAMINATION OF THE CONSPIRATORS

The National Intelligencer, Thurs., Oct. 27, 1859

CHARLESTOWN (VA.), OCTOBER [25], 1859.

The Magistrates' Court assembled here this morning to examine the prisoners captured in the recent insurrection. The following magistrates were on the bench: Col. DAVENPORT, Presiding Justice; Dr. Alexander, John J. Lock, John F. Smith, Thomas H. Willis, George W. Eichelberger, Charles H. Lewis, and Moses W. Burr.

At half-past 10 o'clock the Sheriff was directed to bring in the prisoners, who were conducted from jail under a guard of eighty armed men. A guard was also stationed around the court-house.

CHARLES B. HARDING, Esq., attorney for the county, was assisted by ANDREW HUNTER, counsel for the Commonwealth.

The prisoners were brought in amidst profound silence. Capt. Brown and Edwin Coppoc were manacled together. Brown seemed weak and haggard, with his eyes swollen from the effects of the wounds on his head. Coppoc is uninjured. Stevens seemed less injured than Brown, but looked haggard and depressed. He has also a number of wounds on the head. John Copeland is a bright mulatto, about twenty-five years of age. Green is a dark negro, about thirty years of age.

Sheriff CAMPBELL read the commitment of the prisoners on the charge of treason and murder, when Mr. HARDING, the State's attorney, asked that the Court might assign counsel for the prisoners if they had none.

The Court inquired if the prisoners had counsel, when Brown addressed the Court as follows:

"Virginians: I did not ask for any quarter at the time I was taken. I did not ask to have myself spared. The Governor of the State of Virginia tendered me his assurance that I should have a fair trial; and under no circumstances whatever will I be able to attend to a trial. If you seek my blood you can have it at any moment without the mockery of a trial. I have had no counsel. I have not been able to advise with one. I know nothing about the feelings of my fellow-prisoners, and am utterly unable to attend in any way to my own defence. My memory don't [*sic*] serve me. My health is insufficient, although improving. There are mitigating circumstances, if a fair trial is to be allowed us, that I would urge in our favor. But if we are to be forced, with a mere form of a trial, to execution, you might spare yourselves that trouble. I am ready for my fate. I do not ask a trial. I plead for no mockery of a trial—no insult—nothing but that which conscience gives or cowardice would drive you to practice. I ask to be excused from the mockery of a trial. I do not know what the design of this examination is. I do not know what is to be the benefit of it to the Commonwealth. I have now little to ask other than that I be not publicly insulted as cowardly barbarians insult those who fall into their hands."

The Court assigned Messrs. CHARLES J. FAULKNER and LAW-SON BOTTS as counsel for the prisoners.

After some consultation with the prisoners, MR. FAULKNER, addressing the Court, said:

"I was about to remark to the court that although I feel at any time willing to discharge any duty which the court can legally and by authority of law devolve upon me, I am not, in the first place, aware of any authority which this court has, sitting as an examining court, to assign counsel for the defence. Besides, it is manifest, from the remarks just made by one of the prisoners, that he regards the appearance of counsel under such circumstances not as a *bona fide* act, but rather as mockery. Under these circumstances I do not feel disposed to assume the responsibility of that position. I have other reasons for declining the position, connected with my having been at the place of action, and hearing all the admissions of the prisoners, which render it improper and *inexpedient* for me to act as counsel. . . ."

Mr. Botts said he did not feel it his duty to decline the appointment of the court. . . .

Capt. Brown: There were certain men, I think Mr. Botts was one of them, who declined acting as counsel, but I am not positive about it; I cannot remember whether he was one, because I have heard so many names. I am a stranger here and do not know the disposition or character of the gentlemen named. I have applied for counsel of my own, and doubtless could have them if I am not, as I said before, to be hurried to execution before they can reach here. But if that is the disposition that is to be made of me, all this trouble and expense can be saved.

Mr. Harding: The question is, do you desire the aid of Messrs. Faulkner and Botts as your counsel? Please to answer yes or no.

Capt Brown: I cannot regard this as an examination under any circumstances. I would prefer that they should exercise their own pleasure. I feel as if it was a matter of little account to me. If they had designed to assist me as counsel, I should have wanted an opportunity to consult with them at my leisure. . . .

Mr. Harding then addressed each of the other prisoners separately, and each stated his willingness to be defended by the counsel named.

EXAMINATION OF WITNESSES

Col. Washington was the first witness examined. He related the particulars . . . of his being taken and conveyed with his negroes to the Armory and of subsequent events up to the attack by the marines. . . .

Mr. Kitzmiller gave the particulars of his being taken prisoner and locked up. He subsequently had several interviews with Brown, who always treated them with a great deal of respect and courtesy. . . . [He] went out with Stevens with a flag of truce . . . on Monday afternoon. . . . Recognized in court only Brown and Stevens; he counted 22 men early in the morning armed with Sharps rifles. When Stevens was lying wounded he remarked to witness, "I have been cruelly deceived."

Col. Washington recalled. In conversation with Gov. Wise, Brown . . . [said] that he had nothing to conceal, had no favors to ask, and that he had arms enough for two thousand men, and could get enough for five thousand if wanted.

Armistead Ball stated the particulars of his arrest . . . ; had an interview after his arrest with Brown, who stated . . . that his object was not to make war against the people, and they would not be injured if they remained quiet; his object was to place the United States arms in the hands of black men, and he proposed then to free all slaves in the vicinity. . . .

Mr. John Allstadt, who was brought into the Armory with his slaves, detailed the particulars of battering down his doors and his seizure by six armed men. Thinks Brown fired several times; knows that he saw him with a gun levelled; saw all of the prisoners except the yellow man Copeland.

Alexander Kelly detailed particulars of collision with insurgents, and the exchanging of several shots; could not identify any of the prisoners.

William Johnson testified to the arrest of Copeland, the yellow man, who was attempting to escape across the river; he was armed with a spear and rifle, and was arrested in the middle of the Shenandoah; he said he had been placed in charge of Hall's rifle factory by Capt. Brown.

Andrew Kennedy was at the jail when Copeland was brought in, and questioned him; he said he had come from the Western Reserve of Ohio; that Brown came there in August and employed him at twenty dollars per month.

. . . Copeland said their object was to release the slaves of this country; that he knew of nineteen in the party, but there were several others he did not know.

Joseph A. Brua was one of the prisoners in the engine-house, and was permitted to go out several times with a flag of truce; during the firing Coppoc fired twice, and at the second fire Brown remarked, "That man is down"; witness then asked permission to go out, and found that Beckham had just been shot; has no doubt that Coppoc shot him.

Mr. Allstadt recalled. Thinks that Captain Brown shot the marine who was killed; saw him fire.

The preliminary examination being concluded, the court remanded the prisoners for trial before the Circuit Court.

PROCEEDINGS IN THE CIRCUIT COURT

CIRCUIT COURT, Jefferson county, Virginia—Judge RICHARD PARKER on the Bench.

The Court assembled at two o'clock. The Grand Jury were called and the Magistrate's Court reported the result of the examination in the case of Captain Brown and the other prisoners. The Grand Jury then retired, and the witnesses for the State were sent before them. At five o'clock the Jury returned . . . and stated that they had not completed the examination of witnesses. They were discharged until tomorrow morning at ten o'clock. The trial will commence tomorrow morning. . . . Captain Brown's object in refusing counsel is said to be that if he has counsel he will not be allowed to speak himself, and Southern counsel will not be willing to express his views. The reason being given for hurrying the trial is that the people of the whole county are kept in a state of excitement, and that a large armed force is required to prevent attempts at rescue.

CHAMBERSBURG (PA.), OCT. 26—Capt. Cook, the confederate of Brown . . . , was arrested about eight miles from this place last evening. . . .

HARRISBURG (PA.), OCT. 26—Governor Packer today ordered Capt. John E. Cook, now in jail at Chambersburg, and Albert Hazlett, now confined in Carlisle, to be delivered up to the Virginia authorities, on the requisition of Governor Wise, for trial.

No. 60
The National Intelligencer, Sat., Oct. 29, 1859

CHARLESTOWN (VA.), OCT. 26, 1859

Charlestown is full to overflowing with people, and the excitement . . . is intense. Mr. Johnson, United States Marshal at Cleveland, Ohio, arrived this morning. He . . . identified the negro Copeland as a fugitive from justice in Ohio. . . .

CIRCUIT COURT, Jefferson County, Va.,—Judge Parker on the bench. The Court met at ten o'clock. . . . At twelve o'clock the Grand Jury returned bills of indictment against the prisoners and were immediately discharged. Charles B. Harding, Esq., assisted by Andrew Hunter, Esq., appear for the State; and Charles J. Faulkner and Lawson Botts, Esq., for the prisoners. The indictments against each prisoner were read: First, for conspiring with negroes to create an insurrection; second, for treason against the Commonwealth of Virginia; third, for murder. The prisoners were brought into court. . . . Captain Brown looked somewhat better, his eye not being so much swollen. Stevens had to be supported, and was placed on a mattress on the floor of the courtroom, evidently unable to sit. He has the appearance almost of a dying man. . . .

Before the reading of the indictments, Mr. Hunter called the attention of the Court to the necessity of appointing additional counsel for the prisoners. . . . After consulting with Capt. Brown, Mr. Botts said that the prisoner retained him and desired to have Mr. Green assist him. . . . The Court requested Mr. Green to act as counsel for prisoners, and he consented to do so.

Capt. Brown then rose and said: I do not intend to detain the Court but barely wish to say that, as I have been promised a fair trial, I am not now in circumstances that enable me to attend to a fair trial, owing to the state of my health. I have a severe injury in the back . . . which enfeebles me very much, but . . . I only ask for a very short delay of my trial. . . . I merely ask this that . . . "the devil may have his dues," no more. . . . [My] hearing is impaired . . . in consequence of the wounds I have about my head. . . . I could not hear what the court has said this morning. . . .

Mr. Hunter said that the arraignment could be made, and this question could then be considered.

The Court ordered the indictment to be read so that the prisoners could plead guilty or not guilty, and said it would then consider Brown's request. The prisoners were compelled to stand during the arraignment —Capt. Brown standing with difficulty and Stevens being held upright by two bailiffs. The reading of the indictments occupied about twenty minutes. The prisoners each responded to the usual question, "Not Guilty," and desired to be tried separately.

Mr. HUNTER. The State elects to try John Brown first.

The COURT. His condition must first be inquired into.

Mr. BOTTS. . . . Brown . . . is mentally and physically unable to proceed with his trial at this time. He has heard today that counsel of his own choice will be here soon, whom he will of course prefer. He asks only for a delay of two or three days . . . and I hope the Court will grant it.

Mr. HUNTER. I do not think it the duty of the prosecutor . . . to oppose anything that justice requires. . . . Yet . . . to delay the trial of John Brown for one, two, or three days, they deemed it their duty that the Court, before determining the matter, should be put in possession of all the facts . . . , judicially, that they were aware of in the line of their duties as prosecutors. His own opinion was that it was not proper to delay the trial of this prisoner a single day. . . . He alluded to the circumstances by which they were now surrounded being such as rendered it dangerous, to say nothing of exceeding pressure upon the physical resources of our community growing out of the . . . affair for which the prisoners were to be tried; and that the State law, in making special provisions for allowing a briefer time than usual in the case of conviction of such offenders, within the discretion of the Court, between condemnation and execution, evidently indicates indirectly the necessity of acting promptly and decisively, though always justly, in proceedings of this kind. . . . [He] asked the Court not to receive the unsupported statements of the prisoner . . . but that the jailor and *physician* be examined. . . . [No] impediment had been thrown in the way of the prisoners procuring such counsel as they desired. . . . Able and intelligent counsel had been assigned to them here, and . . . there was but little reason to expect the attendance of those gentlemen from the North who had been written to. There was also a public duty resting upon them to avoid . . . the introduction of anything likely to weaken our present position and give strength to our enemies abroad, whether it issues from the jury in time or . . . comes from the mouth of prisoners or any other source. It was their position that had been imperilled and jeoparded, as they suppose, by enemies.

Mr. HARDING concurred in the objections of Mr. Hunter. . . .

Mr. GREEN, counsel for the prisoners, remarked that he had enjoyed no opportunity for consulting with the prisoners or of preparing for the defence. The letters for Northern counsel had been sent off, but sufficient time had not been afforded to receive answers. Under the circumstances he thought a short delay was desirable.

Mr. BOTTS added that at present the excitement was so great as perhaps to deter Northern counsel from coming, but now that it had been promised that the prisoners were to have a fair and impartial trial, he presumed that they would come and take part in the case.

The COURT stated that if physical inability was shown a reasonable delay must be granted. . . . [The] expectation of other counsel . . . did not constitute a sufficient cause for delay, as there was no certainty about their coming. . . .

Dr. MASON was then sworn. He thought Brown as able to go on understandingly with his trial. . . . Had heard him complain of debility, but not of hardness of hearing.

Mr. COCKRILL, one of the guards at the jail, said that Brown had always been able to converse freely.

Mr. AVIS, jailor, sworn. Has heard Brown frequently say . . . that his mind was confused and his hearing affected. Would not like to give any opinion as to his ability to stand his trial.

After [this testimony] the Court refused to postpone the trial.

WEDNESDAY—AFTERNOON SESSION

At two o'clock the jailor was ordered to bring Brown into court. He found him in bed, and [Brown] declared himself unable to rise. He was brought into court on a cot, which was set down within the bar. The prisoner laid most of the time with his eyes closed and the counterpane drawn up close under his chin. He is apparently not much injured but is determined to resist the pushing of his trial by all the means in his power.

The jury were then called and sworn. The jurors were questioned as to having formed or expressed any opinion that would prevent them from deciding the case impartially. . . . The Court excluded those who were present . . . during the insurrection. . . . The jurors called were all from distant parts of the county, mostly farmers, some of them owning a few slaves and others none. The examination of the jurors was continued until twenty-four were decided by the Court and counsel to be competent jurors. Out of these twenty-four, the counsel for the prisoner has a right to strike off eight, and then twelve are drawn by ballot out of the remaining sixteen. . . . The jury were not sworn in the case, but the Judge charged them not to converse upon the case, or to permit others to converse with them. They were at five o'clock dismissed, the prisoner was carried over to the jail on his cot, and the court adjourned until Thursday morning.

CHARLESTOWN (VA.), Oct. 27, 1859.
SECOND DAY—THURSDAY

Captain Brown was brought into Court this morning walking, but on reaching the bar he laid down at full length on his cot. He looked considerably better. . . .

Mr. BOTTS read the following despatch received by him this morning:/Akron, Ohio, Oct. 26, 1859/To C. J. Faulkner and Lawson Botts, Esqs./ John Brown, the leader of the insurrection at Harper's Ferry, Va., and several of his family, have resided in this county many years. Insanity is hereditary in that family. His mother and sister died with it, and a daughter of that sister has been two years in the Lunatic Asylum. A son and daughter of his mother's brother have also been confined . . . and another son of that brother is now insane and under close restraint. These facts can be conclusively proved by witnesses residing here, who will doubtless attend the trial if desired. [A. H. Lewis]. Mr. Wm. C. Allen, the telegraphic operator at the Akron office, adds to the above dispatch that A. H. Lewis is a resident of that place, and his statements are entitled to implicit credit.

Mr. BOTTS said that on receiving the above despatch he went to the jail with his associate, Mr. Green, and read it to Capt. Brown, and was desired by the latter to say that in his father's family there has never been any insanity at all. On his mother's side there have been repeated instances of it, and . . . his first wife showed symptoms of it, which was also evident in his first and second sons by that wife. Some portions of the statements in the despatch he knows to be correct, but of other portions he is ignorant. . . . Capt. Brown also desired his counsel to say that he does not put in any plea of insanity, and if he has ever been at all insane, he is totally unconscious of it. . . .

Capt. BROWN raised himself up in bed and said: I will add, if the Court will allow me, that I look upon it as a miserable artifice and pretext of those who ought to take a different course in regard to me . . . and I view it with contempt more than otherwise, as I remarked to Mr. Green. . . .

Mr. BOTTS stated that he was further instructed by Capt. Brown to say that, rejecting this plea of insanity entirely, and seeking no delay for that reason, he does repeat to the Court his request made yesterday that time be given for foreign counsel to arrive, whom he now has reason to expect. Yesterday afternoon a despatch was received from Cleveland, Ohio, signed by D. Tilden and dated the 26th instant, asking of Capt. Brown whether it would be of use for counsel to leave last night. To this despatch an answer was returned that the jury would be sworn this morning, and Capt. Brown desired the counsel to come at once. The counsel might reach here by 12 or 1 o'clock to-night. . . .

Mr. HUNTER observed that . . . the question now was whether there was sufficient grounds in this additional information to change the decision announced by the Court yesterday on the same motion. Before a decision was made, [he] deemed it his duty to call attention to two or three matters connected with this affair. Though desirous to avoid forestalling the trial of this case . . . , they were prepared to prove that he had made open, repeated, and constant acknowledgment of everything charged against him. He had gloried in it, and we have but an exhibition of the same spirit and the same purpose in what he announced, that he would permit no defence on the plea of insanity to be put in. What does he mean by wishing for delay for the purpose of having a fair trial? . . . [There] could be no right to claim delay, except so far as the prisoner could show, in a reliable form, that such delay was necessary to do justice in a particular case according to the law and policy of the State of Virginia. In regard to the telegram read, we know not who this Mr. Lewis is; we know not whether he is to come here as counsel for the prisoner or . . . wants to head a band of desperadoes to rescue the prisoner. . . . While commending the earnestness and zeal of the prisoner's counsel, he must ask the Court to reject the motion and proceed with the trial at once.

Mr. HARDING . . . fully concurred; . . . He referred also to the fact that Captain Brown pretended yesterday afternoon that he was unable to walk and was brought into court on a bed. Yet he walked back to jail after the close of the court without difficulty. . . .

Mr. GREEN remarked that one day's delay would be sufficient to ascertain whether the expected counsel would come or not. . . . [Furthermore] he did not believe the prisoner had made any acknowledgment upon which he could be convicted. All the acknowledgments made, so far as he knew . . . , referred to the charge of treason; and those confessions, according to our law, are insufficient to convict a party who may have acknowledged the fact in the plainest manner to a hundred witnesses; for if that is all the evidence upon which the Commonwealth relies, the prisoner cannot be convicted, because our code provides that such confession shall be made in open court, and the prisoner has denied it in open court by putting in the plea of "Not Guilty." . . .

The Court stated that it must see to it . . . that a proper cause for delay was made out before granting such an application. In the present case he could not see that the "telegram" gave any assurance that the additional counsel intended to come. The prisoner is now defended by [conscientious] counsel. . . . The Court could not see that any proper cause was made out. The expected counsel might arrive before the case was concluded and could then see all the testimony taken, and thus the prisoner might have the benefit of their advice, although the case should now proceed. As to the matter of insanity, it was not presented in a reliable form. Instead of mere statements, we should have affidavits, or something of that character. He thought, therefore, that the . . . trial should proceed.

The Jury having been sworn to fairly and impartially try the prisoner, the Court directed that the prisoner might forego the form of standing while being arraigned. . . . Mr. Botts put the inquiry to the prisoner, and he continued to be prostrate in his seat while the long indictment, filling seven closely-written foolscap pages, was read; the first count being *insurrection;* the second, *treason;* and the third, *murder.*

Mr. HARDING . . . then addressed the jury and presented the facts of the case, detailing the scenes at the Armory; the killing of the bridge-keeper and the subsequent killing of citizens named in the indictment; the seizing of Messrs. Lewis Washington and Allstadt with their slaves; the forming of a government within the limits of the Commonwealth; holding citizens as prisoners of war and their subsequent capture, &c. He read the law on the subject of treason and levying war against the State; giving comfort to its enemies, or establishing any other government within its limits, offences punishable by death; the murder of citizens, and in connection with these the punishment for rape; [penalty for] several of the charges of the indictment, if proven, being death. All these charges would be distinctly proven beyond the possibility of a doubt on the mind of the jury. . . .

Mr. GREEN . . . next addressed the jury, giving to them the law applicable to the case. He said that the jury must bear in mind that . . . if they have any doubt as to the law and the fact, and that if they have any doubt as to the law or fact affecting the guilt of the prisoner, they are to give the prisoner the benefit of that doubt. The first charge of treason, as a specific act of treason, must be proven. It must be proven that he attempted to establish a separate and distinct government. . . .

Second, conspiring with slaves to rebel and make insurrection. The jury must be satisfied that such conspiracy was done within the State of Virginia. . . . If done in Maryland this Court could not punish the act, as also if done within the limits of the Armory at Harper's Ferry. . . . Attorney-General Cushing had decided this point with regard to the Armory grounds . . . (which opinion was read to the jury), showing that persons residing within the limits of the Armory cannot even be taxed by Virginia, and that crimes committed within the said limits are punishable by the Federal Courts. Although the jury may doubt about the law on this subject, they must give the prisoner the benefit of that doubt.

Upon the third count, that of murder—if it was committed within the limits of the Armory, this Court has no jurisdiction. And in the case of Beckham, if killed on the railroad bridge, it was committed within the State of Maryland, which State claims jurisdiction up to the Armory grounds. Although he may be guilty of murder, it must be proven willful, deliberate, and premeditated murder to make it a capital offence. If otherwise, the killing was murder in the second degree, punishable by imprisonment. If there is any doubt on these points, you must give that doubt to the prisoner. He was satisfied that the jury will not allow any outside excitement to affect them; that they will do their duty. . . .

Mr. BOTTS impressively addressed the jury. The case, he said, was an unusual one. The crimes charged were in many respects unknown to jury trial—calling for calm, unimpassioned deliberation. . . . The jury must rise morally above all prejudices and influences . . . and bear in mind that the mission of the law is not to wreak vengeance. . . . It was due to the prisoner, he said, to state that he believed himself to be actuated by the highest and noblest feeling that ever coursed through a human breast. . . . [Those] gentlemen who were prisoners . . . were treated with respect. . . . These facts must be taken into consideration. . . .

Mr. HUNTER followed. . . . First, as to high treason, this was probably the first case of high treason against the State that had ever been tried by our State courts, and he fervently hoped it would be the last . . . ; and probably in some degree, not only upon our decision, but upon our *prompt decision* of this case, will that result depend. He thought his friends on the other side were totally mistaken in their view that the law, as it now stands on statute-books in reference to overt acts, was, either in language or substance, that contained in the Constitution of the United States. On the contrary, the phraseology had been varied from the Constitution, and, as he conceived, for a plain and palpable purpose. All the powers vested in the Federal Government were given with great jealousy. This was a historical fact, perfectly familiar, and consequently, while treason against the United States consists only in levying war against them, or in adhering to their enemies or giving them aid and comfort, and there is provision that no person shall be convicted of treason unless on testimony of two witnesses of some overt act, or confession in open court, yet the State law is more full, and includes within its definition of treason also the establishing, without authority of the Legislature, any government within its limits separate from the existing government, or holding or executing of such usurped government any office professing allegiance or fidelity to it or resisting the execution of the laws under color of its authority. And it goes on to declare that such treason, if proved by the testimony of two witnesses to the same overt act, or by confession in court, shall be punished by death. . . . The prisoner had attempted to break down the existing government of the Commonwealth and establish on the ruins a new government. . . .

Mr. Hunter then adverted to the question of jurisdiction. . . . Attorney General Cushing . . . was an able man, but came from a region of country where opinions were very different from ours in relation to the powers of the Federal Government as affecting State rights. Our courts have decided adversely to Mr. Cushing's views. . . . [Twentynine] years ago . . . an atrocious murder was committed between the very shops in front of which those men fought their battle, and the criminal was tried here, convicted, and executed under our laws. There was a broad distinction between the cession of jurisdiction by Virginia to the Federal Government and the mere assent of the State that the Federal Government should become a landholder within its limits. The law of Virginia by virtue of which the grounds at Harper's Ferry were purchased by the Federal Government ceded no jurisdiction.

Captain Brown was also guilty on his own notorious confession of advising a conspiracy. In regard to the charge of murder, the proof will be that this man was not only actually engaged in murdering our citizens, but that he was chief director of the whole movement. No matter whether he was present on the spot or a mile off, he is equally guilty. . . .

AFTERNOON SESSION

Dr. STARRY testified.—On Sunday night he heard a shot fired at the Ferry and heard a cry; he looked out and saw two men passing from the bridge towards the Armory gate; a tall man came from the

Armory gate; two men from the cars cried, "There he goes now"; the man stopped and, raising his rifle, fired; they followed him to the Armory gate and exchanged shots with him; Conductor Phelps was one of those men who afterwards found the black man, Hayward, dying in the railroad office; and said he was commanded to stop by the men on the bridge, and refusing to do so they fired upon him; saw several men patrolling during the night and go into the bridge; did not know what to make of it; and went to inquire of the Armory watchmen what it meant; met a man who levelled a rifle at him; asked him where the watchman was; said he was not there, but that there was "a few of us here"; afterwards, towards morning, saw a wagon pass with three armed men following; witness then went to Mr. Kitzmiller and Mr. Ball, and told them that an armed body of men had possession of the Armory, and not to go near it; also, gave information to other persons employed in the Armory; saw also three of them at Hall's works; did not see more than thirty during the night; could recognize them by a peculiar hat they wore . . . ; did not see nor recognize Brown there at all.

Cross-examined by Mr. GREEN.—As I rode past the Armory armed men were at the gates; they did not attempt to stop me, and I was determined not to be stopped.

Conductor PHELPS sworn.—On Sunday night . . . my train arrived at the Ferry at 1:25, bound East; saw no watchman at the bridge, and thought it strange; . . . was in the act of starting ahead again, when the watchman came up to me much excited, and stated that he had been attacked on the bridge by men having rifles; . . . the baggage master and a passenger accompanied me with lights, and when they entered the bridge some one said, "Stand and deliver"; had previously told engineer to follow him slowly, but immediately saw the muzzles of four rifles pointed at us, resting on the railing; told the engineer to back off, as something was wrong in the bridge, which he did. As I got out on the trestling I heard the report of a gun, and Heywood, the colored man, came running to me and said "Captain, I am shot"; . . . carried him to the railroad office and started for a doctor, and saw one man come out of the bridge and go towards the Armory gate; remarked, "There he goes now," and Throckmorton, clerk of the Wager House, fired at him; the shot was returned by two men at the Armory gate; I was close behind Throckmorton, who exchanged several shots with them; . . . heard men loading their rifles again; the reports were very loud, and I wondered why the people were not aroused; walked back to the railroad office, and one of the parties in the bridge came out; he said, "You can come over the bridge with your train"; I replied, "I would rather not, after these proceedings," . . . . I then felt alarmed for the safety of self and passengers and concluded to wait until daylight; men were passing back and forward from the bridge to the gate of the armory, each wrapped in a blanket; . . . I went to the back of the train and saw from twenty to thirty men in and about the engine-house; about four o'clock I saw a wagon driven into the yard and nearly a dozen men jumped out of it; also a carriage; did not see any one get out of it; saw men go backward and forward, who seemed to be putting something in a wagon; they were also going up and down the street leading from the Armory, and all seemed busy at something; this continued until nearly daylight, when the wagon left the yard and passed over the bridge to the Maryland side. About 3 o'clock, before the wagon left, an old gentleman came to me and said, "The Parties who have arrested me have allowed me to come out on condition that I would tell you that you might cross the bridge with your train"; I afterwards learned that this was Mr. Grist, a citizen of the town; . . . afterwards saw man coming down Shenandoah Street with a lantern, and an armed man arrested him; after this saw a short stout negro walking with a staff with one of these men; . . . afterwards a black boy brought a note to the clerk of the Wager House, ordering breakfast for forty-seven men. I . . . met a man, whom I now recognize as Coppoc, and asked what they meant; he replied, "We do not want to injure you or detain your train—you could have gone at 3 o'clock—all we want is to free the negroes"; I then asked if my train could now start, and went to the guard at the gate, who said, "There is Capt. Smith, he can tell you . . ." I walked to the engine-house, . . . ; I asked [Smith] if "I could cross the bridge," . . . and he said, "Why, I sent you word at three o'clock that you could pass"; . . . I then asked him what security I would have that my train could pass safely . . . ; he called a large stout man to accompany him. . . . Brown and his companion both had rifles, and as we crossed the bridge the three armed men were still in their places. When we got across Brown said to me, "You no doubt wonder that a man of my age should be here with a band of armed men, but if you knew my past history you would not wonder at it so much"; my train was then through the bridge, and I bid him good morning, jumped on my train and left him. . . .

Mr. GREEN . . . here interrupted the witness, and said to the Court that he had just received a despatch from Cleveland announcing that counsel was coming for the prisoner, and would almost certainly be here tonight. As this was a very important witness, and as it was now late, he would ask the Court to adjourn until the morning. . . .

The Court decided that the witness should proceed.

Cross-examined by Mr. GREEN.—In the conversation Brown said it was not his intention to harm anybody, and was sorry that men had been killed; it was not by his orders or his approbation, and would not occur again provided people were peaceable and quiet. . . .

Col. LEWIS W. WASHINGTON sworn.—This witness detailed the circumstances as already published.

Cross-examined by Mr. GREEN.—Cannot say whether the marines fired after they broke into the engine-house; the noise was great and several shouted from the inside that one surrendered; the prisoners were kept in the rear of the engine-house and allowed to seek the safest position; saw no effort to endanger us; Brown's conduct was not rude or insulting towards us.

By Mr. HUNTER.—Was present at the conversation with Governor Wise on Tuesday; Gov. Wise asked Brown if he had not selected Harper's Ferry as a border place . . . for the establishment of a provisional government, and he said certainly; he avowed his object to be to free the Southern states, and said his party consisted of twenty-two, nineteen of whom came over with him; he said he had two hundred Sharps rifles, two hundred revolvers, and witness does not remember how many spears; Brown said that he had enough to arm about 1500 men. The Governor asked if he expected that number. He said double that number, or 5000, if he wanted them. . . . Cook said that Brown had been studying this subject twenty or thirty years; had reconnoitered Harper's Ferry repeatedly.

By Mr. BOTTS.—The prisoners were allowed to go out and assure their families of their safety; Brown went out several times and told his men not to return the fire from the dwelling-houses; there were numerous shots from the dwelling-houses; there were also numerous shots from Brown's party towards the tank where Beckham was killed. . . .

By Mr. HUNTER.—While a prisoner in the engine-house overheard a conversation between Stevens and another of the party not known about slave-holding. Stevens asked the man if he was in favor of slavery; he said yes, although not himself a slave-holder; Stevens said, "You are the first man I would have."

By Mr. HARDING.—. . . All the negroes were armed with spears while in the Armory. They walked about the Armory yard and one came and warmed himself; no negroes from this vicinity appeared to take

up arms voluntarily; saw no wounded men dragged into the Armory.
At seven o'clock the Court adjourned until Friday morning.

No. 61

The Baltimore Weekly Sun, Sat., Nov. 5, 1859

THIRD DAY—FRIDAY

The Court met at 11 o'clock, when Brown was led over
from the jail walking, but very feeble. He laid down on the cot as
on yesterday. . . . Before the trial commenced Brown remarked that
the testimony of Mr. Washington and Conductor Phelps yesterday was
strictly truthful. . . .

Mr. Botts announced the arrival of Mr. Hoyt, who had come here
to assist as counsel for the prisoner. At present, however, he did not
feel disposed to take part in the case; whenever he should feel disposed
he would do so. Mr. Hunter suggested that he had better be qualified as
a member of the bar on the production of proof from Boston. . . . The
Court said that strict legal proof of the fact was not required. Any
citizen's evidence would answer. Mr. Green said that his partner had
received letters from fellow-students of Mr. Hoyt's alluding to him as
a member of the bar. Mr. Hoyt then took the customary oath, and the
testimony was resumed.

By Mr. BOTTS. Conductor Phelps recalled. A question was put to
him prepared by Brown, to which he answered: the firing was commenced by those men on the bridge who shot Hayward; the next
firing was by Throckmorton; does not know whether the firing at
Hayward was intentional. There was no attack made on Brown's men
until after Hayward was shot; he was shot by armed men in the Winchester span of the bridge; the sound of a gun was in the bridge.

By Mr. BOTTS.—Lewis Washington recalled. Negotiations were opening with Brown for the release of the prisoners before the general firing
commenced on Monday. . . . At the opening of the negotiations Brown
frequently suggested that the prisoners should cross the bridge with
him to the second canal lock, his party not to be fired upon until after
they reached that point; no objection was made by any of the prisoners
to the proposition. . . . Heard Capt. Brown frequently complain of the
bad faith of the people in firing on a flag of truce; heard him make
no threat or even any expressions of vindictiveness against the people.
Mr. Brua went out and brought in a promise that the people would
not fire while the negotiations were pending. Cannot say that all the

firing of Capt. Brown or his men was in self-defence. Heard Brown
give frequent orders not to fire on unarmed citizens. The first firing
was against the engine-house. Brown said the people appeared to pay
but little regard to the lives of citizens, and we must take our chances
with them. After the first attack on the engine-house by the marines
there was not a general cry of surrender. . . .

Mr. HUNTER laid before the Jury the printed constitution and
ordinances of the provisional government, reading the two first clauses
of the preamble, and the 75th, 45th, and 48th articles, and briefly sum-
ming up other portions. . . . A large bundle of letters was produced,
each . . . handed to Brown, who at the first glance replied to each, in
a loud voice, "Yes, that is mine." These papers and letters were about
fifty in number.

On receiving a list of the members of the convention Mr. Hunter
read it. It was headed William Charles Morris, president of the convention, and H. Kagi, secretary. . . . On handing the list to Brown,
he exclaimed, with a groan, "That's my signature." In reference to
another paper he said, "I have nothing to say about that." A letter was
next read from J. R. Giddings acknowledging the receipt of a letter
from Brown, and stating that he would be pleased to see him at his
house during the summer. Mr. Hunter then read the letter from
Gerrit Smith about "Kansas work," as already published; it is dated
June, 1859, and endorsed on the back in Brown's writing.

Mr. BOTTS here insisted on the right of examining the letters before they were read.

ARMISTEAD BALL, master machinist of the Armory, testified that
on Monday, early in the morning, he was aroused by Benjamin Hobbs,
announcing that persons were at the Armory carrying off Government
property; when he reached the gates he was accosted by two armed men,
and seized as a prisoner; they refused to make any explanation until
he had been taken within the Armory yard; . . . Capt. Brown . . .
told him the object was to free the slaves—not to make war on the
people; that my person and private property would be safe; that his
war was against the accursed system of slavery; that he had power to
do it, and would carry it out; it was no child's play he had undertaken;
he then gave me permission to return to my family to assure them of
my safety and get breakfast; . . . breakfast not being ready, went back,
and was allowed to return home again, under escort, at a later hour;
. . . Captain Brown said it was his determination to seize the arms
and munitions of the Government to arm the blacks, to defend themselves against their masters; Brown also made a proposition to himself

and other officers of the Armory to deliver into his possession the munitions of war belonging to the Government; we replied that they were already in his possession, as we were; Brown frequently told us that our safety depended on the good conduct of our citizens; when the firing commenced all felt we were in danger, and almost any proposition that was made was accepted to secure our safety; . . . Brown made but one proposition, to go to the canal lock, give up their prisoners and fight it out with the military; at daylight on Tuesday morning witness appealed to Brown . . . not to persist in spilling more blood; Brown replied that . . . he was already proclaimed an outlaw, and 3500 dollars was on his head; with regard to the killing of Beckham, one of Brown's party had fired in that direction several times; remonstrated with him when levelling his rifle at an old man named Griess that he was not a combatant, and he desisted; afterwards saw him fire and heard him say, "I dropped him" . . . ; Capt. Brown made active preparations for resisting the marines; he was always in arms, but I do not think I saw him fire. (The other portion of Mr. Ball's testimony was merely in corroboration of Mr. Washington's.)

Cross-examined by Mr. GREEN.—We, as prisoners, agreed to such terms of capitulation as our citizens were willing to accept. A proposal was written by Mr. Daingerfield, dictated by Brown; does not know whether Brown's son and Stevens were wounded while they accompanied the citizens with a flag of truce; . . . Brown repeatedly said he would injure no one, only in self-defence; Coppoc frequently urged us to seek places of safety, but Brown did not; . . . and at the time of the charge of the marines told us we must equally occupy the post of danger with themselves; there were three or four slaves in the engine-house; they had spears, but all seemed badly scared; Mr. Washington's "Phil" was ordered by Mr. Brown to cut a port-hole through the brick wall; he continued until a brisk fire commenced outside, when he said, "It's getting too hot for Phil," and he squatted; Brown then took up the tools and finished the hole.

JOHN ALLSTADT sworn.—On Morning morning, about three o'clock, was aroused from sleep; asked who was at the door, and the reply was, "Get up quick or we will burn you"; asked what they intended to do; they said, "Free the country of slavery"; told me they were going to take me to Harper's Ferry; . . . [They] had all my blacks, seven in number; we were all put into a wagon; the negroes were then armed with pikes; we went to the Armory yard, where I was put in charge of one of Brown's party; afterwards we were ordered into the watch-house; I saw Colonel Washington there. Brown came and spoke to us about our getting two negroes to take our place, and then he would release us; nothing further was said about that; Brown's rifle was cocked all the time; . . . witness was afterwards transferred to the engine-house; several negroes were there; saw "Phil" making port-holes by Brown's order; the other negroes were doing nothing, and had dropped their spears; some of them were asleep nearly all the time [laughter]; when the marines made the assault Brown's party took a position behind the engines and aimed at the door; Brown was in front squatting; he fired at the marines and my opinion is that he killed that marine.

By Mr. GREEN.—Did not see any others shoot; cannot state certainly by what shot the marine was killed. . . .

ALEXANDER KELLY sworn.—Witness described the manner of Thomas Boerley's being killed on Monday; Brown's party fired at witness and witness returned the fire; Mr. Boerley was with witness and was armed with a gun; saw him soon after he was shot. . . .

ALBERT GRIST sworn.—On Sunday night had been to [prayer] meeting with my son; on coming home across Shenandoah bridge was seized by two men with rifles; . . . they told me I should not be hurt, and asked me whether there were many slave-holders about Harper's Ferry; I told them no; Brown came up and observed, "You have got some prisoners"; they took us to the Armory; we found some citizens there; being tired, witness laid down; Brown said the object was to free the slaves; told him there was not many there; he replied the book says we are all free and equal, and said if we were peaceable we would not be hurt; if not, the town would be taken and laid in ashes; when the cars came down there was some firing; afterwards, about 3 o'clock, witness was sent to tell the conductor that the train might pass unmolested; saw Mr. Beckham, and delivered the message; Brown then dismissed me, but witness did not go home, being afraid of some of Brown's men, not knowing this, might shoot me; saw Hayward brought in wounded.

Mr. KELLY recalled.—Saw George W. Turner killed on High Street; he was shot while in the act of levelling his gun; the shot came from the corner of Shenandoah and High streets; the men who fired had rifles, and one had a shawl on.

AFTERNOON SESSION

. . . HENRY HUNTER sworn.—Went to the Ferry with the Charlestown Guards, but stayed in the bridge; left my company and went off, fighting on my own hook; saw Beckham fall . . . ; thinks Beckham had a pistol in his coat pocket . . . ; don't think the people from the Armory yard saw it. . . .

BENJAMIN F. BEALL sworn.—Went to Harper's Ferry armed; did not join the military, but was stationed at the Galt House in Capt. Botts's company; in the evening walked out on the platform of the railroad; saw Mr. Beckham shot; went as near him as was safe, but perceived he was not breathing; there was firing from the engine-house toward the railroad; Mr. Young, one of the Jefferson Guards, was wounded while making a charge against the insurgents; saw others shot. . . .

Cross-examined.—There was a general firing in almost every direction; McCabe was about firing when he was shot; there were 25 or 30 men firing at the engine-house when McCabe and Young were wounded. . . .

TESTIMONY FOR THE DEFENCE

. . . JOS. A. BRUA . . . testified that he was one of the prisoners in the engine-house. . . . Brown remarked that the prisoners should share their danger; they were allowed to shelter themselves as they could. Mr. Cross went out with a flag of truce; another went out in the same manner and came back wounded. Stevens and Kitzmiller went out, and Stevens was shot. After that it commenced raining very hard. . . . Witness was allowed to go and assist Stevens into the hotel; he returned, according to his pledge, to the engine-house. Was sent several times by Brown to request the citizens not to shoot, as the lives of the prisoners were being endangered. . . . Brown proposed that he should retain possession of what he held, including the Armory and negroes. Col. Washington and all seemed to acquiesce. . . . Mr. Cross was sent out to confer with Mr. Beckham and others on the subject; a guard went with him, who were fired on. After that Stevens wanted to shoot, but Kitzmiller appealed to him, and they went out together to stop the firing; when they did not return Brown seemed to show temper, and there was a change in his arrangements. After that Brown said he had it in his power to destroy that place in half an hour, but he would not do it unless resisted. . . . The special object of witness going out was to stop the firing from the tank, which was annoying those in the guard-house.

A. M. KITZMILLER sworn.—Made repeated endeavors to communicate the state of affairs to Brown. He said his object there was to free the slaves from bondage, and, if necessary, to fight pro-slavery men for that purpose. . . . I had no flag of truce, and did not consider myself bearer of a flag of truce. I descried the rifle company on the bridge, saw they were our own men, and waved my handkerchief, and told Stevens and the other man to remain. I soon heard firing very close; Stevens fired in reply to a shot which struck him from a house on the side of the Winchester railroad. Stevens fell and the other man returned. . . . Thompson . . . was taken prisoner and was shot on the bridge. (Capt. Brown here cried out, "Describe the circumstances connected with the death of Thompson!") I was not there; did not see it; the last I saw of Thompson he was a prisoner with the Ferry people on the bridge; Moore, Burkhard, and Anderson, and twenty or thirty others were there; Mr. Beckham was killed at or about the time Thompson was taken; did not return to the engine-house; the object of witness was to prevent unnecessary shedding of blood; went out at request of Brown to use his influence for that purpose. . . .

Mr. GREEN here stated to the Court that he desired to bring out testimony relating to the shooting of Thompson, one of the insurgents on the bridge, but the State objected to it unless Brown had a knowledge of that shooting.

Mr. HUNTER said that a vast deal of testimony about Brown's forbearance and not shooting citizens had been adduced, but it had no more to do with this case than the dead languages. If he understood the affair, it was to show that . . . Thompson was dispatched after Beckham's death under circumstances perhaps which he himself should not at all approve. . . .

The COURT thought those facts . . . admissible as evidence.

HENRY HUNTER.—I am related to Mr. Beckham . . . ; when he was shot I . . . started with Mr. Chambers to the room where . . . Thompson was confined. . . . We . . . levelled our guns at him, when Mr. Foulk's sister threw herself before him . . . ; we then caught hold of him and dragged him out by the throat; he cried out, "Though you may take my life, thousands and millions will rise up to avenge me and carry out my purpose of giving liberty to the slaves"; we carried him to the bridge, and two of us levelled our guns, and at this moment of wild exasperation . . . a dozen more balls were buried in him; we then threw his body off the trestle . . . and returned to bring out Stevens, intending to serve him in the same way. We found him suffering from wounds, and probably dying, and concluded to spare him. . . .

REZIN CROSS sworn.—I prepared the proposition that Brown should retain possession of the Armory, that he should release us, and that the firing should stop. . . . [There] was another paper prepared by Kitzmiller and some others. I went out to stop the firing; a man went

with me; they took him prisoner and tied him. This was Thompson.
. . . Brown's treatment to me was kind and respectful. . . .

Several witnesses for the prisoner were here called and did not answer.
It was stated that the subpoenas had not been returned. Capt. Brown
here rose from his mattress, evidently excited. Starting upon his feet,
he addressed the Court as follows: "May it please the Court, . . . I
gave the names, as soon as I could get them, of the persons I wished
to have called . . . and was assured they should be subpoenaed. I wrote
down a memorandum to that effect, saying where these parties were.
But it appears that they have not been summoned, so far as I can
learn. And now I ask, if I am to have anything at all deserving the
name or the shadow of a fair trial, that this proceeding be deferred
until tomorrow morning, for I have no counsel, as I have before
stated, on whom I feel that I can rely. But I am in hopes that counsel
may arrive. . . . I have nobody to do any errand for me, for my
money was taken from me when I was sacked and stabbed, and I
have now not a dime. . . ." Brown then laid down again, drew his
blanket over him and closed his eyes, and appeared to sink in a tranquil
slumber.

Mr. HOYT, of Boston, who had been sitting quietly all day at the
side of Mr. Botts, now rose, amid great sensation, and addressed the
Court as follows:

May it please the Court, I would add my voice to the appeal of
Capt. Brown, although I have had no consultation with him, that a
further hearing of the case be postponed until morning. He said he
would state the reason for this request. He was informed and had
reason to believe that Judge Tilden, of Ohio, was on the way to
Charlestown, and would undoubtedly arrive . . . tonight. . . . He had
taken measures to secure that gentleman's arrival at this place tonight
if he reached the Ferry. For himself, he had come from Boston,
travelling night and day, to volunteer his services in the defence of
Capt. Brown, but he could not take the responsibility of undertaking
his defence as now situated. . . . I have not read the indictment through;
have not, except so far as I have listened to this case and heard the
counsel this morning, got any idea of the line of defence proposed. I
have no knowledge of the criminal code of Virginia, and have had
no time to read it. . . . For all these reasons I ask a continuance of
the case till morning.

Mr. BOTTS. . . . [On] first being assigned as counsel for Capt.
Brown, I conferred with him, and at his instance took down a list
of the witnesses he desired subpoenaed. In his behalf, though late at

night, I called up the Sheriff and informed him that I wished subpoenas issued early in the morning. This was done, and these are here— Messrs. Phelps, Williams, and Grist, who have been examined.

Sheriff CAMPBELL stated that the subpoenas were placed in the hands of the officers with the request to serve them at once, and they must have served them, as some of the witnesses are here. The processes not returned may have been sent by private hands and failed to arrive. . . .

Mr. HUNTER. . . . I beg leave to say, in reference to this application, that I suppose the court, even under these circumstances, will have to be satisfied in some way, through the counsel or otherwise, that this testimony is material. . . . So far as any of the witnesses have been examined, the evidence relates to the conduct of Captain Brown in treating his prisoners with leniency, respect, and courtesy, and . . . that his flags of truce . . . were not respected by the citizens. . . . If the defence take this course we are perfectly willing to admit these facts. . . . Unless the court shall be satisfied that this testimony—every particle of which, I have no doubt, is here that could be got—is material to the defence, I submit that the application for delay on that score ought not to be granted. . . . I simply suggest that it is due, in justice to the Commonwealth, . . . that information be given the court showing that the additional testimony wanted is relevant to the issue. The simple statement of counsel I do not think would be sufficient.

Mr. GREEN rose to state that Mr. Botts and himself would both now withdraw from the case, and could no longer act in behalf of the prisoner, he having got up and declared that he has no confidence in the counsel who have been assigned. . . .

Mr. HARDING.—We have been delayed from time to time by similar applications . . . until we now have reached a point of time when we are ready to submit the case to the jury upon the evidence and law, when another application arises. . . . The very witness that they now consider material, Mr. Daingerfield, came here summoned by ourselves, but deeming that we had testimony enough, we did not examine him.

Mr. BOTTS. . . . [There] is now here a gentleman from Boston who has come on to volunteer his services for the prisoner. I suggest to the court to allow him this night for preparation. My notes, my office, and my services shall be at his command. I will sit up with him all night. . . . I cannot do more; and in the meantime the sheriff can be directed to have the other witnesses here tomorrow. . . .

The COURT would not compel the gentlemen to remain on the case,

and accordingly granted the request . . . and at 6 o'clock adjourned.
. . . There is great excitement. . . . The conduct [of the defense] is
to gain time.

No. 62
The National Intelligencer, Tues., Nov. 1, 1859

FOURTH DAY—SATURDAY

The Court met at 10 o'clock. . . . The arrival of H. Griswold, Esq., from Cleveland, Ohio, to take part with Geo. H. Hoyt, Esq.,
of Boston, in the defence, has increased the excitement. Samuel Chilton,
Esq., of Washington, who arrived this morning, will also join the
defence. At 11 o'clock the prisoner was brought into Court and laid
down on his cot. Mr. Hoyt . . . entered . . . accompanied by H. Griswold and Samuel Chilton, Esqs., the latter two gentlemen taking the
oath as attorneys in this Court.

Mr. CHILTON.— . . . I was yesterday very unexpectedly called upon
to come here and take part. . . . I took some time . . . to consider the
proposition, and finally agreed to come on under the expectation of
finding Messrs. Botts and Green still in the case. On arriving here,
however, I learned for the first time the course the case had taken last
evening. These circumstances would render it impossible for him to
discharge the full duty of counsel, not having had time to read the
indictment or examine the evidence already taken. . . . A short delay
of a few hours . . . would enable them to make preparation.

The COURT decided that the trial must go on. Counsel had been
assigned to the prisoner here, of his own selection, who had labored
zealously in his behalf, and had withdrawn because the prisoner had,
yesterday evening, declared in open court, that he had no confidence
in them. . . . Several similar cases remain to be disposed of. This term
will very soon end. . . . The trial must therefore proceed.

Mr. HOYT remarked that yesterday the Attorney for the Commonwealth produced various papers in court which were identified . . .
some as being in Capt. Brown's hand-writing and some as bearing his
endorsement. He had hastily examined those papers, and wished to
object to some. . . . [He said] I desire to know the object of counsel
in introducing those papers.

Mr. HUNTER.—The papers speak for themselves. . . .

MR. HOYT.—I object to the autobiography of Captain Brown as
having no bearing on this case.

Mr. HUNTER.—I withdraw it.

Mr. HOYT.—I object to the letter of Gerrit Smith.

Mr. HUNTER.—I withdraw that, too.

Mr. HOYT.—I handed to the clerk last night a list of names we wished summoned as witnesses: Samuel Strider, Henry Ault, Benjamin F. Mills, John E. P. Daingerfield, and Capt. Simms. I got a despatch just now informing me that Capt. Simms had gone to Frederick, but would return in the first train this morning. I would like to inquire whether the process had reached Captain Simms. . . .

Mr. HUNTER.—He was here yesterday; I hope we will proceed with some other[s].

JOHN E. P. DAINGERFIELD called and testified that he was an officer of the Armory; he was a prisoner . . . at the engine-house; negotiations were going on for the release of all the prisoners before the firing commenced; about a dozen black men were there armed with pikes, which they carried most awkwardly and unwillingly; during the firing they were lying about asleep, some of them having crawled under the [fire] engines; . . . he had no personal fear from [Brown] or his men during his confinement; saw one of the men shot in the engine-house . . . and he died in a few moments; this he learned was one of Capt. Brown's sons; saw . . . come in wounded [another] son of Capt. Brown, . . . wounded whilst out with Mr. Kitzmiller; the prisoner complained frequently of his men being shot down whilst carrying a flag of truce.

Mr. HUNTER complained of going over again the same facts. . . .

Mr. HOYT stated that he regarded it as the only feasible line of defence. . . . It was the duty of counsel if possible to show that Capt. Brown was not guilty of treason, murder, or insurrection, according to the terms of this indictment. We hope to prove the absence of malicious intention. . . . [The] course being pursued was not only in accordance with their conviction of duty, but in accordance with the express commands of their client. . . .

Mr. DAINGERFIELD resumed.—Heard some conversation by Capt. Brown as to having it in his power to lay the town in ashes and carrying off the women and children, but that he had refrained from so doing; . . . the only threat . . . was at the commencement of the storming of the engine-house; he then said that we must all take equal shares with him . . . [but] made no attempt to deprive us of the places we had taken; Brown promised safety to all . . . property except slave property; at the time of the assault by the marines one of the men cried out for quarter; he had heard the same man, in a conversation with Brown during the night, ask him if he was committing treason against his country in resisting the marines, to which Brown replied that he was; the man then said, "I will fight no longer," that he thought he was merely fighting to liberate the slaves . . . ; after the first attack Capt. Brown cried out to surrender, but he was not heard; did not see him fire afterwards; saw Coppoc attempt to fire twice, but the caps exploded; witness saw Capt. Brown wounded by a thrust. . . . Captain Brown appeared to be shielding himself with his head down, but making no resistance; the parties outside appeared to be firing as they pleased.

Mr. MILLS, master armorer. . . . —Witness was . . . confined in the engine-house; before the general firing commenced negotiations were pending for the release of the prisoners; a paper was drawn up which witness refused to sign; another paper was drawn up embracing certain terms and borne by Mr. Brua to the citizens outside; the terms were not agreed to; the last time Mr. Brua was out there was severe firing, which, I suppose, prevented his return; Brown's son went out with a flag of truce, and was shot; . . . heard Brown frequently complain that the citizens had acted in a barbarous manner; he did not appear to have any malicious feeling; he undoubtedly seemed to expect reinforcements; said it would soon be night and he would have more assistance; his intentions were to shoot nobody unless they were carrying or using arms; "If you do, let them have it"; this was while the firing was going on. (Capt. Brown here asked witness whether he saw any firing on his part which was not purely defensive.) It might be considered in that light perhaps; the balls came into the engine-house pretty thick. (Question by Counsel: Did you not frequently go to the door of the engine-house?) No, indeed. (*Laughter*).

A general colloquy ensued between the prisoner, lying on his cot, and the witness. . . . No objection was made to Brown's asking . . . questions . . . , and interposing verbal explanations. . . . Witness's wife and daughter were permitted to visit him unmolested, and free verbal communication was allowed with those outside; we were treated kindly, but we were compelled to stay where we did not want to be; Brown appeared anxious to effect a compromise.

SAMUEL STRIDER sworn.—This witness proceeded to detail all the circumstances of the two days, with what he thought, etc.; nothing new was elicited. He confirmed . . . that Brown endeavored to protect his hostages, etc. . . .

AFTERNOON SESSION

Capt. SIMMS, Commander of a volunteer company of Frederick,

Maryland, was sworn.—The rumor came to Frederick that 750 blacks
and abolitionists had seized Harper's Ferry; witness started for the
Ferry with the volunteers, under command of Col. Shriver . . . ; after
he reached there on Monday afternoon the door of the engine-house
was partly open, and witness was hailed from there . . . and went in;
he met Mr. Daingerfield and others there; Capt. Brown said to witness
. . . that he wanted to be allowed to go over the bridge unmolested,
and that we then might take him if we could; he had fought Uncle
Sam before, and was willing to do it again; Brown complained that
his men had been shot down like dogs while bearing a flag of truce;
told [Brown] that they must expect to be shot down like dogs if they
take up arms in that way; said he had full possession of the town
and could have massacred the inhabitants . . . had he thought proper
. . . so he thought he was entitled to some terms; Brown said he had
shot no one who had not carried arms; . . . he seemed sorry to hear
of [Beckham's] death, and said, "I fight only those who fight me."
Witness then told the prisoner that he did not think any compromise
could be effected. Brown said he kept the hostages for his own safety;
they did not appear to fear any injury from him or his men . . . ;
every man had a gun, and four-fifths of them were under no command.
The military had ceased firing for the night, but men who were
intoxicated were firing their guns in the air, and others at the engine-
house. Brown or any of his men could not have ventured outside of
the door . . . that night without being shot; saw Stevens in the hotel
after he had been wounded, and shamed some young men who were
endeavoring to shoot him as he laid in his bed apparently dying; told
them if the man could stand on his feet with a pistol in his hand they
would all jump out of the window. . . . He had no sympathy for the
acts of the prisoner or his movement . . . but he regarded Capt. Brown
as a brave man, and . . . as a Southern man he came here to state
the facts about the case, so that Northern men would have no opportunity of saying that Southern men were unwilling to appear as
witnesses in behalf of one whose principles they abhorred. . . .

Here the defense closed their testimony. None of the witnesses for
the defense were cross-examined by the State.

Mr. CHILTON, for the prisoner, rose and submitted a motion that
the prosecution in this case be compelled to elect one of the counts in
the indictment and abandon the others. The indictment consists of
four counts, and is endorsed thus: An indictment for treason, advising
and conspiring with slaves and others to rebel, and for murder. The
charge for murder is laid in two of the counts, the third and fourth.

The charge of treason is in the first, and the second count alleges a charge different from that which is endorsed on the back of the indictment, and which is upon record. The second count is under the following statute:

"If a free person advise or conspire with a slave to rebel or make an insurrection, he shall be punished with death, whether such rebellion or insurrection be made or not."

But the second count in the indictment is that these parties who are charged by the indictment conspired together, and with other persons, to induce certain slaves, the property of Messrs. Allstadt and Washington, to make rebellion and insurrection. There is a broad distinction between advising and conspiring with slaves to rebel, and advising and conspiring with others to induce slaves to rebel. Whether he was to avail himself of this irregularity by instructions from the Court to the jury to disregard this second count entirely, or whether it would be proper to wait until the conclusion of the trial and then move an arrest of judgment, he left to his Honor to decide. He proceeded to argue the motion that the prosecution be compelled to elect one count and abandon another, quoting Archbold's Criminal Pleading in support of his view. He further alluded to the hardship which rests upon the prisoner to meet various and distinct charges in the same trial. From the authority he read it would be seen that in case of treason different descriptions of treason could not be united in the same indictment. High treason could not be associated with other treason. If an inferior grade of an offence of the same character could not be included in separate counts, still less can an offence of a different character. Treason in this country is high treason; treason against the State of Virginia is treason against her sovereignty. We have no other description of treason, because treason can only be committed against sovereignty, whether that of the United States or of a sovereign State.

Mr. HARDING could not see the force of the objection made by the learned counsel of the other side. In regard to the separate offences being charged, they were but different parts of one transaction. Treason against the Government is properly made the subject of one of the counts; but we also have a count of murder, for it can hardly be supposed that treason can exist without being followed or accompanied by murder. Murder arose out of this treason, and was the natural result of this bloody conspiracy. Yet now, after all the evidence has been given on all these points, the objection is made that we must confine ourselves to a single one of them. He hoped that no such motion would be granted.

Mr. HUNTER followed on the same side. He replied to the argument of Mr. Chilton, saying that the discretion of the court in compelling the prosecution to elect one count in the indictment is only exercised where great embarrassment would otherwise result to the prisoner. As applied to this particular case it involved this point, that, notwithstanding the transaction, as has been disclosed in the evidence, be one transaction, a continued, closely-connected series of acts, which, according to our apprehension of the law of the land, involve the three great offences of treason, conspiring with and advising slaves to make insurrection, and the perpetration of murder,—yet in a case of this character, we are told it is not only right but proper to put the prosecution upon their election as to one of the three, and bar us from the investigation of the two others entirely, although they relate to facts involved in one grand fact. Notwithstanding the multiplicity of duties involved upon the prosecutor and assistant prosecutor, yet we have found time to be guarded and careful in regard to the mode of framing the indictment. It is my work, and I propose to defend it as right and proper.

Mr. Hunter then proceeded to quote Chitty's Criminal Law and 3 [sic] Robinson's Practice, to prove that the discretion of the court there spoken of is only to be exercised in reference to the furtherance of the great object in view—the attainment of justice. Where the prisoner is not embarrassed in making his defence, this discretion is not to be exercised by the court, and no case can be shown that it has been thus exercised where the whole ground of the indictment referred to one and the same transaction. This very case would show the absurdity of the principle, if it were as broad as contended for by his learned friend. As for the other point of objection, it was too refined and subtle for his poor intellect.

Mr. CHILTON responded.—In order to ascertain what a party is tried for, we must go to the finding of the Grand Jury. If the grand jury return an indictment charging the party with murder, finding a true bill for that, and he should be indicted for manslaughter or any other offence, the court would not have jurisdiction to try him on that count in the indictment; and the whole question turns on the construction of the section of the statute which has been read, viz., whether or not advising or conspiring with slaves to rebel is a separate and distinct offence from conspiring with other persons to induce slaves to rebel.

The COURT said that the difference might perhaps be taken advantage of to move an arrest of judgment, but the jury had been charged and had been sworn to try the prisoner on the indictment as drawn. The trial must go on, and counsel could afterwards move an arrest of judgment. As to the other objection, the Court made this answer: The very fact that one offence can be charged in different counts, varying the language and circumstances, is based upon the idea that distinct offences may be charged in the same indictment. Prisoners are to be tried on the various counts as if they were various transactions. There is no legal objection against charging various crimes in the same indictment. The practice has been to put a party upon election where the prisoner would be embarrassed in his defence; but that is not the law. In this case these offences charged are all part of the same transaction, and no case is made out for the Court to interfere and put the parties upon an election.

Mr. CHILTON said he would reserve the motion as a basis for a motion of arrest of judgment.

ANOTHER MOTION FOR TIME

Mr. GRISWOLD remarked that the position of all the present counsel for the prisoner was one of very great embarrassment. They had no disposition to interfere with the course of practice, but it was the desire of the defendant that the case should be argued. He supposed that counsel could obtain sufficient knowledge of the evidence previously taken by reading the notes of it. But it was now nearly dark. He supposed, if it was to be argued at all, the argument for the Commonwealth would probably occupy the attention of the Court until the usual hour of adjournment, unless it was the intention to continue a late evening session. From what had heretofore transpired, he felt a delicacy in making any request of the Court, but knowing that the case was now ended, except for mere argument, he did not think it would be asking too much for the Court to adjourn after the opening argument on behalf of the presentation.

Mr. HUNTER.— . . . He was bound to remember, and respectfully to remind the Court, that the state of things which place counsel in a somewhat embarrassing position in conducting the defence was purely and entirely the act of the prisoner. His counsel will not be responsible for it; the Court is not responsible for it; but the unfortunate prisoner is responsible for his own act in dismissing his faithful, skillful, able, and zealous counsel on yesterday afternoon. . . . Not only were the jurors kept away from their families by these delays, but there was not a female in this county who, whether with good cause or not, was not trembling with anxiety and apprehension. . . . and it was for his Honor to weigh these in opposite scales, and determine whether we should not go on and bring this case to a close tonight. We had until 12 o'clock to do it in.

Mr. CHILTON said their client desired that they should argue his case. It was impossible for him to do so now, and he could not allow himself to make an attempt at argument on a case about which he knew so little. . . . He would be the last man in the world to subject the jurors to inconvenience unnecessarily; but although the prisoner may have been to blame, . . . he could not see that he should therefore be forced to have his case submitted without argument. In a trial for life and death we should not be precipitate.

The COURT here consulted the jurors, who expressed themselves very anxious to get home. His Honor said that he was desirous of trying this case precisely as he would try another, without any reference to outside feeling. . . .

COMMENCEMENT OF ARGUMENT

Mr. HARDING then commenced the opening argument for the Commonwealth, and spoke only for about forty minutes. He reviewed the testimony . . . and dwelt for some time on the absurdity of the claim . . . of the prisoner that he should have been treated according to the rules of honorable warfare. He seemed to have lost sight of the fact that he was in command of a band of murderers and thieves and had forfeited all title to protection of any kind.

The Court then adjourned . . . to meet again at 10 o'clock on Monday morning, when Mr. Chilton will deliver the opening speech for the prisoner.

No. 63　　CONVICTION OF CAPTAIN BROWN

The National Intelligencer, Thurs., Nov. 3, 1859

FIFTH DAY—MONDAY

The Court met at 9 o'clock. The prisoner was brought in, and the trial proceeded without delay. Brown looks better than heretofore, and his health is evidently improving. He laid on his bed, as usual.

OPENING FOR THE DEFENCE

Mr. GRISWOLD, of Ohio, opened for the defence, taking up the several charges of the indictment . . . With regard to the charge of treason . . . Mr. Griswold argued that Brown could not be guilty of treason, as he was not a citizen of this Commonwealth, and none but a citizen of the Commonwealth could commit treason. Never having sworn allegiance to Virginia, he could not be a rebel against her authority. He was also charged with levying war against the State, but the evidence given did not support the charge. There was a great difference between levying war and resisting authority. Men congregate together to perpetrate crime and have their rules and regulations, and when assailed they defend their lives to the utmost—sacrificing and intending to sacrifice the lives of others; but that was resistance, not levying war. He would not shrink from the admission, and the prisoner openly admitted it, that these men came for the purpose of running away slaves. That was the crime under the laws of Virginia for which the prisoner was amenable to punishment to the extent of those laws. In carrying out that purpose he temporarily took possession of the arsenal at Harper's Ferry, and while there attempts were made to arrest him. Mr. Griswold had no complaint to make about that, but it was in resisting those attempts that this blood was shed and lives taken, and not in levying war against the Commonwealth. It was resisting that which was claimed to be the legal authority of Virginia seeking to arrest those men assembled in violation of law. Such things have often happened. Jails have been broken open, and men taken thence and executed in defiance of law, after being acquitted by a jury of their countrymen, and the power of the Sheriff trampled under foot. Neither does it necessarily constitute levying war if murder ensues; because the commission of the offence, or shedding of blood, may not have been contemplated.

It is said here was an organized movement, and a pamphlet is referred to as evidence of that fact; but it does not necessarily follow that the overthrow of the Commonwealth of Virginia was contemplated by any thing that appeared in that book. The most harmless organizations in the country have been created with all the outside forms and machinery of government. In debating societies governments have been established, a congress created, resolutions and laws discussed; and anyone reading the bulletins of these associations and knowing nothing about them, would suppose them miniature governments organized within the limits of existing governments. No matter what names, what officers they may have, that of itself is not sufficient. Bands of robbers and desperadoes have their rules and regulations, their officers, and they have prescribed death as a punishment for the violation of their laws; but that does not imply that they contemplate the overthrow of the legitimate government. It is only an association and government to control themselves in their intercourse with each other. . . . [The] jury could not find Captain Brown guilty of treason unless they find him guilty of associating with others to organize a government to subvert and overthrow the government of Virginia. But if the pamphlet proved anything it shows that the attempt was to organize a government in opposition to the Government of the United States, and not of Virginia, for all the terms used and all officers appointed have reference to a government like that of the United States. But it was in vague, un-meaning language, which really proves nothing at all. However, there was a clause in it which must be taken, for it was all in evidence, making a distinct and positive statement that it contemplated no overthrow of the General or State Governments, but simply amendment and repeal of obnoxious laws in a constitutional manner. The learned attorney who opened the case seemed to omit this ground entirely. . . .

Mr. Griswold proceeded to discuss the charge of conspiring with slaves. He said there was a manifest distinction between an effort to run off slaves or steal slaves and a conspiring to induce them to rebel. Rebellion and insurrection was a rising up, not to run away, although freedom might be the ultimate object, but a rising up against their masters, against the whites, against the State. It contemplates murder, rapine, arson, and all crimes which follow an insurrection, more es-pecially a servile insurrection. The question was as to the object and intention of the parties. Has any man testified aught going to show that Brown or any one with him said or did one thing to induce the slaves to rise in rebellion, or perpetrate any offence out of which re-bellion grows? Slaves were taken possession of for a temporary purpose and placed in the arsenal; but Col. Washington . . . testified that not a slave took part in the matter except Phil. . . . That was not done for the purpose of insurrection or rebellion, but to protect themselves. True, they were engaged in an unlawful act, but it was not the act charged. They were amenable to punishment, but not as indicated. They are punishable in some ways, but not as charged.

The counsel next proceeded to consider the count charging murder in the first degree. This was a crime involving premeditated murder, but he argued that no such malice had been shown. First, Heywood was killed. . . . Whether it was an accidental or an intentional killing does not appear in the evidence, or by whom it was committed. . . . He could only say, as Brown said to him, "Why should we shoot a negro? . . ." He did not justify these men in staying there and resisting the authority of the country, but he said they were there protecting themselves from arrest. Guns were fired in all directions, and they fired, or intended to fire, only on armed men. Without excusing that conduct for one moment, he would remark that it refuted the idea of premeditated malice. They had not time for the thought and reflection which the law contemplates; not that he would say these men should be allowed to come within the Commonwealth of Virginia, perpetrate these crimes, and go unwhipt of justice, but charge and convict them according to their own law. Virginia has laws and institutions sufficient for her protection, and she has thrown over the lives of her citizens every safeguard that she deems necessary and essential. . . . Capt. Brown knew he was committing an offence against the laws for the protection of slave property . . . and is willing to abide the consequences; but . . . do not convict him of an offence he never dreamed of committing. . . . If a man of the indomitable energy and perseverance of Capt. Brown could be engaged for five months prosecuting such an enterprise, and only gather throughout the United States twenty-one men, black and white, when there was nothing in the world to oppose him, how, in Heaven's name, can it be supposed . . . that there is the remotest danger of another scheme akin to this? . . . .

Mr. CHILTON spoke of the embarrassment with which he undertook the case. . . . He had no sympathy with the prisoner. His own birth and residence until a few years past, had been in Virginia. . . . Although now a resident of the District of Columbia, he had returned to his native State to spend the remainder of his days and mingle his dust with her soil. No other motive operated on him than that of discharging a disinterested duty faithfully. He regretted only the excitement respecting the case. . . . He could not understand . . . on what ground the charges against the prisoner were attempted to be sustained. . . . There were three distinct charges—first, of treason. This was an offence at common law. The word is derived from a French word signifying betrayal. Treason means betrayal of trust or confidence; the violation of fidelity or allegiance to the Commonwealth. He maintained that treason could not be committed against the Commonwealth except by a citizen thereof. In the present case the whole proof shows that this prisoner is not a citizen of Virginia, and therefore cannot be found guilty of treason. The indictment charges the prisoner with committing every act comprising treason. They are charged with levying war against the State and exciting slaves to insurrection, but there was no proof that they committed these acts. There was no proof that they resisted any process issued against them. . . . Hence, under the authority of the Commonwealth, they were rather guilty of resisting *colleo,* which was a resistance of the Federal Government, and not of the Commonwealth.

He had read carefully the prepared provisional constitution, and he regarded it as ridiculous nonsense, a wild chimerical production which could only be produced by men of unsound minds. It defines no territory over which it is intended to operate. . . . It did not even undertake to levy taxes, which is essential to any government. It does not appear that this association was to be established in Virginia, or where it was to go into effect. This was not treason. Is it the adoption of a constitution and the establishment of a government? By no means. These parties had a mere imaginary government to govern themselves, and nobody else—just like rules governing a military company or debating society. Even if they intended to set up a government over others they did not do it. . . . Now, look at the 46th article . . . , which expressly declares that the foregoing articles shall not be construed so as to encourage overthrow of any State government or the General Government, and looks to no dissolution of the Union, but simply amendment and repeal. . . .

Again, the prisoner is charged with conspiring with slaves to make an insurrection. No proof had been shown that the slaves had entered into a conspiracy, and unless that was the case, where was the conspiracy? One party cannot conspire alone. Each charge is to be considered alone by the jury. If they believe the evidence does not warrant a conviction on the charge of treason, they must consider the charge of conspiracy just as if no charge of treason had been made. One count in the indictment was not to be brought in to aid another. He considered that the prisoner had a right to be tried one charge at a time, and entirely disconnected with any other. The Court had, however, overruled the motion made on Saturday, and hence the importance of making this point clear to the jury, so that they might not confuse the various offences and the evidence relating to each.

Next, as to the charge of murder. It was a very singular way of doing business. By the indictment five prisoners are charged with the murder of four men. That they might have done it jointly, he could understand. But they could not severally have done it. . . . [It] was almost impossible for the prisoner to make a defence against such a charge. It was too loose and vague. By the laws of Virginia there was but one specific grade of murder punishable with death, and that was deliberate, premeditated murder. The prosecution charges the prisoner with murder in the first degree, but . . . the evidence . . . does not sustain the charge. The prisoner's conduct in the engine-house showed that there was no malice. . . . The subsequent conflict resulted in the loss of life, but the prisoner endeavored to avoid that conflict, for the purpose of saving life, and therefore could not have been actuated by malice, which is necessary to constitute murder in the first degree. Even if the prisoner was guilty of murder in the second degree or manslaughter, yet that was not a capital crime, and not the crime charged in the indictment. . . . Captain Brown was justified in returning fire when he was fired upon under such circumstances. It was a sort of self-defence; and very probably had a little more time been allowed, these men could have been taken into custody without loss of life. . . .

Mr. HUNTER now rose to close . . . for the prosecution. . . . [He] proceeded to remove the objections that might have been made as to the power of the court to try the case founded on the place where the offence was committed. It was hardly necessary to show that it was within the county of Jefferson, and within the jurisdiction of this court. There was a law in Virginia declaring the bounds of the Commonwealth, making the Potomac river the boundary between Maryland and Virginia, and giving either of the States powers, by a plain compact, to execute a criminal process to the farthest bank. These matters, which are contained in the code of Virginia, it was unnecessary to prove by witnesses. The jury could read the code for themselves. Another law defined the limits of Jefferson county, showing that it embraced the locality where these events occurred, and giving jurisdiction to this court. It was hinted in the preliminary stage of the proceedings and an attempt made to argue that the United States held exclusive jurisdiction over the Armory grounds. But no stress was laid on that point because no one murder out of the four lives taken was committed on the Armory ground.

Mr. Hunter then took up the argument respecting the charge of treason, which he understood to be that none but an attaché of the Commonwealth can commit treason against it. That position he would broadly deny. Our statute defines treason: it is limited to no parties. It does not require that the offender should be a citizen according to our system of government and the complicated machinery of the Federal and State Governments under which we live. In some respects we are unfortunately bound to recognize as citizens of Virginia those who have proven themselves within our borders, as in this case, and without them as in others, our deadliest enemies. The Constitution of the United States provides that citizens of each State shall be entitled to all the privileges of citizens in the several States. Captain Brown came here with immunities given by the Constitution. But did he come divested of the responsibilities belonging to those immunities? Let the word treason mean breach of trust. Did he not betray that trust then—*quasi* consent—with which he is invested when within our borders? By the operation of the Federal Constitution, he was a citizen when he was here, and did that bond of union, which may ultimately prove a bad bond to us in the South, allow him to come into the bosom of the Commonwealth with the deadly purpose of applying the torch to our buildings and shedding the blood of our citizens? But, again, our code defines who are citizens of Virginia. All free white persons born in any other State of this Union who may become residents here are citizens of this State.

The evidence in this case shows that there is no shadow of question that when this man came to Virginia and planted his feet in Harper's Ferry, he came to reside there and hold a place of residence permanently. True, he occupied a farm four or five miles off in Maryland a short time since, but not for the legitimate purpose of establishing a domicile there. It was for a nefarious and hellish purpose—to rally forces to invade this commonwealth and establish himself at Harper's Ferry as a starting-point for a new government. Whatever it was, whether tragical or farcical, and ridiculous as his counsel have presented it, his conduct showed it, if his declarations were insufficient, that it was not alone for the purpose of carrying off slaves that he came here. His provisional government was a real thing, and no debating society, as his counsel would have us believe; and in holding office under it and executing its functions he was clearly guilty of treason. The 46th section has been referred to as showing it as not treasonable; but he supposed that that meant that the new government was to be a Union of the separate States like the present, with the difference that all were to be free States. The whole document must be taken together. The property of slaveholders was to be confiscated all over the South, and any man found in arms was to be shot down. Their conduct at Harper's Ferry looked like insanity, but there was too much method in Brown's madness. His purposes were too well matured. And he and his party declared that there were thousands in the North ready to join them. . . .

Now, as to the charge of conspiring with slaves to rebel, the law says the prisoners are equally guilty whether insurrection is made or not. Advice may be given by actions as well as words. When you put pikes in the hands of slaves and have their masters taken captive, that is advice to the slaves to rebel, and is punishable with death. The law does not require positive evidence, but only enough to remove every reasonable doubt as to the guilt of a party. Sometimes circumstantial evidence is the strongest kind, for witnesses may perjure themselves or be mistaken.

The defence say they do not know who killed the negro Hayward . . . and the supposition is that Hayward was killed by mistake. They say Brown shot no unarmed men; but Beckham was killed when unarmed, and he therefore thought the whole case had been proved by a mass of evidence. With regard to the question of *malice,* the law was that if a party perpetrated a felony and undesignedly takes life, it is conclusive proof of malice. If Brown was only intending to steal negroes, and in doing that took life, it was murder with malice prepense. So the law expressly lays down that killing committed in resisting officers in attempting to quell a riot or to arrest the perpetrator of a criminal offence is murder in the first degree. Then what need of all this delay to prove that Brown treated his prisoners with leniency, and did not want to shed blood? Brown wanted the citizens of Virginia calmly to fold their arms and let him usurp the government, manumit the slaves, confiscate the property of slaveholders, and without drawing a trigger or shedding blood, permit him to take possession of the Commonwealth and make it another Haiti. Such an idea was too abhorrent to pursue. So, too, the idea that Brown shed blood only in self-defence. It was too absurd to require argument. He gloried in coming here to violate our laws. He says he had counted the risk and knew what he was about, and was ready to abide the consequences. That proves malice—thus admitting every thing charged. He knew his life was forfeited if he failed. Then is not the case made out beyond all reasonable doubt—even beyond any unreasonable doubt? We, therefore, ask for his conviction to vindicate the majesty of the law.

Mr. HUNTER closed at 1½ o'clock. During most of the argument Brown lay on his back with his eyes closed.

Mr. CHILTON asked the Court to instruct the jury that if they believed the prisoner was not a citizen of Virginia, but of another State, they cannot convict him on the count of treason.

The COURT declined, saying the Constitution did not give rights and immunities alone, but it also imposed responsibilities.

Mr. CHILTON then asked for another instruction to the effect that the jury must be satisfied that the place where the offence was committed was within the boundaries of Jefferson county, which the Court granted.

A recess was taken for half an hour.

When the jury came in with their verdict an intense excitement prevailed.

Brown sat up in bed while the verdict was rendered as follows:

"The jury find the prisoner guilty of treason in advising and conspiring with slaves and others to rebel, and of murder in the first degree."

Brown laid down quickly and said nothing. There was no demonstration of any kind.

Mr. CHILTON moved an arrest of judgment, both on account of errors in the indictment and an error in the verdict. The points will be argued to-morrow.

Brown was remanded to jail.

Mr. HARDING announced that he was ready to proceed with the trial of Coppoc, who was brought in and took his seat between Messrs. Griswold and Hoyt, who appeared as his counsel.

The remainder of the day was spent in endeavoring to obtain a jury, but the panel was not complete when, at 5 o'clock, the Court adjourned.

No. 64

The Baltimore Weekly Sun
The National Intelligencer
Sat., Nov. 5, 1859

Edwin Coppoc was brought in and placed at the bar for trial. . . . Previous to proceeding . . . , Mr. Griswold stated the points on which an arrest of judgment was asked in Brown's case. In addition to the reasons mentioned yesterday . . . he argued that treason could not be committed against a State . . . , citing the authority of Judge Story. Also, that the jury had not found the prisoner guilty of the crimes as charged in the indictment . . . but . . . of offenses not charged. They find him guilty of murder in the first degree, when the indictment doesn't charge him with offenses constituting that crime.

Mr. Hunter replied, quoting the Virginia code, to the effect that technicalities should not arrest the administration of justice. As to the jurisdiction of the State in case of treason, it was sufficient to say that Virginia has passed a law assuming that jurisdiction, and defining what constitutes that crime.

The Court reserved its decision. . . . It is supposed that if a new trial is refused, an appeal will be taken to a higher court.

CHARLESTOWN, Nov. 2, 1859.

. . . Captain Brown was . . . brought in. . . . The COURT gave its decision on the motion for an arrest of judgment, overruling the objections made. In regard to the objection that treason cannot be committed against the State, the Court ruled that wherever allegiance is due, treason can be committed. Most of the States have passed laws against treason. The objection as to the form of the verdict rendered the Court also regarded as insufficient.

The CLERK now asked the prisoner if he had anything to say why sentence should not be pronounced against him. Capt. Brown stood up and in a clear . . . voice said: "I have, may it please the Court, a few words to say. In the first place, I deny everything but what I have all along admitted, of a design on my part to free slaves. I intended certainly to have made a clear thing of that matter, as I did when I went last winter into Missouri and there took slaves without the snapping of a gun on either side, moved them through the country, and finally left them in Canada. I designed to have done the same thing again on a larger scale. That was all I intended. I never did intend murder, or treason, or the destruction of property, or to incite slaves to rebellion, or to make insurrection.

"I have another objection, and that is, it is unjust that I should suffer such a penalty. Had I interfered in the manner which I admit, and which I admit has been fairly proved, . . . had I so interfered on behalf of the rich and powerful, the intelligent, the so-called great, or in behalf of any of their friends, either father or mother, brother or sister, wife or children, or any of that class, and suffered and sacrificed what I have in this interference, it would have been all right, and every man in this Court would have deemed it an act worthy of reward, rather than punishment.

"This Court acknowledged too, as I suppose, the validity of the law of God. I see a book kissed here which I suppose to be the Bible, or at least the New Testament. That teaches me that all things 'whatsoever I would men should do to me I should do even so to them.' It teaches me, further, to 'remember them that are in bonds as bonded with them.' I endeavored to act up to these instructions. I say I am yet too young to understand that God is any respecter of persons. I believe that to have interfered as I have done, in behalf of his despised poor, was no wrong, but right. Now, if it is deemed necessary that I should forfeit my life for the furtherance of the ends of justice, and mingle my blood further with the blood of my children, and with the blood of the millions in this slave country whose rights are disregarded by wicked, cruel, and unjust enactments, I submit. So let it be done!

"Let me say one word further. I feel entirely satisfied with the treatment I have received on my trial. Considering the circumstances, it has been more generous than I expected, but I feel no consciousness of guilt. I have stated from the first what was my intention and what was not. I have never had any design against the life of any person, nor any disposition to commit treason or excite the slaves to rebel or make any general insurrection. I never encouraged any man to do so, but always discouraged any idea of that kind.

"Let me say also a word in regard to the statements made by some of those connected with me. I fear that it has been stated by some of them that I have induced them to join me. But the contrary is true. I do not say this to injure them, but as regretting their weakness. There is not one of them but joined me of his own accord, and the greater part of them at their own expense. A number of them I never saw and never had a word of conversation with till the day they came to me, and that was for the purpose I have stated.

"Now I have done."

While Brown was speaking, perfect quiet prevailed. When he had finished, the Court, after some preliminary remarks in which the Judge said that no reasonable doubt could exist as to the prisoner's guilt, sentenced him "to be hung in public on Friday, the 2nd of December."

Brown received the sentence with composure, and the only demonstration made was a clapping of hands by a man in the crowd who is not a resident of Jefferson County. This indecorum was promptly suppressed. . . .

No. 65   CLOSE OF THE TRIALS AND SENTENCE OF THE PRISONERS

The National Intelligencer, Tues., Nov. 15, 1859

Charlestown, Nov. 11, 1859.

The proceedings of the Circuit Court for Jefferson County were brought to a close yesterday morning, after a session of three weeks, which was occupied exclusively in the trial of the Harper's Ferry conspirators. The Circuit Court of Frederick County, over which Judge Parker presides, commences today, and hence the necessity of the closing of the term for this county. The term will long be remembered . . . here, five men having been tried and found guilty of the highest crimes known to our laws.

The convicts—Cook, Coppoc, Copeland, and Green—were brought out yesterday to receive the sentence of Judge Parker. . . . The prisoners . . . were asked if they had anything to say why sentence should not be passed upon them.

Cook and Coppoc proceeded to deliver short addresses, the former being somewhat vehement . . . whilst the latter made a firm impression by his quiet and collected style of delivery. Both protested their ignorance of the attack on Harper's Ferry until the Sabbath of the night before the attack, when they were called on to swear to obey the orders of their commander, Brown. Coppoc stated that he knew he should be punished for his foolhardy attempt, but he thought it should have been lighter than had been adjudged. The negroes denied saying anything.

Judge Parker then proceeded to deliver sentence. . . . "[The] sentence of the law is that you, and each one of you, . . . be hanged by the neck until you be dead—and that execution of this judgment be made and done . . . on Friday, the sixteenth of December next, upon you Shields Green and John Copeland, between the hours of eight in the forenoon and twelve noon of that day; and upon you, John E. Cook, and Edwin Coppoc, between the hours of twelve noon and five in the afternoon of same day . . . and may God have mercy upon the soul of each one of you."

No. 66

The Richmond Enquirer, Tues., Nov. 8, 1859

Shall John Brown be pardoned? The law of Virginia, Chap. 17, sec. 18, provides: "The Governor shall not grant a pardon in any case before conviction nor to any person convicted of TREASON against the Commonwealth, EXCEPT WITH THE CONSENT OF THE GENERAL ASSEMBLY, DECLARED BY JOINT RESOLUTION. Neither shall he grant a reprieve to any person convicted of treason for a longer period than until the end of the session of the General Assembly, during which it may be granted or than until the end of the succeeding session, when it is granted during the recess." Here, then is an end to all pardon by the Executive. . . .

No. 67   GOVERNOR'S MESSAGE TO THE LEGIS-LATURE OF VIRGINIA [DEC. 5, 1859]

The Richmond Enquirer, Tues., Dec. 6, 1859

. . . our peace has been disturbed; our citizens . . . imprisoned, robbed and murdered; the sanctity of their dwellings . . . violated; their persons . . . outraged; their property . . . seized by force of arms. . . .

This was no result of ordinary crimes. . . . It was an extraordinary and actual invasion, by a sectional organization. . . .

Sudden, surprising, shocking as this invasion has been, it is not more so than the rapidity and rancor of the causes which have prompted and put it in motion. . . . Causes and influences lie behind it. . . . For a series of years social and sectional difference have been growing up, unhappily. . . . An evil spirit of fanaticism has seized upon negro slavery as the one subject of social reform, and the one idea of its abolition has seemed to madden whole masses of one entire section of the country. It enters into their religion, into their education, into their politics and prayers, into their courts of justice, into their business, into their Legislatures, . . . It has been taught by the Atheism of a "higher law" than that of a regular government bound by constitutions and statutes. . . . It has been inflamed by prostituted teachers and preachers and presses. . . . It has established spies everywhere and has secret agents . . . and secret associations and "underground railroads" in every free State . . . It has openly and secretly threatened vengeance on the execution of our laws. And since their violation it has definitely proclaimed aloud that *"insurrection is the lesson of the hour"*—not of slaves only, but all are to be free to rise up against fixed government. . . .

During the trial of [the Harper's Ferry raiders] and since, appeals and threats of every sort . . . have been made to the Executive.—I lay before you the mass of these, it being impossible to enter into their details. Though the laws do not permit me to pardon in cases of treason, yet pardons and reprieves have been demanded on the grounds of, 1st: insanity; 2nd: magnanimity; 3rd: the policy of not making martyrs.

As to the first, the parties themselves or counsel put in no plea of insanity. No insanity was feigned even; the prisoner Brown spurned it. . . . As to the second ground . . . : I know of no magnanimity which is inhumane, and no inhumanity could well exceed that to our society, *our slaves* as well as their masters, which would turn felons like these . . . loose again on a border already torn by a fanatical and sectional strife. . . . As to the third ground . . . ; To hang would be no more martyrdom than to incarcerate the fanatic. The sympathy would have asked on and on for liberation, and to nurse and soothe him, while life lasted, in prison. His state of health would have been heralded weekly, as from a palace . . . ; the work of his hands would have been sought as holy relics. . . . There was no middle ground of mitigation. To pardon or reprieve at all was to proclaim a licensed impunity to the thousand fanatics who are mad only in the guilt and folly of setting up their individual supremacy over life, law, property, and civil liberty itself. The sympathy with the leader was worse than the invasion itself.

The appeal was: it is policy to make *no martyrs,* but disarm murderers, traitors, robbers, insurrectionists, by *free pardon* for wanton, malicious, unprovoked felons! . . . .

HENRY A. WISE.

TOPICS FOR ESSAYS

SUGGESTED LENGTH (words):

(1) *Tactics of the Defense* (including Brown)   300
(2) *Brown in the Courtroom*   300
(3) *Was the Verdict Just?* (Consult, as well,
    Caleb Cushing in "The Rostrum," Ch. IV, below)   500

TOPICS FOR LIBRARY RESEARCH

BIBLIOGRAPHY:

John Allstadt	H. Griswold	Hon. Richard Parker
Lawson Botts	Charles D. Harding	Heywood Shepherd
Samuel Chilton	George W. Hoyt	Samuel Strider
Edwin Coppoc	Andrew Hunter	George W. Turner
Charles J. Faulkner		

SUPPLEMENTARY RESEARCH:

(1) Haiti and Harper's Ferry—were they parallel attempts, as Mr. Hunter suggested?   500-1500

(2) Availing yourself of whatever materials (books, articles, newspaper files, and legal documents) your library has, write a documented essay on the legal history of the John Brown case *after* the sentence—that is, the appeal, grounds for its rejection, reaction to the rejection, or other aspects.
500-1500

THE EXECUTIONS—AND SOME
OTHER MATTERS

No. 68 INTELLIGENCE FROM CHARLESTOWN

Correspondence of the *Baltimore American* in *The National Intelligencer,* Sat., Dec. 3, 1859

CHARLESTOWN, DEC. 1, 1859.

After an absence of five weeks I yesterday returned to this excited and panic-stricken town; and, although the panic portion of the programme has died out, the excitement has rather increased. There is no falling off in the number of miraculous stories of armed invaders, mysterious despatches, and wonderful combinations against the peace and good order of the old Commonwealth, but the people have become so used to them that they calmly await a confirmation of the story before they send in their petitions to the commanding officer to order more troops from Richmond. The panic among the women and children is, however, most intense, especially in the rural portions of the country. The burning of so many stock yards and farm buildings has caused a feeling of insecurity and alarm that is quite natural, and people retire to their beds in doubt and uncertainty whether they will not be aroused before morning by the torch of the incendiary.

Martial law has not been proclaimed here yet, though I cannot see what additional rigors could be enforced on this most unfortunate people. Even the citizens of the town cannot pass through the suburbs without being arrested and carried off to headquarters. Persons coming into the town have to be detained an hour or more, and then marched by an armed guard to the presence of the military authorities to give an account of themselves. On leaving they have to obtain a pass, and run the gauntlet of a dozen sentinels to return to their homes again. Yesterday, as I entered the town, I saw the venerable Edward Ruffin, the famous Virginian agriculturist, with his flowing locks, being marched to headquarters between two armed guards, and even the Hon. Andrew Hunter has been subjected to the same species of military discipline. On entering the cars at Harper's Ferry we were fortunate in meeting the chief of police at Charlestown, who accompanied us and passed us through the line of military that surrounded the depot awaiting the arrival of the train. No one was allowed to leave the cars unless vouched for by some one in authority; and those who were not so fortunate were marched to headquarters to give an account of themselves. . . .

154

Sheriff Campbell informs me that Capt. Brown admits his participation in the Kansas massacre, as charged upon him by the *Herald of Freedom,* but offers various excuses and palliations for his conduct. The feeling produced against him by Mrs. Doyle's letter—the charge of murdering her husband and two sons not being denied by him—is most intense. He is no longer admired for his truthfulness and bravery, but is now regarded as a hardened and unprincipled hypocrite. He is understood to be endeavoring to explain in his letters and statements he is writing the motives that governed him in his Kansas work.

The work of erecting the scaffold was commenced yesterday. . . . It is in a position where the execution can be seen by all . . . but the military lines will be formed at such distance as to preclude . . . hearing anything the prisoner may say. . . . The prisoner, I learn, spent a quiet night, and to all outward appearances seemed less cheerful, but quite resigned. He refuses to receive any spiritual advice. I learn that orders for the execution will be issued this morning. The only persons within the line will be the sheriff, jailor, and surgeon. The nearest line of military will be one hundred feet from the scaffold, and the other line two hundred feet, outside of which the civic spectators will be allowed. . . .

The following letter to John Brown . . . is communicated to the New York *Express* by the Hon. Andrew Hunter . . . , who believes it to be genuine. It may have been written at the instance of Mrs. Doyle, but not by her, as we remember to have seen "her mark" appended to other papers bearing her name:

CHATTANOOGA, Tennessee, Nov. 20, 1859

Sir: Although vengeance is not mine, I confess that I do feel grateful to hear that you were stopped in your fiendish career at Harper's Ferry. With the loss of your two sons you can now appreciate my distress in Kansas when you, then and there, entered my house at midnight and arrested my husband and two boys, and took them out of the yard and in cold blood shot them dead in my hearing. You can't say you did it to free our slaves. We had none and never expected to own one. It has only made me a poor disconsolate widow, with helpless children. While I feel for your folly, I do hope and trust that you will meet your just reward. Oh! how it pained my heart to hear the dying groans of my husband and children. If this scrawl gives you any consolation you are welcome to it.

MAHALA DOYLE.

N.B. My son, John Doyle, whose life I begged of you, is now grown up, and is very desirous to be in Charlestown on the day of your execution, and would certainly be there if his means would permit it.

No. 69
The National Intelligencer, Sat., Dec. 3, 1859

CHARLESTOWN, DEC. 1—By permission of the State authorities the wife of John Brown arrived here this afternoon in a carriage from Harper's Ferry, escorted by mounted troops. . . . The troops formed in a hollow square in front of the jail when she alighted. The interview of the husband and wife took place in present of the sheriff. . . . She returned under escort to Harper's Ferry this evening . . . where she will await the reception of the body of her husband tomorrow.

No. 70
Correspondence of the *Baltimore American* in *The Richmond Enquirer*, Tues., Dec. 6, 1859

CHARLESTOWN, VA., DEC. 1—[It] is the intention to allow Mrs. Brown to remain with her husband until nine o'clock this morning, when she will . . . proceed under an armed escort to Harper's Ferry, to await the arrival of his remains in the evening. After the execution his body will be placed in a coffin and conducted under an armed cavalry escort to await the arrival of the midnight train for Baltimore, and from thence to Philadelphia, New York, and, it is thought, to Boston. The people here are rather averse to giving up his body to be canonized at the North, but all admit that the appeal of his wife could not be disregarded by the Governor. . . .

Mrs. Brown . . . stated that she had not seen [Brown] since last June . . . , and that they had been separated, with the exception of a few days, for nearly two years. They had, however, corresponded. . . .

I learn from Captain Avis, the jailor, that the interview between the prisoner and his wife was characteristic of the man. . . . The prisoner said he contemplated his death with composure and calmness. . . . It was doubtless best that he should be legally murdered for the good of the cause, and he was prepared to submit to His will without a murmur.

In regard to his execution, he said he desired no religious ceremonies, either in the jail or on the scaffold, from ministers who either consent to or approve of the enslavement of their fellow-creatures—that he would prefer to be accompanied on the scaffold by a dozen slave children and a good old slave mother, with their appeal to God for blessings on his soul, than all the eloquence of the whole clergy of the Commonwealth combined.

No. 71

Correspondence of the *Baltimore American* in *The Richmond Enquirer*, Tues., Dec. 6, 1859

CHARLESTOWN, DEC. 2, P.M.—. . . . The prisoner was brought out of jail at 11 o'clock. . . . Sheriff Campbell bid the prisoner farewell in his cell, and Brown returned his thanks to him for his kindness, and spoke of Captain Pate as a brave man. He was then conducted to the cells of his fellow prisoners, desiring to take his leave of them. Entering the cell of Copeland and Green, he told them to stand up like men and not betray their friends. He handed each a quarter of a dollar, saying that he had no more use for money, and having said this, he bid them a final farewell!

Next he visited Cook and Coppoc who were chained together. Addressing Cook, he remarked, "You have made false statements." Cook asked, "What do you mean?" Brown replied, "Why, in stating that I sent you to Harper's Ferry." Cook replied, "Did you not tell me in Pittsburg to come to Harper's Ferry and see if Forbes had made disclosures?" Captain Brown, "No, sir! You know I protested against your coming." To this Cook only responded: "Captain Brown, we remember differently." As he said this he dropped his head, and Brown, as if in contempt, turned away, and, addressing Coppoc, said: "Coppoc, you also made false statements, but I am glad to hear you have contradicted them. Stand up like a man." Brown also handed Coppoc a quarter, and then shaking both by the hand, parted with them.

The prisoner was next taken to Stevens' cell, and kindly interchanged with him a goodbye. Stevens said: "Goodbye, Captain—I know you are going to a better land." Brown replied: "I know I am," and urged Stevens to bear up, and not betray his friends. He also gave Stevens a quarter, and then took leave of him. He did not visit Hazlett, as he has always persisted in denying any knowledge of him.

At the door of the jail an open wagon, with a pine box in which was a fine oak coffin, was waiting for him. He looked around and spoke to several persons whom he recognized, and walking down the steps, was assisted to enter the wagon, and took his seat on the box containing his coffin, along with jailor Avis. He looked with interest on the fine military display, but made no remark. The wagon moved off as soon as he had taken his seat, flanked with two files of riflemen in close order.

On reaching the field the military had already full possession, and pickets were stationed at various points. The citizens were kept back at the point of the bayonet from taking any position except that assigned them—nearly a quarter of a mile from the scaffold.

On his way to the scaffold, Mr. Sadler, the undertaker, remarked to Capt. Brown, "You are a game man, Captain." To which Capt. Brown replied: "Yes, I was so trained—it was one of the lessons of my mother; but it is hard to part from friends, though newly made." Then he remarked—"This is a beautiful country—I never had the pleasure of seeing it before." On reaching the field on which the gallows was erected, Brown said: "Why are none but military allowed in the enclosure? I am sorry the citizens have been kept out."

As he reached the gallows he observed Wm. Hunter and Mayor Green standing near, to whom he said, "Gentlemen, goodbye," his voice not faltering in the least.

While on the scaffold Sheriff Campbell asked if he would take a handkerchief in his hand to drop as a signal when he was ready. He replied, "No—I do not want it. . . ." The prisoner walked up the steps firmly, and was the first man on the gallows. Jailor Avis and Sheriff Campbell stood by his side, and after shaking hands and bidding an affectionate adieu, thanked them for their kindness. He then put the cap over his face and the rope around his neck. Mr. Avis then asked him to step forward on the trap. He replied, "You must lead me, for I cannot see." The rope now being adjusted and the military order given, the soldiers marched and countermarched, and took their position as if an enemy was in sight. Nearly ten minutes was thus occupied, the prisoner standing meanwhile. Mr. Avis inquired if he was not tired? Brown replied, "No—but don't keep me waiting longer than necessary."

At fifteen minutes past eleven the trap fell. A slight grasping of the hands and twitching of the muscles was visible, and then all was quiet.

The body was several times examined, and his pulse did not cease beating for thirty-five minutes. It was then cut down and placed in a coffin, and conveyed under a military escort to Harper's Ferry by special train at four o'clock.

The whole arrangements were carried out with a precision and military strictness that was most annoying. . . .

No. 72

Mary Anna Jackson, in *Memoirs of Stonewall Jackson*
(Louisville, 1895), pp. 130-132

"December 2d. John Brown was hung today at about half-
past eleven A.M. He behaved with unflinching firmness. The arrangements were well made and well executed under the direction of Colonel
Smith. The gibbet was erected in a large field, southeast of the town.
Brown rode on the head of his coffin from his prison to the place of
execution. The coffin was of black walnut, enclosed in a box of poplar of
the same shape as the coffin. He was dressed in a black frock-coat, black
pantaloons, black vest, black slouch hat, white socks, and slippers of
predominating red. . . . The open wagon in which he rode was strongly
guarded on all sides. . . . Brown had his arms tied behind him and
ascended the scaffold with apparent cheerfulness. After reaching the top
. . . he shook hands with several. . . . The sheriff placed the rope
around his neck, then threw a white cap over his head, and asked him
if he wished a signal. . . . He replied that it made no difference,
provided he was not kept waiting too long. In this condition he stood
for about ten minutes on the trap-door, which was supported on one
side by hinges and on the other (the south side) by a rope. Colonel
Smith then announced to the sheriff 'all ready'—which apparently was
not comprehended by him, and the colonel had to repeat the order, when
the rope was cut by a single blow, and Brown fell through about five
inches, his knees falling on a level with the position occupied by his
feet before the rope was cut. With the fall his arms, below the elbows,
flew up horizontally, his hands clinched, and his arms gradually fell,
but by spasmodic motions. There was very little motion of his person
for several moments, and soon the wind blew his lifeless body to and
fro. . . . I hope that he was prepared to die, but I am doubtful. He
refused to have a minister with him. . . . His body was taken back
to the jail, and at six o'clock P.M. was sent to his wife at Harper's
Ferry. When it arrived, the coffin was opened, and his wife saw the
remains, after which it was again opened at the depot . . . lest there
should be an imposition. . . ."

No. 73

James Redpath, *The Public Life of John Brown* (Boston, 1860), pp. 396-397

At eleven o'clock, John Brown came out of jail. An eye witness said of his appearance at this solemn moment: "He seemed to walk out of the Gates of Fame. . . ." His face was even joyous, and a forgiving smile rested upon his lips. His was the lightest heart . . . in the whole of Charlestown that day. . . . He stood in the midst of that organized mob, from whose despotic hearts petty tyranny seemed for the nonce eliminated by . . . admiration. . . .

As he stepped out of the door, a black woman, with a little child in her arms, stood near his way. The twain were of the despised race for whose emancipation and elevation to the dignity of children of God he was about to lay down his life. His thoughts at that moment none can know except as his acts interpret them. He stopped for a moment in his course, stooped over, and with the tenderness of one whose love is as broad as the brotherhood of man, kissed it affectionately. That mother will be proud of that mark of distinction for her offspring; and some day, when over the ashes of John Brown the temple of Virginia liberty is reared, she may join in the joyful song of praise which on that soil will do justice to his memory. As he passed along, a black woman, with a child in her arms, ejaculated, "God bless you, old man; I wish I could help you, but I cannot." He heard her, and as he looked at her, a tear stood in his eye.

No. 74

F. B. Sanborn, *Memoirs of John Brown* (Concord, 1878), p. 94

Except a codicil to his will, and a note to his wife inclosing it, the very last paper written by John Brown was this sentence, which he handed to one of his guards in the jail on the morning of his execution:

[CHARLESTOWN, VA., Dec. 2, 1859]
"I, John Brown, am now quite *certain* that the crimes of this *guilty land* will never be purged away but with *blood*. I had, as I now think,

vainly flattered myself that without very much bloodshed it might be done."

A week before this, Brown's friend and supporter in his Virginia campaign, Theodore Parker, had written from Rome, to Francis Jackson, in Boston, the same declaration, to the truth of which history has fully borne witness. "A few years ago," wrote Parker, on the 24th of November, 1859, "it did not seem difficult first to check slavery, and then to end it, without any bloodshed. I think this cannot be done now, nor ever in the future. All the great charters of humanity have been writ in blood. I once hoped that of American democracy would be engrossed in less costly ink; but it is plain now that our pilgrimage must lead through a Red sea, wherein many a Pharaoh will go under and perish."

No. 75

Thomas Drew, *The John Brown Invasion* (Boston, 1860), pp. 73-79

The Brown Farm at North Elba [New York] is on the highest arable spot of land in the state, . . . soil . . . hard and sterile. . . . Mr. Brown . . . had come there in pursuance of the great purpose of his life. This land formerly belonged to Gerrit Smith, and lies near to those large tracts which Mr. Smith had presented . . . to certain colored people; and it was to aid these colored people . . . that he had originally come to a place so unpromising. . . .

The next morning . . . on opening the front door, a glorious sight saluted me. Directly in front . . . looms up a rugged chain of the Adirondacks, broken, jagged, massive, and wonderfully picturesque. Off the left stands, in solitary grandeur, the towering pyramid called "White Face." . . . The Saranac and Ausable flow at each side of it; and just at its base, they tell us, is Lake Placid, a sheet of water famed . . . for its exquisite beauty. . . . Just the country . . . for the heroic soul of John Brown, and a proper place to be the receptacle of his ashes. . . .

As the body was lowered into the grave, a gush of grief . . . burst from the family, and Mr. Young [the minister] stood forth to comfort them. Raising his deep and mellow voice, and quoting the words written to Timothy by Paul . . . , he said: "I have fought a good fight; I have finished my course; I have kept the faith; henceforth there is laid up for me a crown of righteousness which the Lord, the righteous

judge, shall give me . . ."; which words he followed with the bene-
diction. . . . He added nothing more. The words seemed to fall like
balm on all. . . .

Mr. Brown had expressed a desire that his body should be laid in
the shadow of a great rock, not far from his house. This rock . . .
was the first object to arrest my attention. It stands . . . about eight
feet in height, and from fifteen to twenty feet square. It is a very striking
and picturesque object. . . .

No. 76   THE EXECUTIONS AT CHARLESTOWN

Correspondence of *The Baltimore Sun* in *The Richmond
Enquirer*, Tues., Dec. 20, 1859

CHARLESTOWN, Dec. 16, 1859

. . . The crowd . . . was . . . at least five times as numerous as on the occasion of Brown's execution. . . . After a brief prayer
by the clergyman, the caps were drawn over the heads of [Green and
Copeland], and the ropes affixed. . . . Copeland remained quiet, but
Green was engaged in earnest prayer up to the moment the trap was
drawn. . . . The bodies . . . will be interred tomorrow . . . though
there is a party of medical students here from Winchester, who will
doubtless not allow them to remain there long. . . .

When called upon by the sheriff, [Cook and Coppoc] stood calm and
. . . were helped into the wagon and took their seats on their coffins.
Their appearance was . . . of hopeless despair. . . . On the gallows
they shook hands and bid each other good bye. After the caps were
drawn, Cook said, "Stop a minute—where is Edwin's hand?" Cook
said, "God bless you," and Coppoc said in a loud tone, "Be quick as
possible." . . .

No. 77

The Richmond Enquirer, Tues., Feb. 7, 1860

CHARLESTOWN, VA., FEB. 6, 1860

Stevens has been found guilty. The jury were absent about
fifteen minutes. . . . The trial of Hazlett commenced today. . . .

No. 78

The National Intelligencer, Sat., Feb. 11, 1860

The grand jury at Charlestown (Va.) have found bills of indictment against Owen Brown, Francis J. Meriam, and Jeremiah Anderson, charging them with conspiring with slaves to create insurrection. The persons here named are a portion of John Brown's men who have thus far escaped arrest.

No. 79

The National Intelligencer, Thurs., Feb. 16, 1860

VIRGINIA—On the 13th instant Governor Letcher, of Virginia, transmitted to the Legislature of the State a message complaining of the course of Governor Kirkwood, of the State of Iowa, in declining to grant compliance with [his] requisition for the delivery of Barclay Coppoc, a fugitive from justice, who had been engaged in the Harper's Ferry raid. This refusal was upon merely technical grounds—first, for want of authentication of the notarial seal; secondly, that the demand for the requisition was not accompanied "by the copy of an indictment found or an affidavit before a magistrate"; and, thirdly, that "it is not stated, unless it be inferentially, that Coppoc committed the acts charged in the State of Virginia."

No. 80

The National Intelligencer, Fri., Mar. 17, 1860

VIRGINIA AND OHIO—Gov. Letcher laid before the Legislature of Virginia, on the 14th instant, a communication on the subject of the refusal of Gov. Dennison, of Ohio, to surrender, as fugitives from justice, Francis Meriam and Owen Brown, two of John Brown's . . . conspirators. The ground of refusal appears to be that "no enactment of this State [Ohio] has clothed the Governor with authority to surrender to another State fugitives from its justice seeking refuge here." And it is urged that, under the power claimed by virtue of the Constitution of the United States, the conditions on which the requisition is based are defective in not stating with precision where the offence was committed. Governor Letcher cites a case in which, on the 22d of February last, Governor Dennison makes a requisition upon *him* for the surrender of a fugitive from justice. He concludes . . . : "If the course which has been pursued by the authorities of the States of Ohio and Iowa is to become the settled policy of the non-slaveholding States towards us, we must adopt such measures for protection against these gross outrages upon our rights as will be suited to the case. We must adopt retaliatory measures. . . . What these . . . shall be I leave to the wisdom of the General Assembly."

CHARLESTOWN (VA.), MARCH 16, 1860.

The town was thronged with visitors today and several military companies arrived. Stevens and Hazlett were hung at noon. . . . Both exhibited great firmness and resignation. There were no religious exercises on the gallows, as they persisted in refusing all . . . kindly offices. . . . They were both spiritualists. . . .

TOPICS FOR ESSAYS

SUGGESTED LENGTH (*words*):

(1) *John Brown's Last Day*   500
(2) *John Brown's Plan of Operations*   500

TOPICS FOR LIBRARY RESEARCH

BIBLIOGRAPHY:

Governor Dennison	Governor Kirkwood
Mahala Doyle	Governor Letcher
Thomas Drew	James Redpath
Stonewall Jackson	Edmund Ruffin

Chapter IV

THE REACTION

No. 81 [THE LIBERATOR (BOSTON)]
Fri., Nov. 4, 1859

At a meeting of the Executive Committee of the American Anti-Slavery Society held in Boston Nov. 1st, the following Resolution was Adopted: "Resolved that it is recommended to the friends of impartial freedom . . . in case of the execution of Capt. John Brown, now on trial . . . , to observe that tragical event, ON THE DAY OF ITS OCCURRENCE, in such manner as by them may be deemed most appropriate in their various localities—whether by public meetings and addresses . . . or any other justifiable mode of action—for the furtherance of the Anti-Slavery cause, and renewedly to consecrate themselves to the patriotic and Christian work of effecting the abolition of that most dangerous, unnatural, cruel and impious system of slavery, which is the fruitful source of all our sectional heart-burnings and conflicts, which . . . tends to promote servile insurrections and civil war, . . . which is a burning disgrace and fearful curse . . . , and by the speedy extinction of which alone can the land be saved from violence, blood, and utter demoralization./ In behalf of the Executive Committee . . . /WM. LLOYD GARRISON, President/ WENDELL PHILLIPS, CHARLES C. BURLEIGH, Secretaries."

No suggestion more timely and more important than this could be made; and now that sentence of death has been pronounced against the brave martyr . . . , let the day of his execution . . . be the occasion of such a public moral demonstration against the bloody and merciless slave system as the land has never witnessed. Friends of freedom everywhere! Begin at once to make the necessary arrangements. . . .

No. 82 [THE BOSTON TRANSCRIPT]
Reprinted in *The Liberator*, Nov. 4, 1859

. . . . The extraordinary course of some Northern newspapers in attempting to fasten the late miserable affair upon the leaders of the Republican party is simply absurd and contemptible. Nor will the respectable press at the South, or sensible men anywhere thank them for any such course, for if it be true that a party which is numerically the strongest in the country is indeed favorable to a servile insurrection, then the days of slavery are indeed numbered, and when the negroes are once convinced of the fact, there will be little peace or safety at the South.

The really wise men at the South will treat the whole affair as a most foolish, impracticable and unfortunate scheme, planned and led on by a brave, simple-hearted, unselfish, and modest monomaniac, whose heart has been lacerated by his own sufferings, and whose brain, touched by hereditary insanity, has at length become really affected and diseased. What true wisdom, humanity and good sense require to be done in this case is very plain. But it is not very probable that any such course will be taken. Where men are angry, and particularly, where they are *frightened,* there is small hope of wisdom or humanity. And the course pursued at the trial of Old Brown is a disgrace to the civilization of the age. Can any one read his simple, touching, and yet plucky appeal for delay, without a tear?

He asked no favors. He scouted the defence of insanity. He made no denial of facts. But he was exhausted, wounded, partially deaf, and *simply desired to communicate with his friends.* Did any one ever before know a case where a man was on trial for his life, and was denied such a request? Never, certainly, where the common law prevails. Never, in a Protestant country. And so the trial is going on in hot haste, and this old man is brought into court daily on his bed, and is defended by men whom he never saw or heard of until he was taken. Whatever may be his guilt or folly, a man convicted under such circumstances . . . will be the most terrible fruit that slavery has ever borne, and will excite the execration of the whole civilized world.

There may be an excuse in some minds for this state of things, from the alarm and excitement in Virginia; but is there any excuse here at the North for the expression of sentiments . . . like this: "The nearest tree would be the fittest mode of exit from this scene of mischief." "Had the guilty parties been sent forthwith to execution by sentence of a drum-head court-martial, it would have been a fitting doom for murderers taken in hot blood. . . ." This language is not used in Austria by Haynau, but in Boston by —————!

No. 83   [THE BOSTON POST]
Reprinted in *The Liberator,* Nov. 4, 1859

. . . It will not do to allege that the preachers of civil war are ultras of the Garrison school, and that the Republican leaders have nothing to do with such theorists. Garrison, Phillips, and Gerrit Smith will not serve as scapegoats to bear off this load of crime. What, as for years Democrats have justly alleged, can such arraignments of slaveholders as the acknowledged Republican leaders habitually make, result in but civil war? Does not Brown profess the same principles that Seward and Chase and Wilson and Gillette profess. . . ? Is the irrepressible conflict speech of Senator Seward . . . a myth? Did Senator Wilson never write his emancipation letter to the Garrisonians? Are the terrible words . . . used by Senators Wade, Chase, and Gillette on the floor of the Senate forgeries? No. . . . Was ever cause and effect more clearly traced than it is in this terrible outbreak? . . . . How can political leaders, with such affinities, shake off the terrible responsibility of such work as that at Harper's Ferry? Let them first stop their denunciation of slaveholders; then let the Republicans shake off Giddings. . . . For the good of our country, we hope this occurrence will open the eyes of the North to the evil of anti-slavery agitation and will lead good citizens to frown upon it and all its works.

No. 84   [THE SALEM (Mass.) REGISTER]
Reprinted in *The Liberator,* Nov. 4, 1859

W. W. Throckmorton, the clerk in the Wager Hotel at Harper's Ferry, . . . reveals the following "chivalric" conduct of the F. F. V's . . . : "Stevens, the wounded man, was then brought in, and another fellow named Thompson was brought in a prisoner, and placed in the parlor tied hand and foot. All this time a sharp firing was kept up. When Beckham was shot, our men became almost frantic. They rushed in here, where the prisoner (Thompson) was, crying, 'Shoot him!' 'Kill him!' and had it not been for a lady who was in the room (Miss Christine Fouke, sister of the landlord), he would have been killed on the spot. They cocked their guns, and pointed at him, crowding around, but she stood over him, telling them, 'For God's sake, save him! Don't kill him in that way, but let the law take its course!'

She said they had him a prisoner, bound, and he could not get away, and begged that they would not kill him. The man said he was willing to die; knew he had to die; and wanted to be shot. *They finally got hold of him, took him out on the platform, and shot him. He had more than forty balls fired into him. . . .* The crowd also tried to get hold of Stevens, who was wounded, and was lying in bed upstairs, but Miss Fouke prevented it, and finally a guard was placed over him." Is this a specimen of Virginia "Chivalry" of which we have heard so much? A prisoner, tied hand and foot, deliberately taken out and riddled . . . while a woman stands by and implores the infuriated men not to kill him in that way . . . ! Such conduct might do for "border ruffians" and "Kansas shriekers," but for sons of the Mother of Presidents! Oh! Virginia, blush! . . . .

The telegraph represents that . . . the prisoners were brought into court . . . under a guard of *eighty armed men*—Brown and Coppoc manacled together, Brown weak and haggard, . . . Stevens haggard and depressed . . . , and guards stationed around the court house, and bayonets glistening on all sides, in the heart of Old Virginia, where everything is so quiet and contented and beautiful!

No. 85　　[THE EASTERN TIMES (Me. Dem.)]

Reprinted in *The National Intelligencer,*
Tues., Nov. 1, 1859

. . . that any sane men of any party deliberately counselled that movement, with a view permanently to embarrass the South or to strengthen Northern sentiment, is too preposterous to be believed. . . . Still, Republicanism cannot escape its share of responsibility. . . . That the Republican party have *designed* to encourage such acts we do not charge; but that their speeches, their doctrines, and their actions have stimulated them we have no sort of doubt. And . . . we charge an equal amount of responsibility upon the hotspurs of the South. . . . Northern fanaticism and abolitionism are today being nourished and fattened on the untenable demands of the South. . . . Forbearance is needed on both sides. . . .

No. 86   [THE PROVIDENCE (R.I.) JOURNAL (Rep.)]

Reprinted in *The National Intelligencer,* Nov. 1, 1859

We are told . . . that the Republicans have instigated and perpetrated the recent atrocious folly and wickedness at Harper's Ferry . . . that it is for such violence . . . that the Republican party has been organized . . . and in effect by Northern papers that a majority of the Northern people are incendiaries and murders . . . that the objects of all these is to ravage the Southern portion of the Confederacy with fire and sword. Could there be a more atrocious calumny . . . ?

No. 87   [THE PROVIDENCE (R.I.) POST (Dem.)]

Reprinted in *The National Intelligencer,* Nov. 1, 1859

That John Brown and his associates are fanatics is plain enough, but that they are insane . . . cannot be for a moment pretended. They are just as insane as Garrison is, but having less caution . . . or of sincerity . . . they are involved in difficulties from which he has escaped. The most that can be said for them is that they are men . . . who have allowed a single purpose to take possession of their minds. . . .

No. 88   [THE BATH (Me.) DAILY TIMES]

Reprinted in *The Richmond Enquirer,* Tues., Nov. 15, 1859

We have also said that the Harper's Ferry affair has developed a fact creditable to the Virginia character. . . . In how many portions of our country would Judge Lynch have arbitrated in the case of Brown and his confederates, before the regular judicial process could have been made available? We doubt if in our own State the burning indignation and revenge of our people could have been stayed, when vengeance was being called for by so many . . . tongues of our neighbors and friends, laid low in death by the brutality of the invader of their rights. . . . And after trial, after virtual confession, when the verdict was rendered and the sentence passed, there was no excitement, no demonstration of applause. . . . We ask if, in these facts, we do not see exhibited a trait of character . . . worthy of admiration?

No. 89   [HARPER'S WEEKLY]

Oct. 29, 1859, p. 690

A week ago people were astounded by news that a servile insurrection had broken out at Harper's Ferry. . . . It is now well understood that . . . the insurrection was merely the work of a half-crazed white, whose views and aims were, to say the least, extremely vague and indefinite. Osawatomie Brown, as he loved to be called, was an old soldier of fortune, who had fallen upon evil days in Kansas, where he lost two of seven sons; misfortune had embittered his temper and turned his brain; he fancied he was charged with the mission of liberating slaves by force; and the sad recurrence of Harper's Ferry, with the loss of life which it occasioned, is the miserable result.

It is hardly necessary to add that the event will possess marked political significance at the present time. The admitted affiliations between Gerrit Smith and old Brown, and the peculiar sympathy expressed for him and his friends by certain organs of the Republican party, are likely to increase the vote against the Republican candidates this fall.

For, whatever opinions a man may hold in reference to the slavery controversies . . . , all are unanimous against any thing like compulsory emancipation and servile revolts. The horrors of servile war . . . are vividly realized by men of all parties; even the warmest friends of the slave . . . would, like Mr. Everett, shoulder a musket at any time to prevent such atrocities. And though the leading Republican politicians and papers may and do repudiate the acts of Brown and his associates, it is likely that a large section of the people of this country will hold them responsible for what has happened. It will be said that men of Brown's stamp would never have ventured upon the outrages they have committed but for the open sympathy expressed by persons of high standing with the cause they espoused. . . .

No. 90   [HARPER'S WEEKLY]

Dec. 10, 1859, p. 786

Congress meets next week, and, as usual, men of property are uneasy on the subject. Judging from the newspapers, one might fairly expect a dissolution of the Union before the end of the session. We do not look for that event quite so soon.

It is probable that the Republicans will control the House of Representatives. . . . It seems to be supposed in some quarters in the South that the supremacy of the Republican party will naturally lead to a ferocious attack on the vested rights of the Southern States. We confess that we do not look for any thing of the kind. It is quite likely that a large number of very severe speeches will be made against slavery by Northern members. But . . . the chances are that various money bills and nice private jobs will be quietly smuggled through; after which it is likely that the Northern members will be found less uncompromising on the subject of slavery. Poor John Brown will doubtless be a staple topic; but if the honest men are not sharp, he will serve as a cover for grants of various kinds, and in the fury of sectional strife Congressional rogues will reap a handsome harvest.

As to disunion, both parties know too much for any thing of the kind. Party newspapers in both sections . . . prate about dissolving the Union; but the military force which quelled the Harper's Ferry émeute —twelve United States Marines—is quite sufficient to keep the real disunionists in check. . . . Whatever people may think, the destinies of this nation are not yet at the mercy of a few country editors.

The practical questions which will be brought before Congress next session relate to the tariff and the banks. . . . It remains to be seen whether the slavery discussion and the private jobs will leave room for their proper ventilation. . . .

No. 91   [THE NEW YORK COURIER AND ENQUIRER (Rep.)]

Reprinted in *The National Intelligencer,*
Tues., Nov. 15, 1859

. . . The North, the Centre, and the West—the great heart and most efficient limbs of the Confederacy—are all true to the Union and the Constitution; and should disunion raise its head at the South, John Brown has taught the world how much opposition from that quarter is really worth. If seventeen fanatics, led on by a madman, could hold in subjection a town containing 2000 Virginians, and keep at bay whole regiments of Virginia militia, who even under the eye of their Governor dared not attack their invaders, but stood by and saw twelve United States marines make the assault and capture in ten minutes—what would those same boastful soldiers do when confronted by Northern valor . . . ?

No. 92   [THE NEW YORK JOURNAL OF COMMERCE]
Reprinted in *The National Intelligencer,*
Tues., Dec. 6, 1859

. . . The present is not the first instance when the Union has apparently trembled upon the verge of dissolution. . . . While the Republic was yet in its infancy . . . , partisanship and sectional hate racked the nation, . . . and seemed to portend its inevitable destruction. Matters were then in apparently far greater extremity than now. . . . Then it was that Washington, almost despairing, said: "I can never believe that Providence, which has guided us so long . . . , will withdraw its protection at this crisis." And it did not. . . .

We are now on the eve of one of the most important Presidential elections . . . and one apparently involving deeper interests. . . . It is not unusual to hear expressions of earnest desire that a Washington was now living to guide . . . us in this emergency. . . . His name is not yet forgotten . . . but such is the bitterness of partisanship and sectionalism that even the "Father of his Country" would at present fail to reconcile the differences of his wrangling children. . . .

No. 93   [THE BUFFALO COMMERCIAL ADVERTISER]
Reprinted in *The National Intelligencer,*
Tues., Nov. 1, 1859

. . . it is impossible to close the book of Old John Brown's life without a sigh of pitiful admiration for the blind heroism, the stupid zeal, he has manifested during all the four or five stormy years since he left his farm in Montgomery County, in this State, to resist by violence the introduction of slavery into Kansas. He was one of the few brave men among the horde who went out to Kansas . . . He believed in it, and it is fair to suppose that he had become a monomaniac on the subject. . . .

We are sorry to see in the Democratic press a pitiful attempt to make political capital out of these events, and to represent the crimes of a crazy fanatic as the sins of a party. . . .

No. 94   [THE NEW YORK EVENING POST (Rep.)]
Reprinted in *The National Intelligencer,*
Tues., Nov. 1, 1859

. . . there is no party to whose policy and principles the
schemes of Old Brown are more abhorrent than the Republicans, and
. . . the Democratic office-holders and the abolitionists are the only
parties who have the slightest reason to encourage the Kansas madman,
or who can make capital out of enterprises like his.

Because the majority at the North are opposed to slavery, shall they
be accused of inciting the men who clap the torch to the house of the
slave-owner and arm the negro for insurrection? . . . .

No. 95   [THE WASHINGTON REPUBLIC (Rep.)]
Reprinted in *The National Intelligencer,*
Tues., Nov. 1, 1859

. . . Brown . . . was evidently insane; but of such insanity,
shooting or hanging is doubtless the only legitimate cure. . . . His gang
must have been composed of men either as insane as himself, or woe-
fully deficient in intellect and intelligence. . . . Most of them, however,
have paid the utmost penalty of their fatuity. . . .

No. 96   [THE PHILADELPHIA LEDGER]
Reprinted in *The National Intelligencer,*
Tues., Oct. 25, 1859

. . . that miserable fracas . . . shows us some of our military advantages, . . . the importance of railroads, and steamboats, and
telegraphs in a military point of view. About eighty miles from Baltimore and a hundred from Washington, a band of madmen, outlaws,
and rebels most unexpectedly seize the . . . arsenal . . . But . . . in
twenty-four hours troops are congregated from a distance, in some cases,
of one hundred and fifty miles, at a moment's notice, cannon and
military stores are transported, and the whole insurrection is quelled.
. . . We have not had before such an exhibition of military promptness
and efficiency. . . . So unexpected a rising, at so unexpected a point,
could hardly have been conceived; and yet such are the advantages of

railroads and telegraphs, though built entirely for the purposes of peace, that in an instant they place all military and volunteer forces within a hundred and fifty miles in such proximity as this to the seat of war —Cabinet Councils are assembled, military officers summoned, troops gathered by telegraph, and conveyed by steam to the seat of war with a celerity inconceivable fifty years ago. . . .

No. 97   [THE BALTIMORE WEEKLY SUN]
Sat., Oct. 22, 1859

On Monday morning our city was startled with intelligence of an insurrection of a most formidable character, which had broken out suddenly at Harper's Ferry, Va. . . . [On] Tuesday morning the whole insurrection was suppressed. Thus the short, sharp, terrible drama, provoked by a handful of enthusiasts, fanatics, adventurers, or by whatsoever term they may be designated, was brought suddenly to a close. A fearful retribution dealt out in the subjugation of the insurgents has left but little for the civil officers of the law to do in vindication of this grievous outrage against society. . . .

The whole movement—in its origin, its mode of demonstration, the absurd pretences developed in documents found upon the prisoners and the dead, the weakness of the parties in the attempt to carry out their apparent design, and their miserable end—is degraded beneath sympathy, and excites nothing but contempt as a miserable caricature of insurrectionary ambition. Yet it is impossible to contemplate the inevitable fate which these deluded fanatics have brought upon themselves, without a sentiment of commiseration towards them, as the victims of that social and political error with which a large proportion of the northern mind is indoctrinated and imbued. These poor wretches have only carried out to its practical absurdity a theory which is gradually diffusing itself, under the false pretence of a political sentiment among the people, and presumes to invite co-operation even in the Southern states.

Intelligent men, however, will learn in time that there can be no compromises with a thing, in itself, hostile to the spirit of our national compact. It may take more subtle and insidious forms than that in which the fanatics at Harper's Ferry have exhibited it, but it is the same thing, however its hideous deformity may be disguised to serve the ends of political ambition; and its fruits must be repulsive sectionalism and internecine strife. The lesson is timely. . . .

THE PRESS—*THE SOUTH*

No. 98 [THE RICHMOND ENQUIRER]
Fri., Oct. 21, 1859

The "irrepressible conflict" was initiated at Harper's Ferry, and though there, for the time suppressed, yet no man is able to say when or where it will begin again or where it will end. The extent of this iniquitous plot cannot be estimated by the number of men detected and killed or captured . . . ; the localities from whence these men came— . . . New England, . . . Iowa, . . . Ohio, . . . Kansas—show an extent of country embracing the whole Northern section of the Union, as involved in the attempt at instigating servile insurrection in Virginia. Alarming as is the fact that so extended a conspiracy has been detected, a yet more serious circumstance is presented in the amount of pecuniary means at the disposal of these leaders.

. . . *"tents, blankets, spades, and about fifteen hundred Sharps Rifles with ammunition." From whence came the money to buy these things?* . . . . "Fifteen hundred Sharps Rifles and ammunition," must have cost $15,000. When the known economy of our *Northern brethren* is considered, the fact that so large a sum has been furnished for the pillage of our property and the murder of our persons, will give some idea of what the South may expect ere the "irrepressible conflict" just begun is finally ended, either by our triumph or subjugation. . . .

The Harper's Ferry *émeute* failed by a mistaken idea of the temper of Virginia slaves.—The late effort was made after passing into a slave State; but how long before the Abolition fanatics of Cincinnati may seize Newport, in Kentucky, away from the Marines at Washington, and within hailing distance of the depot of Western Abolitionism? Virginia has been assailed. All the memories of her sacrifices for the Union availed nothing to protect the soil that gave permanency to the Union.—The name and family of Washington offered no protection from the assaults of these fanatics. Since these things are patent, what safety has Kentucky from the hordes that swarm upon her border on the Ohio side? The aid of the Federal Government was near Harper's Ferry, and was in hands faithful to the Constitution, but another year may place that aid in the hands of our assailants, and the "higher law" of an "irrepressible conflict" urge on and strengthen the hands that murder our families and pillage our property. Is there no remedy? Shall the South, divided by useless conflicts about Federal politics, fall as single victims to marauding bands of Northern fanatics? Can there

176

be no union of council, actions and *arms* among States so vitally interested in the integrity of each? . . . .

No. 99　[THE RICHMOND ENQUIRER]
Tues., Oct. 25, 1859

. . . It is but just that a disclaimer should be made by the
Northern press; but . . . the voice of the *people* at the North, through
the polls, is necessary to restore confidence and to dispel the belief that
the Northern people have aided and abetted this treasonable invasion
of a Southern State.

If the success of a party is of more importance than the restoration
of good feeling and attachment to the Union, let that fact go forth
from the polls of New York at her approaching election. Upon her
soil, the treason, if not planned, was perfected; the money of her
citizens gave vitality to the plot; the voice of her people should speak
words of encouragement to the outraged sovereignty of a sister State.
The vile clamor of party, the struggle of Republicanism for power,
has given an impetus to the abolition zeal of old Brown and his comrades, that impelled them forward in their mad career of treason and
bloodshed. The leader of the Republican forces gave utterance to the
treasonable declaration of "an irrepressible conflict," and if the people
of New York really repudiate [that] dogma let them send from the
polls greetings of overthrow that shall, if possible, restore confidence,
and cement the broken fragments of attachment for the Union. . . .

The Harper's Ferry invasion has advanced the cause of Disunion
more than any other event . . . since the formation of the Government;
it has rallied to that standard men who formerly looked upon it with
horror; it has revived, with ten-fold strength, the desire of a Southern
Confederacy. The heretofore most determined friends of the Union
may now be heard saying, "if under the form of a Confederacy our
peace is disturbed, our State invaded, its peaceful citizens cruelly
murdered . . . by those who should be our warmest friends . . . *and
the people of the North sustain the outrage,* then let disunion
come." . . . .

No. 100

Reprinted in *The Richmond Enquirer,* Tues., Nov. 15, from an unspecified newspaper in Charleston, S.C., dated Nov. 7, 1859

With all due reverence to the memory of our forefathers, I think the time has arrived in our history for a separation from the North. . . . The Constitution . . . has been violated . . . , if the Union stands we have no security either for life or property . . . , emissaries are in our midst, sent here by a party which claims to have the good of the country at heart, but in fact are assassins . . . , there are papers in the South, supported by Abolition money. . . . We must separate, unless we are willing to see our daughters and wives become the victims of a barbarous passion and worse insult.

With five millions of negroes turned loose in the South, what would be the state of society? It would be worse than the "Reign of Terror" . . . . The day of compromise is passed. . . . We should not listen to the words of Northern men who are continually telling us we are safe, while they attempt to ridicule this "Harper's Ferry business." Watch those fellows. . . . Gentlemen may cry peace, but there is no peace. Every gale that sweeps from the North brings new instruments of death in our midst. We publish to the world the causes that impel us to a separation, and throw ourselves upon the justice of God. . . . The hour has now come. The curtain falls, and the Republic framed by the hands of Washington and Jefferson fades from the view. Better civil war than injustice and oppression.

No. 101   [THE CHARLESTON MERCURY]

Reprinted in *The National Intelligencer,*
Tues., Dec. 6, 1859

We are satisfied that every intelligent man in the South has been completely disgusted at the broad and pathetic farce that has been played off before the public about the hanging of that hoary villain, "Old Brown," from the five hundred invaders in possession of Harper's Ferry and the 1,000 negroes carried off to the mountains of Pennsylvania . . . ; the marches and countermarches of troops, down to the final climax of military aid offered by Governor Gist, of South Carolina, to the Governor of Virginia for the purpose of making certain the aforesaid hanging . . . , it is a tissue of disgrace, exaggeration, and invention sufficient to stir the gall of any Southerner who has regard for the dignity and respectability of the Southern people. To us it really looks as if those in possession of the telegraph were in league to ridicule the South and make us a laughing-stock to ourselves and before the world. . . .

No. 102   [THE MADISON WEEKLY VISITER (Ga., Whig)]

Reprinted in *The National Intelligencer,*
Tues., Nov. 1, 1859

One of the remarkable features in our State and Federal Government at this time is a greatly diminished regard for the statutes of the land. . . . This state of things is peculiar to no section of this country. . . . The fanaticism of New England, acting upon a higher law than the Constitution to destroy the rights of the South, is not more treasonable in its consequences than the encouragement of unlawful enterprises at the South to override a sacred compact of the past in the revival of the slave trade from the coast of Africa.

The difficulty in bleeding Kansas and the late affair at Harper's Ferry are only additional instances going to show that the law of inclination is being substituted for the law of the land. . . .

The law of retaliation . . . is but the incubation of revolution, and . . . an explosion sudden and overwhelming is destined, at no distant day, to burst upon this country.

No. 103   [THE LEESBURG WASHINGTONIAN (Va., Whig)]

Reprinted in *The National Intelligencer,*
Tues., Nov. 1, 1859

. . . These fanatics have learned by the result that our citizens and slaves are happy and contented, and will resist to the bitter end any interference . . . We in the South have also learned by this . . . tragedy that that band of fanatics known as the abolitionists proper of the North constitute an exceedingly small portion of the Northern people. After a long and diligent effort . . . but *fourteen white men and five free negroes* could be mustered into their service. . . .

THE PRESS—*THE WEST*

No. 104 [THE CLEVELAND DEMOCRAT]
Reprinted in *The Richmond Enquirer*, Fri., Oct. 28, 1859

A bolder or a worse man . . . the world never knew. His single virtue, "linked with a thousand crimes," was bull-dog courage. Fanatic to the highest degree—a pupil, in politics, of the Giddings school—he has been taught to believe that the killing of a slaveholder was an act which God would approve. When in this city last spring, in his lectures, he told of his stealing negroes and running them to Canada—of his stealing horses, which he then had with him for sale—of his shooting down slaveholders, and of other acts equally atrocious. "And now," said Brown, "I wish to know if the people of Cleveland approve of what I have done. . . ." and more than one-half of his audience . . . shouted "aye," whilst not a single "nay" was uttered by any one present.

Such approval as this—and the question was put at all his lectures—gave Brown confidence that his party would sustain him in whatever he might do against the men of the South, and thus emboldened, the miserable wretch, by servile insurrection, sought to overthrow the government and bring himself to its head.

No. 105 [THE ST. LOUIS DEMOCRAT (Free Soil)]
Reprinted in *The Liberator* (Boston), Fri., Nov. 4, 1859

We should be better pleased if Brown and his followers, instead of being shot down like soldiers in battle, were made to die the ignominious death of traitors and murderers. They should have been saved for the gallows—every one of them. Were the slaves themselves to rise in revolt, their guilt, however great, would be light in comparison with the guilt of those white rebels, or rather rapparees. They not only spilled innocent blood, but they did their utmost to draw down destruction on the slave population of Virginia and Maryland, whose good they pretended to have in view, but who would be undoubtedly exterminated in the event of their uprising. Therefore, we say, they were the enemies of black and white. . . . And here we would protest against the weakness of making any plea of abatement, on the ground that 'old Brown' is not in his right mind. The madness engendered as the spirit of unholy vengeance is not a mood on which the Spirit

180

of Mercy can look with a benignant eye. Like the drunkenness which culminates in crime, it is but a preliminary stage of that instigation by the devil, which the law itself makes emphatic mention of.

No. 106 [THE LAWRENCE HERALD OF FREEDOM (Kans., Rep.)]

Sat., Oct. 29, reprinted in *The Richmond Enquirer,* Nov. 15, 1859

. . . who were those men in the Territory at that time [summer of 1857]? There were Walden and Thacher, Ralph and John E. Cooke, Holmes and Kagi, we believe; Phillips and Redpath, Hinton and Conway. They did all in their power to induce the people to keep out of the October elections . . . , but the real interest of the Territory triumphed over their revolutionary plots, and in October we had possession of the Territorial government. . . .

Old John Brown, with his minions, who opened the bloody issue in Kansas, by *murdering* the five heads of families on Pottawatomie Creek, at midnight, on the 25th of May, 1856, appeared and took charge of the marauding forces. . . . Brown was in constant intercourse with men in the East, who declared . . . that "their only hope of abolishing slavery in the United States lay through *revolution".* . . .

Their next point of attack was Virginia. . . . The whole plan had been known in Kansas for a long time. . . . With his few immediate supporters he was to take possession of the Armory, while others, with teams, were to carry the arms and military supplies to the mountains. In those fastnesses he was to erect his independent standard, around which the negroes were to assemble. A secret organization, permeating all sections of the North, with powerful backing in Kansas, was to furnish recruits. Thus strengthened they would be able to bid defiance to State and Federal authority and . . . they would keep alive their movements, acting mostly upon the defensive at first, till the negroes of the Canadas and of the South could give them sufficient strength to justify aggressive moments. . . .

Our present fears are that the Republican party will suffer by the action of these *parasites.* . . .

The first thing the people of Kansas heard of Old John Brown was in the summer of 1855. A meeting of ultra-Abolitionists was held at Cazenovia, N.Y., if we recollect rightly. While in session, Brown . . . appeared in that Convention and made a very fiery speech, during which he said he had four sons in Kansas, and he had three others who were desirous of going there, to aid in fighting the battles of freedom. He could not consent to go unless he could go *armed,* and he would like to arm all his sons, but was not able to do so. Funds were contributed upon the spot—principally by Gerrit Smith.

The four sons had located on Pottawatomie creek, in Lykins county and in the fall of 1855 were joined by the father and other brothers. When the Wakarusa war was pending the old man and four sons arrived in Lawrence, the balance he reported sick. As they drove up in front of the Free State Hotel they were all standing in a small lumber wagon. . . . Each was supplied with a goodly number of firearms, and navy revolvers, and poles were standing endwise around the wagon box with fixed bayonets pointing upwards. They looked really formidable and were received with great éclat. A smart military company was organized at once, and the command was given to Old Brown. From that hour he commenced fomenting difficulties in camp, disregarding the commands of superior officers, and trying to induce the men to go down to Franklin and make an attack on the pro-slavery forces encamped there. The Committee of Public Safety were called upon several times to head off his wild adventure, as the people of Lawrence had planted themselves on the law, claiming that they had not been guilty of its infraction, and that no *armed* body of men should enter the town for any purpose whatever, and that they would not go out of town to attack any such body. Peace was established, and "Old Brown" *retired in disgust.*

When the news of the threatened siege of Lawrence reached John Brown, Jr., who was a member of the Topeka Legislature, he organized a company of about sixty men and marched towards Lawrence. Arriving at Palmyra, he learned of the sacking of the town and the position of the people. He reconnoitered for a time in the vicinity, but finally marched back toward Osawatomie. The night before reaching that place, when only a few miles away, they camped for the night. Old John Brown, who, we believe, was with the party, singled out, with himself, seven men.—These he marched to a point eight miles above the mouth of Pottawatomie Creek, and called from their beds at their several residences, at the hour of midnight, on the 24th of May, Allen Wilkinson, Wm. Sherman, Wm. P. Doyle, Wm. Doyle, and Drury Doyle. All were found the next morning, their heads and sides and their throats cut; others with their skulls split open in two places, with holes in their breasts, and hands cut off; and others had holes through their breasts with their fingers cut off.

No man in Kansas has pretended to deny that Old John Brown led that murderous foray, which massacred those men. Up to that period not a hair of Old John Brown's head, or that of any of his sons, had been injured by the pro-slavery party. It was not until the 30th of August, three months after the Pottawatomie massacre that the attack was made on Osawatomie by the pro-slavery forces, and Frederick Brown, a son of Old John, was killed.

The truth of history requires this statement. If Brown *was* a monomaniac, it dates back anterior to his first visit to Kansas.

No. 107 [THE INDIANAPOLIS JOURNAL]
The National Intelligencer, Thurs., Dec. 29, 1859

We copy from the Cincinnati *Gazette* of Monday last the subjoined extract from the Kansas correspondence of *The Indianapolis Journal.* It will attract attention as associating the late John Brown with an atrocious act in Kansas concerning which there has been recently some controversy in a portion of the public press:

LAWRENCE (KANSAS), DECEMBER 17, 1859.
A "John Brown" anti-slavery meeting was held in Lawrence last evening. . . .

After some of the speakers had lauded Brown as a second Jesus, and one of them alluded to the Pottawatomie massacre, which has been laid at John's door—

MR. STEVENS said he did not believe John Brown had any thing to do with it; but there was a gentleman present who could testify to that fact. "Name him, name him," several called out. "It is Capt. Walker," (now sheriff of Douglas county, and one of the bravest of the Free-State leaders).

Capt. WALKER rose and said, "Gentlemen, there is no use in keeping back the truth or perverting facts. John Brown told me himself that he was present at the murder of those men on Pottawatomie Creek." (This startled like a thunder clap the defenders of Brown.) He proceeded: "I am ready to take an oath that John Brown made such a statement to me. I know more about this matter than I can state, especially as it would implicate as actors in that murder some persons now in this room. John Brown had those men in his power, and he could have kept them prisoners. For himself he never could justify taking a man prisoner and then deliberately cutting his throat. . . ."

Gov. CHARLES ROBINSON also said that he believed John Brown had acknowledged to him he was present and approved of the killing of those men. . . . He had not and could not justify the excesses committed by Free-State men after they had the civil power in their hands.

Dr. ADAIR, a nephew of John Brown . . . said . . . Brown had told him that he was present at the killing of those men. But there were palliating circumstances connected with it.

I may add that there is no question whatever, from what I have heard from persons who know the facts, that John Brown planned and carried out that massacre. The facts come to me from men who stand among the most truthful of any in Kansas. The truth is, the less Republicans lionize Old Brown the better.

TOPICS FOR ESSAYS

SUGGESTED LENGTH (*words*):

(1) *The New England Press and the Raid*	300
(2) *The Middle Atlantic States Press and the Raid*	300
(3) *The Southern Press and the Raid*	300
(4) *The Western Press and the Raid*	300
(5) *The American Press and the Raid*	500
(6) *New Light on John Brown: The Press*	500

TOPICS FOR LIBRARY RESEARCH

BIBLIOGRAPHY:

William L. Garrison   Captain Walker
Governor Gist   The Wakarusa War
Governor Charles Robinson

SUPPLEMENTARY RESEARCH:

Either in your college library or in the newspaper office of the town in or near which your college is located there will probably be old newspaper files of one or more newspapers (other than those used here). Consult them for the dates Oct. 17-Dec. 31, 1859. Then write a documented essay on the editorial reaction of *your* locality to the Raid as an extension or refutation of the corresponding regional sentiments quoted in this book.   500-1500

THE ROSTRUM

No. 108 [HON. CALEB CUSHING]

Speech in Boston, in *The National Intelligencer,*
Sat., Dec. 17, 1859

. . . Gentlemen, it happened to me, while administering the laws of the United States, to render an opinion that the Armory at Harper's Ferry is under the exclusive jurisdiction of the United States. . . . That opinion was true. I know it. . . . To this point of law [raised by Brown's counsel] founded upon my opinion, the counsel for the Commonwealth replied . . . that my opinion was not good law; that it might be good law in Massachusetts, but . . . not . . . in Virginia; and thereupon the trial proceeded. I say that that was an ill-advised suggestion on the part of the counsel for the Commonwealth. . . . I would have presented myself before the Chief Justice of the United States, and I would have obtained from Roger B. Taney a writ of error to appeal that question to the tribunals of the United States. . . . Why did I not? . . . True, acts of murder . . . of treason . . . of burglary . . . of rapine had been perpetrated upon the grounds of the Armory at Harper's Ferry, but not there only; for John Brown, in this most insane . . . most criminal outrage, had been guilty of five violations of law, three of them at least capital felonies by the law of the State of Virginia. . . .

"Extenuation"? What extenuation? . . . [Go] with me to one of those fertile prairies of the far West . . . to the frontier cabin of a pioneer settler of the far West. . . . [Two] husbands are torn from the arms of their wives and ruthlessly slaughtered in cold blood. Nay, their youthful children are brained before their eyes. Methinks I can hear now the wailing cry of that poor woman, Mahala Doyle; of that unhappy Louisa Wilkinson. . . . That evidence exists on record in the report of the committee appointed by the House of Representatives to examine into the disorders of Kansas. I say that murderous act of John Brown was the commencement of bloodshed in Kansas. . . .

But it is said that John Brown was insane. . . . I say . . . there is a handful of men of highly intellectual mind, of the highest culture . . . —Wendell Phillips, Lloyd Garrison, Waldo Emerson, Theodore Parker, and Gerrit Smith—who by constant brooding on a single idea, that idea, if you please, a right one, have become monomaniacs. . . .

No. 109   [RALPH WALDO EMERSON]

Speech in Salem, Mass., on Jan. 6, 1860.
From James Redpath (ed.), *Echoes of Harper's Ferry*
(Boston, 1860), pp. 118-122

. . . John Brown, the founder of liberty in Kansas, was
born in . . . Connecticut in 1800. When he was five years old his
father emigrated to Ohio, and the boy was there set to keep sheep,
and to look after cattle . . . ; he went bareheaded and barefooted, and
clothed in buckskin. He said that he loved rough play, could never
have . . . enough. . . . It chanced that in Pennsylvania, where he was
sent by his father to collect cattle, he fell in with a boy whom he
heartily liked, and whom he looked upon as his superior. This boy
was a slave; he saw him beaten with an iron shovel, and otherwise
maltreated . . . had no friend, and no future. This worked such
indignation in him that he swore an oath of resistance to Slavery as
long as he lived. And thus his enterprise to go into Virginia and run
off 500 or 1000 slaves was not a piece of spite or revenge, a plot of
two years or of twenty years, but the keeping of an oath made to
heaven and earth 47 years before. Forty-seven years at least, though I
incline to accept his own account of the matter, at Charlestown, which
makes the date a little older, when he said, "This was all settled
millions of years before the world was made."

He grew up a religious and manly person in severe poverty; a fair
specimen of the best stock of New England; having that force of
thought and that sense of right which are the warp and woof of
greatness. . . . Thus was formed a romantic character absolutely without any vulgar trait; living to ideal ends, without any mixture of self-
indulgence or compromise. . . .

I am . . . surprised at the easy effrontery with which political gentlemen, in and out of Congress, take it upon them to say that there are
not a thousand men in the North who sympathize with John Brown.
It would be far safer and nearer the truth to say that all people, in
proportion to their sensibility and self-respect, sympathize with him.
. . . All women are drawn to him by their predominance of sentiment.
All gentlemen, of course, are on his side. . . . For what is the oath of
gentle blood and knighthood? What but to protect the weak and lowly
against the strong oppressor. . . . Who makes the Abolitionist? The
Slaveholder. . . .

No. 110 [HON. EDWARD EVERETT]

Speech at the Union Meeting, Boston, Thurs., Dec. 8, 1859, in *The Richmond Enquirer,* Dec. 16, 1859

. . . it seems to me . . . in bad taste at least to try to point a sneer at a State like Virginia. . . . A conflict of such an unprecedented character, in which twelve or fourteen persons on the two sides are shot down in the course of a few hours, appears to me an event at which levity ought to stand rebuked, and a solemn chill to fall upon every right thinking man. . . .

Mr. Chairman, those who look upon the existing excitement at the South as factitious or extravagant have, I fear, formed a very inadequate idea of the nature of such an attempt as that which was made at Harper's Ferry was intended to be, and would have been, had it proved successful. . . . With this wild, but thoroughly matured plan, he provided weapons for those on whose rising he calculated at Harper's Ferry; he seized the national arsenal . . . and he intended, if unable to maintain himself at once in the open country, to retreat to the mountains, and from their fastnesses harass, paralyze, and at length revolutionize the South . . . and when I contemplate the horrors that would have ensued . . . , I am filled with emotions to which no words can do justice. . . . The memory of our Fathers—of those happy days when the men of North and South stood together for the country, on hard fought fields . . . —is all this forgotten? . . . No, fellow citizens, no, a thousand times, no. This glorious Union shall not perish. . . .

No. 111 [WENDELL PHILLIPS] "THE LESSON OF THE HOUR"

Speech at Brooklyn, N.Y., on Nov. 1, 1859, in Redpath (ed.), *Echoes of Harper's Ferry,* pp. 43-66

. . . "The Lesson of the Hour"? I think the lesson of the hour is insurrection. (*Sensation.*) Insurrection of thought always precedes the insurrection of arms. The last twenty years have been an insurrection of thought. We seem to be entering on a new phase of the great American struggle. . . . It seems to me the idea of our civilization . . . is that men do not need any guardian. . . . Institutions . . . are but pasteboard, and intended to be against the thought of the street. Statutes are mere milestones, telling how far yesterday's thought has travelled; and the talk of the sidewalk today is the law of the land. . . . If you said to an American, for instance, anything in regard to . . . slavery . . . in the last twenty years—anything about a principle—he ran back instantly to the safety of such a principle. . . . He had not yet raised himself to the level of daring to trust justice, which is the preliminary consideration to trusting people. . . . Now our object for twenty years has been to educate the . . . American people up to that level of moral life which shall recognize that free speech carried to this extent is God's normal school, educating the American mind. . . . I believe in moral suasion. The age of bullets is over. I think that is the rule of our age. . . . Yet let me say . . . I think you can make a better use of iron than forging it into chains. If you must have the metal, put it into Sharps rifles. It is a great deal better used that way than in fetters; types are better than bullets, but bullets a thousand times rather than a clumsy statue of a mock great man, for hypocrites to kneel down and worship in a state-house yard. (*Loud and renewed cheers and great hissing.*) I am so unused to hisses lately, that I have forgotten what I had to say. . . .

Connecticut has sent out many a schoolmaster to the other thirty States; but never before so grand a teacher as that Litchfield-born schoolmaster at Harper's Ferry, writing as it were upon the Natural Bridge in the face of nations his simple copy: "Resistance to tyrants is obedience to God." (*Loud cheers.*)

I said that the lesson of the hour was insurrection. I ought not to apply that word to John Brown of Osawatomie, for there was no insurrection in his case. It is a great mistake to call him an insurgent. . . . Whatever calls itself a government and refuses that duty [of rendering equal justice between man and man] . . . is no government. It is only a pirate ship. Virginia . . . is a pirate ship, and John Brown sails the sea a Lord High Admiral of the Almighty, with his commission to sink every pirate he meets on God's ocean of the nineteenth century. . . . John Brown has twice as much right to hang Governor Wise as Governor Wise has to hang him. (*Cheers and hisses.*). . . . Harper's Ferry is the Lexington of today. Up to this moment Brown's life has been one unmixed success. . . . Suppose he did fail, in one sense; he has done a great deal still. Why, this is a decent country to live in now. (*Laughter and cheers.*) Actually, in this Sodom of ours, twenty-two men have been found ready to die for an idea. God be thanked for John Brown, that he has discovered or created them. (*Cheers*). . . .

The slaves of our country have not risen, but as in most other cases, redemption will come from the interference of a wiser, higher, more advanced civilization on its exterior. . . . It is the lesson of the age. The first cropping out of it is in such a man as John Brown. . . . What is defeat? Nothing but an education—nothing but the first step to something better. . . .

Thank God, I am not a citizen. You will remember, all of you, citizens of the United States that there was not a Virginia gun fired at John Brown. Hundreds of well-armed Maryland and Virginia troops rushed to Harper's Ferry and—went away! *You* shot him! Sixteen marines, to whom you pay eight dollars a month—your own representatives. . . . Sixteen men, with the Vulture of the Union above them— (*sensation*)—your own representatives! . . . . And the New York press daily prints the accounts of the *trial*. Trial! . . . Wounded, fevered, . . . the trial half finished before his first request for aid had reached his friends,—no list of witnesses or knowledge of them till the crier, calling the name of some assassin of his comrades, wakes him to consciousness; the judge a tool, and the prosecutor seeking popularity by pandering to the mob; no decent form observed, and the essence of a fair trial wholly wanting, our History and Law alike protest against degrading the honored name of *Jury Trial* by leading it to such an outrage as this. . . . This blow, like the first gun at Lexington, "heard around the world,"—this blow at Harper's Ferry reveals men. Watch those about you and you will see more of the temper and unconscious purpose and real moral position of men than you would imagine. . . . Be not in a hurry; action will come enough from this sentiment. . . .

No. 112   [HENRY D. THOREAU] "A PLEA FOR CAPTAIN JOHN BROWN"

Read in Concord, Mass., Oct. 30, and in Boston, Nov. 1, 1859; in Redpath (ed.), *Echoes of Harper's Ferry*, pp. 17-42

. . . [He] went to the great university of the West, where he sedulously pursued the study of Liberty, for which he had early betrayed a fondness, and having taken many degrees, he finally commenced the public practice of Humanity in Kansas, as you all know. . . . I remember, particularly, how, in his speech here, he referred to what his family had suffered in Kansas, without ever giving the least vent to his pent-up fire. . . . Also referring to the . . . Border Ruffians, he said . . . , "They had a perfect right to be hung." . . .

The newspapers seem to ignore . . . that there are at least as many as two or three individuals to a town throughout the North, who think much as [I do] about him and his enterprise. . . . [They] are an important and growing party. . . . "But he won't gain any thing by it." Well, no, I don't suppose he could get four-and-sixpence a day for being hung, take the year round; but then he stands a chance to save a considerable part of his soul . . . when *you* do not. No doubt you can get more in your market for a quart of milk than for a quart of blood, but that is not the market that heroes carry their blood to. . . .

"Served him right"—"A dangerous man"—"He is undoubtedly insane." So they proceed to live their sane, and wise, and altogether admirable lives. . . .

I read all the newspapers I could get within a week after this event, and I do not remember in them a single expression of sympathy for these men. . . . Some voluminous sheets decided not to print the full report of Brown's words. . . . It was as if a publisher should reject the manuscript of the New Testament, and print [Senator] Wilson's last words. . . .

Insane! A father and six sons, and one son-in-law, and . . . as many at least as twelve disciples—all struck with insanity at once; while the sane tyrant holds with a firmer gripe than ever his four million of slaves, and a thousand sane editors . . . are saving their country and their bacon! . . .

The only government that I recognize . . . is that power that establishes justice in the land. . . . What shall we think of a government to which all the truly brave and just men in the land are enemies . . . ? A government that pretends to be Christian and crucifies a million Christs every day!

Treason! Where does such treason take its rise? . . . Can you dry up the fountains of thought? . . . .

The United States have a coffle of four millions of slaves . . . and Massachusetts is one of the confederated overseers to prevent their escape. Such are not all the inhabitants of Massachusetts, but such are they who rule and are obeyed here. It was Massachusetts, as well as Virginia, that put down this insurrection. . . . She sent the marines there, and she will have to pay the penalty. . . .

It was [Brown's] peculiar doctrine that a man has a perfect right to interfere by force with the slaveholder, in order to rescue the slave. I agree with him. . . . I think that for once the Sharps rifles and the revolvers were employed in a righteous cause. The tools were in the hands of one who could use them. . . .

Some eighteen hundred years ago Christ was crucified; this morning, perchance, Captain Brown was hung. These are the two ends of a chain which is not without its links. He is not Old Brown any longer; he is an angel of light. . . .

I foresee the time when the painter will paint [the scene of John Brown telling his captors his views after the taking of the engine-house], no longer going to Rome for a subject; the poet will sing it; the historian record it; and, with the Landing of the Pilgrims and the Declaration of Independence, it will be the ornament of some future national gallery, when at least the present form of slavery shall be no more here. We shall then be at liberty to weep for Captain Brown. Then, and not till then, we will take our revenge.

No. 113 [GOVERNOR WISE]

Speech in Richmond, Va., Fri., Oct. 21, in *The Richmond Enquirer*, Oct. 25, 1859

. . . "Old Brown," the fanatic of Osawatomie and Lawrence and Fort Scott memory, who denounced the Missourians as "Border Ruffians," became himself the Border Ruffian of Virginia, and is now a prisoner of Treason to her authority. The slaves he would incite to insurrection and massacre, would not take up arms against their masters. His spears were untouched by them. And they are themselves mistaken who take him to be a madman. He is a bundle of the best nerves I ever saw, cut and thrust, and bleeding and in bonds. He is a man of clear head, of courage, fortitude, and simple ingenuousness. He is cool, collected and indomitable, and it is but just to him to say, that he was humane to his prisoners, as attested to me by Col. Washington and Mr. Mills; and he inspired me with great trust in his integrity, as a man of truth. He is a fanatic, vain and garrulous, but firm, and truthful, and intelligent. His men, too, who survive, except the free negroes with him, are like him. He professes to be a Christian, in communion with the Congregationalist Church of the North, and openly preaches his purpose of universal emancipation; and the negroes themselves were to be the agents, by means of arms, led on by white commanders. . . . And Col. Washington says that he, Brown, was the coolest and firmest man he ever saw in defying danger and death. With one son dead by his side, and another shot through, he felt the pulse of his dying son with one hand and held his rifle with the other, and commanded his men with the utmost composure, encouraging them to be firm, and to sell their lives as dearly as they could. Of the three white prisoners, Brown, Stevens and Coppoc, it was hard to say which was most firm; and of the two negroes it was hard to say which seemed the most cowardly and false.—The North Carolina negro offered to betray all persons involved in the affair if spared, and the Canada negro, who was, I believe, one of the members of their provisional Congress, was a crouching craven, who lied, as Brown said, for his life.

THE PULPIT

No. 114   [REV. HENRY WARD BEECHER]

Preached at Plymouth Church, Brooklyn, Sun., Oct. 30,
1859, in Redpath (ed.), *Echoes of Harper's Ferry*, pp.
257-279

. . . Seventeen men, white men, without a military base,
without supplies, without artillery, without organization more than a
squad of militia, attacked a State, and undertook to release and lead
away an enslaved race! They do not appear to have been called by
the sufferers, nor to have been welcomed by them. They volunteered
a grace, and sought to enforce its acceptance. Seventeen white men surrounded two thousand, and held them in duress. . . . [Seventeen] white
men overawed a town of two thousand brave Virginians, and held
them captives until the sun had gone, laughing, twice round the
globe! . . .

It was in [Kansas] that Brown received his impulse. A tender father,
. . . he saw his first-born seized like a felon, chained, driven across
the country, . . . and long lying at death's door. Another noble boy,
without warning, without offence, unarmed, in open day, in the midst
of the city, was shot dead! . . . The shot that struck the child's heart,
crazed the father's brain. . . .

I deplore his misfortunes. I sympathize with his sorrows. I mourn
the hiding or obscuration of his reason. I disapprove of his mad and
feeble schemes. I shrink from the folly of the bloody foray, and I
shrink . . . from all anticipations of that judicial bloodshed which,
doubtless, ere long, will follow. . . .

Let no man pray that Brown be spared. Let Virginia make him a
martyr. Now, he has only blundered. His soul was noble; his work
miserable. But a cord and a gibbet would redeem all that, and round
up Brown's failure with a heroic success. . . .

The condition of the slave must be changed, but . . . there must be
change in the law, . . . in the church, . . . in the upper classes, . . . in
the middle classes, and in all classes. Emancipation when it comes will
come either by revolution or by a change of public opinion in the
whole community. . . . The evil is not partial. It cannot be cured by
partial remedies. . . .

No. 115   [REV. GEORGE B. CHEEVER]

Preached in New York, Tues., Nov. 24, 1859, in Redpath,
Echoes of Harper's Ferry, pp. 141-175

. . . The terrible outbreak at Harper's Ferry calls us anew
to the consideration of our own duty, and of the means by which we
may avoid God's judgments, and redeem our country from a wickedness
that threatens to consume us. . . . And a most remarkable thing it
is, that just when the doctrines of the inviolability and sacredness of
slave property had reached their culminating point of audacity and
infamy; when it was becoming a political truism that there could be
no right of intervention against the wrong of human Slavery where
it already exists, but only the right of endeavoring to prevent its extension; when some politicians even, in the only party in the country
imagined to possess any remnant of conscience or of principle, were
setting up a defence of the rights of the South to undisturbed possession of their millions of slaves, as a vested interest and right not
to be meddled with; that just at this juncture, God should have shot
John Brown out of the cannon of his providence right into the bosom
of that vested interest; shot him as a bomb against it, scattering all
the theories of politicians to the winds, and setting all men to a new
discussion, not merely of the right of the slaves themselves to assert
their own freedom, but of the right and duty of all men to help them
to it, in any and every just way that God puts in their power. . . .

[Virginia's] laws are of no more force or validity than the laws of
an association of Thugs, or . . . thieves, or . . . counterfeiters. Com-
modore Decatur might with as much propriety have been . . . hanged
for treason in Algiers, as John Brown for treason in Virginia, for John
Brown owed no more allegiance to Virginia than Decatur owed to
Algiers. . . .

This event must open up the subject. . . . Either Slavery is absolutely
right or wrong. . . . Either slaves are the most sacred of all property,
or the most diabolical of all robbery. If slavery is impious, a government grounded on it, protecting it, making laws in its behalf, is an
exasperation of villainy infinitely atrocious, making not only slaves out
of freemen, but villains out of its own citizens. . . . There can be no
sanction, no justification, for such wickedness. . . . The whole world is
rightfully at war with such iniquity . . . ; no man can possibly commit treason in seeking to overthrow it. . . . If the abolition of the government were necessary for the overthrow of the sin . . . , then the

sooner the government is abolished the better. It were infinitely better that three hundred thousand slaveholders were abolished, struck out of existence, than that four million human beings, with their posterity forever, should be enslaved under them. . . .

No. 116

Editorial of *The Albany* (N.Y.) *Argus* reprinted in *The National Intelligencer*, Thurs., Dec. 28, 1859

It is the fashion to impute to the Clergy, as a body, sympathy with the sectional intolerance of the day. Nothing can be more false or more unjust . . . The divines who preach "killing no murder" are few indeed. In the city of New York, Cheever (who is a pensioner upon the British Anti-Slavery Societies); in Brooklyn, Beecher; in Boston, one or two of the same kidney, and in the interior some scattered imitators, are all of the clergy engaged in this crusade—and these stand in relation to their fellow-clergymen, and judged by their own avowed standards of orthodoxy, in very questionable positions. We venture to say that not more than five in a hundred of the clergy attached to congregations join or sympathize in the preaching of the gospel of insurrection which a few so noisily and wickedly proclaim.

For twenty years the little knot of Abolitionists have been wandering from city to city in the North, repeating the same speeches, delivering the same lectures, making the same appeals. One wonders at the barrenness of their invention. . . . Yet these men, inconsiderable and disregarded, gathering no converts, . . . have had their consequence multiplied and their evil purposes ministered to by a press hostile to them. There are scores of clergymen who preach a purer gospel and a higher morality than Beecher; but who hears of them? . . . No! The sermon of a preacher who is true to the spirit of peace and loyal to his country . . . is not worthy of notice because it is so common. Beecher and Parker obtain audience of the press, because their spasmodic eloquence creates a sensation. . . .

THE POETS

No. 117   OLD JOHN BROWN: A SONG FOR EVERY SOUTHERN MAN

Anonymous broadside (Richmond, 1859); the McGregor Collection, Library of the University of Virginia

Now all you Southern people, just listen to my song,
It's about the Harpers' Ferry affair, it is not very long.
To please you all I do my best, I sung it in other towns,
And while I am in Richmond, I'll tell you about old Brown.
Chorus: Old Ossawattomie Brown! Old Ossawattomie Brown!
That will never pay,/Trying to come away down South,/And run
   the niggers away.

Old Brown and Cook, and a dozen more, to Harpers' Ferry went,
They got into the arsinel [*sic*] there, they did not have no right;
Old Governor Wise heard of this, he started from Richmond town,
He went to Harpers' Ferry, and there he caught old Brown.
   (Chorus, &c.)

They took him down to Charlestown, and into prison throw'd him;
They put two chains upon his legs, Oh yes! it was to hold him,
They put two chains upon his legs and two upon his arms,
The virdict [*sic*] of the jury was, old Brown he should be hung.
   Chorus, &c.). . . .

Now all you Southern people a little advice I give;
Patronize the South and the State in which you live;
And not unto Northern people your money never pay,
They have their agents in the South, to run your slaves away.
   (Chorus, &c.)

Now all you Southern darkies, a word to you I'll say;
Always mind your masters, and never run away,
And don't mind these Northern agents, they tell to you a lie,
They get you at the North, and starve you 'till you die. (Chorus, &c.)

No. 118

Anonymous, in W. W. Scott, "The John Brown Letters," *The Virginia Magazine of History and Biography,* IX (April, 1902), p. 393

. . . I recall from memory, and imperfectly, two stanzas of a song, very popular at that time, in derision of Brown and his attempt. It ran something after this manner:

"In Harper's Ferry section there was an insurrection,
John Brown thought the niggers would sustain him;
But old Massa Wise put his spectacles on his eyes,
And he landed him in the happy land o' Canaan.

CHORUS:

"Ha, ha, ha, and a ha, ha, ha!
The days of Southern Rights am comin',
So it's never mind weather, but get over double trouble,
For I'm bound for the happy land o' Canaan. . . ."

No. 119   "WITH A ROSE"

Louisa May Alcott, in Redpath (ed.), *Echoes of Harper's Ferry,* p. 98

A life so powerful in its truth,/ A nature so complete;
It conquered ruler, judge and priest/ And held them at its feet.
Death seemed proud to take a soul/ So beautifully given,
And the gallows only proved to him/ A stepping-stone to heaven.
Each cheerful word, each valiant act/ So simple, so sublime,
Spoke to us through the reverent hush/ Which sanctified that time.
That moment when the brave old man/ Went so serenely forth,
With footsteps whose unfaltering tread/ Reechoed through the
    North.
The sword he wielded for the right/ Turns to a victor's palm;
His memory sounds forever more/ A spirit-stirring psalm.
No breath of shame can touch his shield,/ Nor ages dim its shine;
Living, he made life beautiful,—/ Dying, made death divine. . . .

No. 120   "THE HERO'S HEART"

L. Maria Child, in Redpath (ed.), *Echoes of Harper's Ferry*, p. 348

A winter sunshine, still and bright,/The Blue Hills bathed with golden light,
And earth seemed smiling to the sky,/When calmly he went forth to die.
Infernal passions festered there,/Where peaceful nature looked so fair;
And fiercely, in the morning sun,/Flashed glittering bayonet and gun.
The old man met no friendly eye,/When last he looked on earth and sky;
But one small child, with timid air,/Was gazing on his silver hair.
As that dark brow to his upturned,/The tender heart within him yearned;
And, fondly stooping o'er her face/He kissed her, for her injured race.
The little one, she knew not why/That kind old man went forth to die;
Nor why, mid all that pomp and stir,/He stooped to give a kiss to *her*.
But Jesus smiled that sight to see,/And said, "He did it unto *me*"!
The golden harps then sweetly rung,/And this the song the Angels sung:
"Who loves the poor doth love the Lord!/Earth cannot dim thy bright reward;
We hover o'er yon gallows high,/And wait to bear thee to the sky."

No. 121   [JOURNAL ENTRY OF LONGFELLOW]

Samuel Longfellow, *The Life of Henry Wadsworth Longfellow* (Boston, 1886) II, p. 396

The second of December, 1859. This will be a great day in our history; the date of a new Revolution,—quite as much needed as the old one. Even now as I write, they are leading old John Brown to execution in Virginia for attempting to rescue slaves! This is sowing the wind to reap the whirlwind, which will come soon.

No. 122   ["THE PORTENT"]
Herman Melville, *Battle Pieces* (New York, 1866), p. 11

Hanging from the beam,
   Slowly swaying (such the law),
Gaunt the shadow on your green,
   Shenandoah!
The cut is on the crown
   (Lo, John Brown),
And the stabs shall heal no more.

Hidden in the cap
   Is the anguish none can draw;
So your future veils its face,
   Shenandoah!
But the streaming beard is shown
   (Weird John Brown),
The meteor of the war.

No. 123   "HOW OLD BROWN TOOK HARPER'S FERRY"
The Poetical Works of Edmund Clarence Stedman (Boston, 1885), pp. 64-70

John Brown in Kansas settled, like a steadfast Yankee farmer,
Brave and godly, with four sons, all stalwart men of might.
There he spoke aloud for freedom, and the Border-strife grew
   warmer,
Till the Rangers fired his dwelling, in his absence in the night. . . .

Then he grasped his trusty rifle, and boldly fought for freedom. . . .

And the Lord *did* aid these men, and they labored day and even,
Saving Kansas from its peril; and their very lives seemed charmed,
Till the ruffians killed one son . . . in cold blood . . . all unarmed;
Then Old Brown,/ Osawatomie Brown,/ Shed not a tear, but . . .
   frowned a terrible frown!

Then they seized another brave boy . . . and they loaded him with
  chains. . . ;
Drove him cruelly, for their sport, and at last blew out his
  brains. . . .

And he swore a fearful oath, by the name of the Almighty,
He would hunt this ravening evil that had scathed and torn him
  so. . . .

'Twas the sixteenth of October, on the evening of a Sunday:
"This good work," declared the captain, "shall be on a holy
  night!" . . . .

Took the guarded armory-building, and the muskets and the can-
  non;
Captured all the county majors and the colonels, one by one;
Scared to death each gallant scion of Virginia they ran on. . . .

. . . [To] storm, with all the forces I have mentioned, was too
  risky;
So they hurried off to Richmond for the Government Marines,
Tore them from their weeping matrons, fired their souls with Bourbon whiskey,
Till they battered down Brown's castle with their ladders and machines. . . .

"Hang Old Brown,/ Osawatomie Brown,"
Said the judge, "and all such rebels!" with his most judicial frown.
But, Virginians, don't do it! for I tell you that the flagon,
Filled with blood of Old Brown's offspring, was first poured by
  Southern hands;

And each drop from Old Brown's life-veins, like the red gore of
  the dragon,
May spring up a vengeful Fury, hissing through your slave-worn
  lands!
And Old Brown,/ Osawatomie Brown,
May trouble you more than ever, when you've nailed his coffin
  down!

[Nov., 1859]

No. 124

Mrs. J. C. Swayze, *Ossawattomie* [sic] *Brown/A Drama in Three Acts* (New York, 1859)

. . . ACT III. SCENE I. *Interior of the Kennedy Farm . . . Brown seated at table with letters.*

Brown. [Reading letter] "It is well known, that in every instance where an enlightened body of men have espoused the cause of the oppressed, and have endeavored to set them free, the result has invariably proved a failure, from sole cause that the would-be liberators depend on the cooperation of those whose battles they are fighting, *but which inevitably fails them at the moment of action.* . . . It is a stubborn fact, recorded in the history of ages. To emancipate at one blow any downtrodden race, you must provide force enough to liberate them *at least without cooperation from,* if not absolutely *against* their will. . . . If, in spite of these arguments, you are still determined to rush on to the attack, I will give you all the pecuniary aid in my power, but remember, *I have no faith in the success of the undertaking. A Philosopher."* [*Speaking*] There's a wet blanket, and from a professed abolitionist! . . .

I have collected arms, unknowing to the people, that, in the hands of outraged men, who are fighting for their freedom, would insure their safety against many thousand. This is no lawless outbreak—we are not here to murder and to rob. God knows I have no thirst for blood. Those weapons are for self-defense—to guard the passage of our rescued band to shores of greater safety—and I have no fear in leaving it to all humanity to justify the act. . . .

SCENE VI. *Prison. Brown lying on a cot.* . . . And so I am to have a visit from a lady. Mrs. Sligo, I know her well by name. It is generous and kind of the good soul to come to me. But I fancy it is not so much the sympathizing woman feeling for one in my desolate position, as the strong minded lady claiming sympathy with the cause. . . .

Enter Mrs. Sligo. . . .

Mrs. Sligo. Oh, my poor, dear, persecuted man. I felt all your sufferings, and I thought I could not better aid the noble cause for which you bleed, than by exerting every influence to get to see you. [Takes out tablet . . . Writing his words down] And you are prepared for the worst? And willing to die a martyr, and all that sort of thing?

Brown. I am willing to follow where the other brave hearts have gone before; I regret the course of events more for others than for myself.

Mrs. Sligo. [Aside] I always said so. What a man, to be sure! He's as calm and collected as if he was not going to be hung, and—and all that sort of thing.

Enter Jailor.

Jailor. Madam, I am sorry, but there is another lady. Prepare yourself, sir, to see— . . . .

No. 125
[Mann Satterwhite Valentine], *The Mock Auction: Ossawatomie* [sic] *Sold* (Richmond, 1860), pp. 228-257

. . . At last, in some sort, by the moon,
He got into ship-shape his platoon;
And swearing oaths both black and blue,
As counting up the twenty-two—
Of that enormous, ardent band,
Who to the rack had come to stand.
The hero mounted the only horse,
And rode forth to view his force;—
Such steed was the epitome
Of all horse animality,
A charger, indeed, for a buzzard—
To make a snack from. . . .
Our outraged leader went to see
The abandoned dupe—Ossawatomie. . . .
There lay the filthy old hyena,
Reposing on his bed of straw;
His raw-boned body broken strangely,
And bestial savageness fully
Starting from his gloating eyes,
As he smother'd up complaining cries. . . .
So dangles Ossawatomie,
From the beam of spirituality;
His neck entangling with a cord,
Of a thousand Isms,—twisted hard,
And strong enough, in their fusion,
To wag and not pretension on. . . .

No. 126   "BROWN OF OSAWATOMIE"

John Greenleaf Whittier, in Redpath (ed.), *Echoes of Harper's Ferry*, pp. 303-304

JOHN BROWN of Osawatomie
Spake on his dying day:
"I will not have, to shrive my soul,
A priest in Slavery's pay;
But, let some poor slave-mother,
Whom I have striven to free,
With her children, from the gallows-stair,
Put up a prayer for me!"

John Brown of Osawatomie,
They led him out to die;
And, lo!—a poor slave mother
With her little child pressed nigh.
Then the bold, blue eye grew tender,
And the old, harsh face grew mild,
As he stooped between the jeering ranks
And kissed the negro's child!

The shadows of his stormy life
That moment fell apart:
Without, the rash and bloody hand,
Within, the loving heart.
That kiss, from all its guilty means,
Redeemed the good intent,
And round the grisly fighter's hair
The martyr's aureole bent!

Perish with him the folly
That seeks through evil, good;
Long live the generous purpose
Unstained with human blood!
Not the raid of midnight terror,
But the thought which underlies;
Not the outlaw's pride of daring,
But the Christian's sacrifice.

Oh! never may yon blue-ridged hills
The Northern rifle hear,
Nor see the light of blazing homes
Flash on the negro's spear.
But let the free-winged angel Truth
Their guarded passes scale,
To teach that Right is more than Might
And Justice more than Mail! . . . .

CONGRESS AND THE ELECTIONS

No. 127

The National Intelligencer, Dec. 6, 1859

[Mon., Dec. 5, 1859]

In Senate

The First Session of the Thirty-sixth Congress commenced this day, conformably to the Constitution. The following is a list of the Senators. . . .

RESOLUTIONS

Mr. MASON submitted the following resolution:

Resolved, that a committee be appointed to inquire into the facts attending the late invasion and seizure of the armory and arsenal of the United States at Harper's Ferry, in Virginia, by a band of armed men, and report—

Whether the same was attended by armed resistance to the authorities and public force of the United States, and by the murder of any of the citizens of Virginia, or of any troops sent there to protect the public property.

Whether such invasion and seizure was made under color of any organization intended to subvert the government of any of the States of the Union; what was the character and extent of any such organization; and whether any citizens of the United States not present were implicated therein, or accessory thereto. . . .

What was the character and extent of the military equipment in the hands or under the control of said armed band, and where, and how, and when the same was obtained and transported to the place so invaded.

And that said committee report whether any and what legislation may, in their opinion, be necessary on the part of the United States for the future preservation of the peace of the country, or for the safety of the public property, and that said committee have power to send for persons and papers. . . .

No. 128

The National Intelligencer, Dec. 10, 1859

[Thurs., Dec. 8, 1859]

House of Representatives

[A Voice:] John Brown was a Black Republican.

Mr. CORWIN [Ohio]: Was he? If so, did it follow that the whole Republican party was ready to march with him to Harper's Ferry? Let them put away all this ill feeling and unjust crimination. . . . As far as he knew the objects of the Republican party, . . . they were the very same as those of the founders of our Government. . . .

Wendell Phillips was an exponent of Republican principles, was he? . . . In all free States Phillips was well known to belong to that school of transcendental philosophers whose ideas rise to the immense and immeasurable heights which the human mind is expected to be capable of attaining fifty centuries hence, who say there is no constitution save that of the pavement, that the United States Constitution is only waste paper; that the Government of Virginia is only an association of piratical men; and that the earth must ascend towards heaven instead of heaven coming down to earth. [*Laughter.*] This was supposed to be a rhetorical figure. . . . He was informed that the next night after he listened to Mr. Phillips's eloquent rhapsody in Brooklyn, [Phillips] went to deliver it in the neighboring State of New Jersey, but they would not hear it, and he had to substitute a lecture on "The Lost Arts." [*Laughter.*] . . . Wendell Phillips said that all Virginia had to offer to the bravest . . . man in the world was a gallows, but the philosopher did not add that Brown could find for his great attributes no better employment than cutting throats. . . .

No. 129

The National Intelligencer, Dec. 17, 1859

[Thurs., Dec. 15, 1859]

House of Representatives

Mr. VALLANDIGHAM [Ohio]: Too many of the North were striving to force the South out of the Union, and too many of the South were anxious to be forced out. The doctrines of Hale, Banks, Seward, Chase, Giddings, and Lincoln, and above all of the New York

Tribune, were the doctrines of a large majority of the North and of a respectable minority of the West, and there was no use in denying it. His colleague (Mr. CORWIN) not only did not represent the sentiments of the Republicans of Ohio, but was not a respectable follower of that party which he professed to head. . . . Throughout the North and the Northwest there were manifestations of sympathy for John Brown. At a meeting in Cleveland ex-judges, ex-congressmen, and other men of distinction joined in shedding tears over his fate; in one county in Ohio the Court of Common Pleas was adjourned on the day of his execution, and even in his own district a court-house bell was tolled on that day. There was a public sentiment behind all this. . . . He assured the gentleman from Tennessee . . . that he was mistaken in supposing that the North is ready to put down agitation; that only a few sympathize with John Brown; or that fugitive slaves could be recaptured in one-half of the free States. . . . New England was a peculiar people, who had dethroned Jehovah and set up a deity of their own; and before a year had passed he predicted they would set up the statue of John Brown in the place of Daniel Webster. . . . [The] South had ample apology in the events of the last few months. War, open war, had been proclaimed against them, and arson and murder had been committed in their streets. The murderer had been executed, but he had risen from the dead a hero and a martyr, and his followers were gathering strength and only awaiting the hour to renew the invasion. . . . [Would] they secede now? . . . . Wait a little while. Let them try again the peaceful remedy of the ballot-box, more potent than the bayonet. . . .

No. 130   LETTER TO COMMITTEE IN NEWARK, N.J.

The National Intelligencer, Jan. 17, 1860

WASHINGTON, DECEMBER 22, 1859.

GENTLEMEN: . . . . You will allow me the expression of my abiding confidence in the patriotism and fidelity of the Southern States, and that, when the excitement of the unhappy, wicked, and greatly to be deprecated events at Harper's Ferry shall have passed away, they will return to their ancient state of feeling, and our country will go on in her accustomed order and propriety . . . WM. PENNINGTON

No. 131
The National Intelligencer, Jan. 21, 1860

[From speech of Rep. Sherman of Ohio, leading candidate for Speaker, after more than thirty unsuccessful attempts to organize the House]

Mr. SHERMAN: In other words, I am charged with being a Republican. . . . Mr. Sherman said that was his offence, and no other. . . . Through this contest he had been patient and quiet. He desired an organization of the House opposed to the Administration, and thought it was their duty to investigate and analyze the mode in which the executive powers . . . have been administered. . . . He came here expecting only a business session, and that the slavery question would not come up at all, and but for the unfortunate affair of John Brown at Harper's Ferry he did not believe there would have been any feeling on the subject. They ought to have met with kindly feelings, no man approving of the act of Brown, and every man willing to say so. . . . If bad blood had been stirred up, those gentlemen on the Democratic side had done it. . . .

No. 132
Reprinted from The Augusta (Ga.) Chronicle in The National Intelligencer, Feb. 9, 1860

At last the Hon. Wm. Pennington, of New Jersey, has been duly elected and installed Speaker of the Thirty-sixth Congress. The announcement creates no unusual stir. . . . There is no manifestation of hostility, we believe, among us to such an election, though, of course, we all would much prefer it had been otherwise. A Southern conservative might have been elected last week by the votes of three Northern Democrats, but they stood out to the last to prevent it; and so the power in the House goes over to the Republicans. If the House never does worse than elect such a man as the present Speaker we shall all probably be able to get along together some years yet. Gov. Pennington, though certainly objectionable, is a very moderate Republican, and not at all violent. He is doubtless conscientious in his *mental* convictions, but without any *feeling* of animosity or hatred towards the South.

No. 133

The National Intelligencer, Feb. 14, 1860

[Speech of Senator Hunter (Va.), Jan. 30, 1860]
. . . Mr. President, is it surprising that these bitter seeds of sectional hate and alienation . . . should have borne their bloody fruit in the raid of John Brown? Is it surprising that men who were taught to look on us as accursed of man and God, and as sustaining institutions which are incapable of palliation or defence, feel that they are justified in attacking us by all the means in their power, no matter what may be the consequence? I know that gentlemen have risen here to disclaim all sympathy or approbation with that attack, and I do not mean, by any means, to impeach their sincerity; but it is to be remarked that in none of the non-slaveholding States where the Republican party have the predominance have the Governors of those States, or as far as I know, the Legislatures, proposed any legislation which was calculated to punish and repress such attacks in the future; and it is also to be remembered that the Republican party at this session chose for its candidate as Speaker of the other House a man who had endorsed a book which preached precisely what John Brown practised; which recommended that they should get up servile war and dissension. . . .

No. 134

The National Intelligencer, Jan. 26, 1860

[Stephen Douglas on Jan. 23 in the Senate said that] He considered the outbreak at Harper's Ferry as a legitimate and logical consequence of the doctrines inculcated by the Republican party, in regard to the "irrepressible conflict" between different social systems in different States. . . . That theory had been promulgated by his Republican competitor in Illinois, Mr. LINCOLN, four months before its enunciation by Mr. SEWARD in his Rochester speech, and was a radical dogma. . . . [He] then proceeded to show that this theory was a novelty, and was certainly disregarded by the framers of the Constitution, and argued that, as long as the Republican party pursued its present aggressive policy there would be danger of future invasions like that of Harper's Ferry unless the Federal Government were clothed with power to keep the peace between the States.

Mr. FESSENDEN expressed his surprise at . . . Mr. Douglas. . . . [He said that] the Republicans were not responsible in any sense for the acts of John Brown or for the existing agitation of the slavery question, which, after being quieted in 1850, had been re-opened by Mr. DOUGLAS in 1854.

No. 135

John G. Nicolay and John Hay, *Complete Works of Abraham Lincoln* (New York, 1905), V, pp. 309-324; italicized commentary from *Campaign Documents, 1860*, n.p., n.d.

[Speech of Abraham Lincoln at the Cooper Union Institute, Feb. 27, 1860]

. . . This is all Republicans ask . . . in relation to slavery. As [our founding fathers] marked it, so let it be again marked, as an evil not to be extended, but to be tolerated and protected only because of, and so far as, its actual presence among us makes that toleration and protection a necessity. (*Loud applause.*) Let all the guaranties those fathers gave it be not grudgingly, but fully and fairly, maintained. . . .

And now . . . I would address a few words to the Southern people. . . . You charge that we stir up insurrections among your slaves. We deny it; and what is your proof? Harper's Ferry! (*Great laughter.*) John Brown! (*Renewed laughter.*) John Brown is no Republican, and you have [yet] to implicate a single Republican in his Harper's Ferry enterprise. (*Loud applause.*) . . . Some of you generously admit that no Republican designedly aided or encouraged the Harper's Ferry affair, but still insist that our doctrines and declarations necessarily lead to such results. We do not believe it. We know we hold to no doctrines and make no declarations which were not held to and made by our fathers who framed the Government under which we live. . . .

Slave insurrections are no more common now than they were before the Republican party was organized. What induced the Southampton insurrection, twenty-eight years ago, in which at least three times as many lives were lost as at Harper's Ferry? You can scarcely stretch your very elastic fancy to the conclusion that Southampton was got up by Black Republicanism. (*Laughter.*) In the present state of things in the United States, I do not think a general or even a very extensive slave insurrection is possible. . . . Much is said by Southern people about the affection of slaves for their masters and mistresses; and a part of it, at least, is true. . . .

In the language of Mr. Jefferson . . . , "it is still in our power to direct the process of emancipation and deportation peaceably, and in such slow degrees as that the evil will wear off insensibly, and their places be, *pari passu,* filled up by free white laborers." (*Loud applause.*) "If, on the contrary, it is left to force itself on, human nature must shudder at the prospect held up." Mr. Jefferson did not mean to say, nor do I, that the power of emancipation is in the Federal Government. He spoke of Virginia; and, as to the power of emancipation, I speak of the slaveholding States only. The Federal Government, however, as we insist, has the power of restraining the extension of the institution— the power to insure that a slave insurrection shall never occur on any American soil which is now free from slavery. (*Applause.*) John Brown's effort . . . was not a slave insurrection. It was an attempt by white men to get up a revolt among slaves, in which the slaves refused to participate. In fact, it was . . . absurd. . . . That affair, in its philosophy, corresponds with the many attempts . . . at the assassination of kings and emperors. An enthusiast broods over the oppression of a people till he fancies himself commissioned by Heaven to liberate them. . . .

But you will not abide the election of a Republican President! In that supposed event, you say, you will destroy the Union, and then, you say, the great crime of having destroyed it will be upon us! . . . .

Let us Republicans . . . do nothing through passion and ill temper. Even though the Southern people will not so much as listen to us, let us calmly consider their demands, and yield to them . . . if we possibly can. . . . Invasions and insurrections are the rage now. Will it satisfy them, if, in the future, we have nothing to do with invasions and insurrections? We know it will not. We so know because we know we never had anything to do with invasions and insurrections; and yet this total abstaining does not exempt us from . . . denunciation. . . .

TOPICS FOR ESSAYS

SUGGESTED LENGTH (*words*):

(1) *John Brown and the Poets*   300
(2) *Wendell Phillips: Facts or Fancy?*   300
(3) *The Pulpit and the Raid*   300
(4) *Reverend Cheever as Historian*   300
(5) *The Rostrum and the Raid*   300
(6) *Congress and the Raid*   500
(7) *John Brown in Kansas*   500

TOPICS FOR LIBRARY RESEARCH

BIBLIOGRAPHY:

Louisa M. Alcott   Edward Everett   Rep. Sherman of Ohio
Elijah Avey   Senator Hunter   Edmund C. Stedman
George B. Cheever   Abraham Lincoln   Mrs. J. C. Swayze
L. Maria Child   H. W. Longfellow   Mann S. Valentine
Caleb Cushing   Herman Melville   Senator Wilson
Mr. Corwin of Ohio   William Pennington   Henry C. Wright
Ralph W. Emerson

SUPPLEMENTARY RESEARCH:

Thoreau and Slavery   500-1500
Wendell Phillips and Slavery   500-1500

Chapter V

EPILOGUE

THE COUNTRY

No. 136 DECLARATION OF CAUSES WHICH INDUCED THE SECESSION OF SOUTH CAROLINA [Dec., 1860]

Frank Moore (ed.), *The Rebellion Record* (New York, 186[?]), I, p. 4

. . . The Constitution . . . in its fourth Article, provides as follows: "No person held to service or labor in one State under the laws thereof, escaping into another, shall, in consequence of any law or regulation therein, be discharged from such service or labor, but shall be delivered up. . . ." This stipulation was so material to the compact [the Constitution] that without it that compact would not have been made. The greater number of the contracting parties held slaves. . . . The States of Maine, New Hampshire, Vermont, Massachusetts, Connecticut, Rhode Island, New York, Pennsylvania, Illinois, Indiana, Michigan, Wisconsin, and Iowa, have enacted laws which either nullify the acts of Congress, or render useless any attempt to execute them. In many of these States the fugitive is discharged from the service of labor claimed. . . . and the States of Ohio and Iowa have refused to surrender to justice fugitives charged with murder, and with inciting servile insurrection in the State of Virginia. Thus the constitutional compact has been deliberately broken and disregarded . . . ; and the consequence follows that South Carolina is released from her obligation. . . .

We affirm that these ends for which this Government was instituted have been defeated. . . . [The non-slaveholding] States have assumed the right of deciding upon the propriety of our domestic institutions; and have denied the rights of property established in fifteen of the States and recognized by the Constitution; they have denounced as sinful the institution of Slavery; they have permitted the open establishment among them of societies whose avowed object is to disturb the peace of and eloin the property of the citizens of other States. They have encouraged and assisted thousands of our slaves to leave their homes; and those who remain have been incited by emissaries, books, and pictures, to servile insurrection.

For twenty-five years this agitation has been steadily increasing, until it has now secured to its aid the power of the common Government. . . . [All the States of the North] have united in the election of a man to the high office of President of the United States whose

214

opinions and purposes are hostile to Slavery. He is to be intrusted with the administration of the common Government, because he has declared that that "Government cannot endure permanently half slave, half free," and that the public mind must rest in the belief that Slavery is in the course of ultimate extinction. . . .

On the 4th of March next this party will take possession of the Government. . . .

Sectional interest and animosity will deepen the irritation; and all hope of remedy is rendered vain, by the fact that the public opinion at the North has invested a great political error with the sanctions of a more erroneous religious belief.

We, therefore, the people of South Carolina, by our delegates in Convention assembled, . . . have solemnly declared that the Union . . . is dissolved. . . .

No. 137   THE EMANCIPATION PROCLAMATION

Statutes at Large of the United States (Boston, 1863), Vol. XII, pp. 1268-1269.

BY THE PRESIDENT OF THE UNITED STATES OF AMERICA: *A Proclamation.*

Whereas on the 22d day of September, A.D. 1862, a proclamation was issued by the President of the United States, containing, among other things, the following, to wit:

"That on the 1st day of January, A.D. 1863, all persons held as slaves within any State or designated part of a State the people whereof shall then be in rebellion against the United States shall be then, thenceforward, and forever free; and the executive government of the United States, including the military and naval authority thereof, will recognize and maintain the freedom of such persons and will do no act or acts to repress such persons, or any of them, in any efforts they may make for their actual freedom.

"That the executive will on the 1st day of January aforesaid, by proclamation, designate the States and parts of States, if any, in which the people thereof, respectively, shall then be in rebellion against the United States; and the fact that any State or the people thereof shall on that day be in good faith represented in the Congress of the United States by members chosen thereto at elections wherein a majority of the qualified voters of such States shall have participated shall, in the absence of strong countervailing testimony, be deemed conclusive evidence that such State and the people thereof are not then in rebellion against the United States."

Now, therefore, I, Abraham Lincoln, President of the United States, by virtue of the power in me vested as Commander-in-Chief of the Army and Navy of the United States in time of actual armed rebellion against the authority and government of the United States, and as a fit and necessary war measure for suppressing said rebellion, do, on this 1st day of January, A.D. 1863, and in accordance with my purpose so to do, publicly proclaimed for the full period of one hundred days from the first day above mentioned, order and designate as the States and parts of States wherein the people thereof, respectively, are this day in rebellion against the United States the following, to wit:

Arkansas, Texas, Louisiana, (except the parishes of. . . .), Mississippi, Alabama, Florida, Georgia, South Carolina, North Carolina, and Virginia (except the forty-eight counties designated as West Virginia, and also the counties of . . .), and which excepted parts are for the present left precisely as if this proclamation were not issued.

And by virtue of the power and for the purpose aforesaid, I do order and declare that all persons held as slaves within said designated States and parts of States are, and henceforward shall be, free; and that the Executive Government of the United States, including the military and naval authorities thereof, will recognize and maintain the freedom of said persons.

And I hereby enjoin upon the people so declared to be free to abstain from all violence, unless in necessary self-defense; and I recommend to them that, in all cases when allowed, they labor faithfully for reasonable wages.

And I further declare and make known that such persons of suitable condition will be received into the armed service of the United States to garrison forts, positions, stations, and other places, and to man vessels of all sorts in said service.

And upon this act, sincerely believed to be an act of justice, warranted by the Constitution upon military necessity, I invoke the considerate judgment of mankind and the gracious favor of Almighty God.

No. 138 [CONSTITUTIONAL AMENDMENTS]

Federal and State Constitutions (Government Printing Office, 1909), I, p. 31

ARTICLE XIII [1865]

SECTION 1. Neither slavery nor involuntary servitude, except as a punishment for crime whereof the party shall have been duly convicted, shall exist in the United States, or any place subject to their jurisdiction. . . .

ARTICLE XIV [1868]

SECTION 1. All persons born or naturalized in the United States, and subject to the jurisdiction thereof, are citizens of the United States and of the State wherein they reside. No state shall make or enforce any law which shall abridge the privileges or immunities of citizens of the United States; nor shall any State deprive any person of life, liberty, or property, without due process of law; nor deny to any person within its jurisdiction the equal protection of the laws. . . .

THE MAN

No. 139

Nathaniel Hawthorne, "Chiefly about War-Matters," *The Atlantic Monthly*, X (July, 1862), p. 54

. . . I shall not pretend to be an admirer of old John Brown, any farther than sympathy with Whittier's excellent ballad about him may go; nor did I expect ever to shrink so unutterably from any apophthegm of a sage, whose happy lips have uttered a hundred golden sentences, as from that saying, (perhaps falsely attributed to so honored a source,) that the death of this blood-stained fanatic has "made the Gallows as venerable as the Cross!" Nobody was ever more justly hanged. He won his martyrdom fairly, and took it firmly. He himself, I am persuaded, (such was his natural integrity,) would have acknowledged that Virginia had a right to take the life which he had staked and lost; although it would have been better for her, in the hour that is fast coming, if she could generously have forgotten the criminality of his attempt in its enormous folly. On the other hand, any common-sensible man, looking at the matter unsentimentally, must have felt a certain intellectual satisfaction in seeing him hanged, if it were only in requital of his preposterous miscalculation of possibilities. (Can it be a son of old Massachusetts who utters this abominable sentiment? For shame!)

But, coolly as I seem to say these things, my Yankee heart stirred triumphantly when I saw the use to which John Brown's fortress and prison-house has now been put. . . . The engine-house is now a place of confinement for Rebel prisoners. . . .

No. 140 THE MASSACHUSETTS JOHN BROWN SONG

L. H[olbrook], in Frank Moore (ed.), *Songs of the Soldiers* (New York, 1864), pp. 125-126

Old John Brown's body is a-mouldering in the dust,
Old John Brown's rifle's red with blood-spots turned to rust,
Old John Brown's pike has made its last, unflinching thrust,
    His soul is marching on!

Glory! Glory! Hallelujah!
"Forward!" calls the Lord, our Captain:

Glory! Glory! Hallelujah!
With him we're marching on.

For treason hung because he struck at treason's root,
When soon palmetto-tree had ripened treason's fruit,
His dust, disquieted, stirred at Sumter's last salute—
His soul is marching on!

Who rides before the army of martyrs to the word?
The heavens grow bright as He makes bare his flaming sword,
The glory fills the earth of the coming of the Lord—
His soul is marching on! . . . .

No. 141   CALL ALL! CALL ALL!

By "Georgia," in Frank Moore (ed.), *Rebel Rhymes and Rhapsodies* (New York, 1864), p. 13

. . . Old Kentucky is caved from under,
Tennessee is split asunder,
Alabama awaits attack,
And Georgia bristles up her back.

Old John Brown is dead and gone!
Still his spirit is marching on,—
Lantern-jawed, and legs, my boys,
Long as an ape's from Illinois! . . . .

No. 142

F. B. Sanborn, *Memoirs of John Brown* (Concord, 1878), pp. 89-97

During the four or five hours after day break, when he might have escaped from the town, he was urged to do so by Kagi, by Stevens, and by others; but for one reason or another he delayed his movements until it was too late. For twelve hours he held the town at his mercy; after that he was firmly caught in the trap he had entered. . . .

His own explanation of his failure is characteristic: it was foreordained to be so. "All our actions," he said to one who visited him in prison, "even all the follies that led to this disaster, were decreed to happen ages before the world was made." He declared at the same time that had he betaken himself to the mountains, he could never have been captured, "for he and his men had studied the country carefully, and knew it a hundred times better than any of the inhabitants." He ascribed his ruin to his weakness in listening to the entreaties of his prisoners and delaying his departure. . . . "It was the first time," somebody reports him as saying, "that I ever lost command of myself, and now I am punished for it." But he soon began to see that this mistake was leading him to his most glorious success, a victory such as he might never have won in his own way. A month after his capture he wrote thus to his old school-master . . . : "I have been a good deal disappointed, as it regards myself, in not keeping up to my own plans; but I now feel entirely reconciled to that, even; for God's plan was infinitely better, no doubt, or I should have kept to my own. Had Samson kept to his determination of not telling Delilah wherein his great strength lay, he would probably *have never overturned the house*. I did not tell Delilah, but I was induced to act very contrary to my better judgment; and I have lost my two noble boys, and other friends, if not my two eyes. But God's will, not mine, be done." . . . .

Standing on the battle-field at Gettysburg . . . , Abraham Lincoln pronounced [Nov. 19, 1863] that immortal eulogy on those who "gave their lives that the nation might live. . . ." Not long afterward Lincoln himself fell, the last great victim in the struggle, as John Brown had been its first great martyr. Henceforth their names will be joined and their words will be remembered together, the speeches of the condemned convict at Charlestown and of the successful statesman at Gettysburg going down to posterity as the highest range of eloquence in our time. . . .

The public murder of John Brown upon a Virginia gallows, following closely after his capture . . . , was the first act in the long tragedy, of which the public murder of Lincoln was the final catastrophe. . . . Nor is it without the deepest reason, in the fitness of things, that the great heart of the people, in all nations, responding to the voice of Nature, joins the names of Brown and Lincoln in the same throb of gratitude. An American lady, who had known intimately both these martyrs of liberty, was spending a few weeks, soon after the emancipation of the Russian serfs, in Moscow, that citadel of ancient oppression. Entering a poor man's shop one day to purchase the *icon* or picture of some Russian saint, and giving the shopkeeper to understand that she was an American, he drew her with enthusiasm into a recess of his dingy rooms, where a lamp was continually burning before rude pictures of his American saints, John Brown and Abraham Lincoln, placed side by side for his daily worship. He had been a serf, one of the millions whom the noble edict of Alexander set free. Along with the czar and his patron saint, he paid religious honors to the two American emancipators, the echoes of whose good fame had reached him, blended in one lofty note, as they came across seas and lands, from the Potomac to the Moskwa.

No. 143

A letter in the George W. Brown Papers of the Kansas State Historical Society, Topeka, Kansas

Fort Scott, Kans.
Aug. 4, 1879

Hon. Eli Thayer
Worcester, Mass.

My Dear Sir: Yours of the 28th ult recd asking for facts in my possession in regard to John Brown's participation in what is known as the Pottawatomie massacre and the raid into Missouri. . . . I was in John Brown's camp at the Trading Post in Linn Co. Kansas early in January A.D. 1859 and had conversations with him in regard to both transactions.

As to the "Massacre" he said he would not say that he was *not* engaged in it, but he *would* say that he advised it and justified it and was willing to take a full share of the responsibility of it. He said that the death of those pro-slavery men had been determined upon at a meeting of free-state settlers the day before—that he was present at that meeting and, I think, presided, and that the executioners were then and there appointed. He said he would not say that he was one of them, but . . . that if it was wrong he was as much to blame as any.

He gave as a reason for the deed that the men were carriers of news to Missourians, that they kept a "grape-vine telegraph" with Missourians and were endangering the settlements by bringing in the invaders. He said it became necessary to make an example, and so strike terror and put an end to that sort of thing.

As to the raid into Missouri—it was made on the 20th Dec. 1858. . . . It was led by Capt. Brown in person . . . and proceeded into Vernon Co. Mo., a distance of three or four miles. The Missouri Democrat of Dec. 30th 1858 gave the Missouri statement of the losses. . . . It states that they "murdered" David Crews (or Cruise), "kidnapped a negro woman," took wagon, horses &c. & robbed Mr. Martin and family of a fine mule—took from the estate of James Lawrence, in possession of his son-in-law five negroes, 2 horses, 1 yoke of cattle and ox-wagon, double-barrel shotgun, saddle and clothing. From Isaac B. La Rue, five negroes, six horses, 1 yoke of cattle, clothing—and took prisoners whom they released. In the conversation to which I have alluded Capt. Brown said he had sent the slaves on to their freedom—that they had earned the property of their masters—and that his young men were entitled to forage to the extent of their subsistence. He denied the current rumor that the slaves had been taken away by violence and against their will. As to the killing of Cruise, he said that he had given strict orders . . . that there should be no firing unless resistance was offered. . . . Cruise was a . . . plain, unoffending farmer. It was reported that he had no weapons on his person. The killing of him was regarded as an unjustifiable outrage—and it subjected our settlements to great danger from retaliatory measures.

I protested to the Captain against this violence. We were settlers—he was not. He could strike a blow and leave. The retaliatory blow would fall on us. Being a free state man, I myself was held personally responsible by pro-slavery ruffians in Ft. Scott for the acts of Capt. Brown. One of these ruffians—Brockett—when they gave me notice to leave the town, said, "When a snake bites me I don't go hunting for that particular snake. I kill the first snake I come to."

I called Capt. Brown's attention to the facts that we were at peace with Missouri—that our Legislature was then in the hands of free state men to make the law—that even in our disturbed Counties of Bourbon and Linn they were in a majority and had elected the officers both to make and execute the laws—that without peace we could have no immigration—that no southern immigration was coming—that agitation such as his was only keeping our northern friends away &c. &c.

The old man replied that it was no pleasure to him—an old man—to be living in the saddle—away from home and family and exposing his life—and if the free state men in Kansas felt that they no longer needed him he would be glad to go.

He seemed very erratic—at war with all our accustomed ideas on the slavery question—but very earnest.

I think the conversation made an impression on him—for he soon after went to his self-sacrifice at Harper's Ferry.

Yours,/ George A. Crawford

P.S. . . . Let me say for Capt. Brown that if alive he would allow no man to apologize for that Pottawatomie affair, or to deny his participation in it. He stood squarely by it.

No. 144
The Daily Journal (Lawrence, Kans.) Dec. 10, 1879

I am a native of . . . Maryland . . . a painter by trade. . . . [On] October 20, 1855, . . . I emigrated to Kansas with my family and settled in Anderson County, on the Pottawatomie Creek, about one mile west of Greeley. I joined the Pottawatomie rifle company at its reorganization in May, 1856, at which time John Brown Jr. was elected captain. . . . About noon [on May] 23d, old John Brown came to me and said he had just received information that trouble was expected on the Pottawatomie, and wanted to know if I would take my team and take him and his boys back so that they could keep watch of what was going on. . . . The party, consisting of old John Brown, Frederick Brown, Owen Brown, Watson Brown, Oliver Brown, Henry Thompson (John Brown's son-in-law), and Mr. Winer . . . started . . . about two o'clock p.m. All of the party, except Mr. Winer, who rode a pony, rode with me in my wagon. When within two or three miles of the Pottawatomie creek we turned off the main road to the right, drove down into the edge of the timber between the two deep ravines and camped about one mile above Dutch Henry's crossing.

After my team was fed and the party had taken supper, John Brown told me for the first time what he proposed to do. He said he wanted me to pilot the company up to the forks of the creek some five or six miles above, into the neighborhood in which I lived, and show them where all the pro-slavery men resided; that he proposed to sweep the creek as he came down of all the pro-slavery men living on it. I positively refused. . . . He insisted . . . , but when he found that I would not go he decided to postpone the expedition until the following night. I then wanted to take my team and go home, but he refused . . . and said I should remain. . . . We remained in camp that night, and all day the next day. Sometime after dark we were ordered to march.

We started, the whole company, in a northerly direction, crossing Mosquito creek above the residence of the Doyles. Soon after crossing the creek someone of the party knocked at the door of a cabin but received no reply. . . . The next place we came to was the residence of the Doyles. . . . The old man Doyle and two sons were called out and marched . . . toward Dutch Henry's in the road, where a halt was made. Old John Brown drew his revolver and shot the old man Doyle in the forehead, and Brown's two youngest sons immediately fell upon the younger Doyles with their short two-edged swords.

One of the young Doyles was stricken down in an instant, but the other attempted to escape, and was pursued a short distance . . . and cut down. The company then proceeded down Mosquito creek to the house of Allen Wilkinson. Here the old man Brown, three of his sons, and son-in-law . . . went to the door and ordered Wilkinson to come out, leaving Frederick Brown, Winer, and myself standing in the road. . . . Wilkinson was taken and marched some distance . . . and slain in the road with a short sword by one of the younger Browns. . . .

We then crossed the Pottawatomie and came to the house of Henry Sherman, generally known as Dutch Henry. Here John Brown and the party, excepting Frederick Brown, Winer, and myself . . . went into the house and brought out one or two persons, talked with them some, and then took them in again. They afterward brought out William Sherman, Dutch Henry's brother, marched him down into the Pottawatomie Creek, where he was slain with swords by Brown's two youngest sons. . . .

I desire . . . to say that I did not then approve of the killing of those men, but Brown said it must be done for the protection of the Free State settlers; that the pro-slavery party must be terrified, and that it was better that a score of bad men should die than that one man who came here to make Kansas a free State should be driven out. . . . That night and the acts then perpetrated are vividly fixed in my memory, and I have thought of them many times since.

I then thought that the transaction was terrible, and have mentioned it to but few persons since. In after time, however, I became satisfied that it resulted in good to the Free State cause, and was especially beneficial to Free State settlers on Pottawatomie Creek. The pro-slavery men *were dreadfully* terrified, and large numbers of them soon left the Territory. It was afterwards said that one Free State man could scare a company of them. I always understood that Geo. W. Grant came to our camp on Ottawa Creek, near Captain Shore's, with a message from his father . . . to John Brown, asking for protection from threatened assaults of the Shermans and other pro-slavery ruffians. But I did not know Geo. W. Grant at the time and do not remember of seeing him. I frequently heard the circumstance mentioned as a fact. . . .

After several days . . . while John Brown was cooking breakfast for the company, James Redpath came into our camp and had some conversation with Captain Brown. I saw Redpath again after the battle of Black Jack . . . , and I desire to say, in this connection, that I never told Redpath at any time that John Brown was not present at the Pottawatomie tragedy. His statement, which has been read to me, to the effect that "two squatters, who aided in the execution," gave him such information, is totally false, so far as I am concerned. As Winer and myself were the only settlers in the neighborhood not members of Brown's family, who were present at the tragedy, I can only conclude he referred to us. . . .

Lane, Kansas, Dec. 6, 1879.   JAMES TOWNSLEY

No. 145

Thomas Hughes, *The Manliness of Christ* (Boston, 1880), pp. 126-129

Now I freely admit that there is no recorded end of a life that I know of more entirely brave and manly than this one of Captain John Brown, of which we know every minutest detail, as it happened in the full glare of our modern life not twenty years ago. About that I think there would scarcely be disagreement anywhere. The very men who allowed him to lie in his bloody clothes till the day of his execution, and then hanged him, recognized this. "You are a game man, Captain Brown," the Southern sheriff said in the wagon. "Yes," he answered, "I was so brought up. It was one of my mother's lessons. From infancy I have not suffered from physical fear. I have suffered a thousand times more from bashfulness"; and then he kissed a negro child in its mother's arms, and walked cheerfully on to the scaffold, thankful that he was "allowed to die for a cause, and not merely to pay the debt of nature, as all must."

There is no simpler or nobler record in the "Book of Martyrs," and . . . I would only remind you that he at least was ready to acknowledge from whence came his strength. "Christ, the great Captain of liberty as well as of salvation," he wrote just before his death, "saw fit to take from me the sword of steel after I had carried it for a time. But He has put another in my hand, the sword of the Spirit, and I pray God to make me a faithful soldier wherever He may send me." And to a friend who left him with the word, "If you can be true to yourself to the end, how glad we shall be," he answered, "I cannot say, but I do not think I shall deny my Lord and Master, Jesus Christ." The old Abolitionist would have been as amazed as any man at such a comparison as we are dealing with, and would have reminded us that, so far from treading the wine-press alone [as Christ did], he was upheld by the sympathy and enthusiasm of all of his own nation, and of the world outside his own nation, for whom he cared.

No. 146

Quoted in Oswald Garrison Villard, *John Brown: A Biography Fifty Years After* [1910] (New York: Alfred A. Knopf, 1943), pp. 670-671; reprinted with the kind permission of the publisher

I, John Avis, a Justice of the Peace of the County of Jefferson, State of West Virginia, under oath do solemnly declare that I was Deputy Sheriff and Jailor of Jefferson County, Virginia, in 1859 during the whole time that Captain John Brown was in prison & on trial for his conduct in what is familiarly known as the Harper's Ferry Raid; that I was with him daily during the whole period; that the personal relations between him and me were of the most pleasant character; that Sheriff James W. Campbell & I escorted him from his cell the morning of his execution one on either side of him; that Sheriff Campbell & I rode with Captain Brown in a wagon from the jail to the scaffold one on either side; that I heard every word that Captain Brown spoke from the time he left the jail till his death; that Sheriff Campbell (now deceased) and I were the only persons with him on the scaffold.

I have this day read, in the early part of Chapter 8 of *The Manliness of Christ* by Thomas Hughes, the following paragraph. . . .

Respecting the statements contained [therein] I solemnly declare:—

First, that Captain John Brown . . . was furnished with a change of clothing as promptly as prisoners in such condition usually are; that he was allowed all the clothing he desired; and that his washing was done at his will without any cost to himself. . . . I saw that he was at all times . . . treated kindly. . . . In further proof of the kindness he received at my hands I will state that Captain Brown in his last written will & testament bequeathed to me his Sharps Rifle and a pistol. Furthermore, on the night before the execution Captain Brown and his wife, upon my invitation, took supper with me and my family at our table in our residence which was a part of the jail building.

2. . . . The only remarks made by Captain Brown between his cell and the scaffold were commonplace remarks about the beauty of the country and the weather.

3. The statement that "he kissed a negro child in his mother's arms" is wholly incorrect. Nothing of the sort occurred . . . for his hands, as usual in such cases, were confined behind him before he left the jail;

he was between Sheriff Campbell and me, and a guard of soldiers surrounded him, and allowed no person to come between them and the prisoner, from the jail to the scaffold, except his escorts.

4. Respecting the statement that he "walked cheerfully to the scaffold," I will say that I did not think his bearing on the scaffold was conspicuous for its heroism, yet not cowardly.

5. Whether he was "thankful that he was allowed to die for a cause and not merely to pay the debt of nature as all must," or not, I cannot say what was in his heart; but if this clause means, as the quotation marks would indicate, that Captain Brown used any such language or said anything on the subject, it is entirely incorrect. Captain Brown said nothing like it. The only thing that he did say at or on the scaffold was to take leave of us & then just about the time the noose was adjusted he said to me: "Be quick."

CHARLESTOWN, W. VA.   (Signed) JOHN AVIS
April 25, 1882.

No. 147   THE WORLD'S HOMAGE

Oliver Wendell Holmes, *Complete Poetical Works* (Boston, 1895), pp. 272-273

[June 14, 1882]
. . . All through the conflict, up and down
Marched Uncle Tom and Old John Brown,
    One ghost, one form ideal;
And which was false and which was true,
And which was mightier of the two,
The wisest sibyl never knew,
    For both alike were real. . . .

TOPICS FOR ESSAYS

SUGGESTED LENGTH (*words*):

(1) Write a history of the affairs of the nation with regard to slavery after Oct. 16, 1859, using the few documents in this section, relating them to John Brown wherever warranted.   300

(2) *John Brown and Abraham Lincoln: Fact and Fancy* 300

(3) *John Brown and the Negro Child* (Use the documents in Chapter II as well.)   300

(4) *The South Carolina "Declaration" and the Virginia Extradition Story* (Use the documents in Chapter II as well.)   500

TOPICS FOR LIBRARY RESEARCH

BIBLIOGRAPHY:

John Avis	O. W. Holmes	Harriet B. Stowe
George A. Crawford	Thomas Hughes	Eli Thayer
Nathaniel Hawthorne	Frank Moore	James Townsley
L. Holbrook		

SUPPLEMENTARY RESEARCH:

Consult three or four histories of the United States. Report on the relationship, if any, that they establish between the Raid and the disruption of the Union.   500-1500

TOPICS FOR FULL-LENGTH ESSAYS

AND RESEARCH PAPERS

TOPICS FOR ESSAYS

INSTRUCTIONS: *Now you are asked to attempt a synthesis drawn from parts of the entire book.*

SUGGESTED LENGTH (*words*):

(1) *The Life of John Brown to Oct., 1859*	1500
(2) *John Brown's Relationship to His Raiders*	1500
(3) *The Raid: A Factual Account*	1500-2500
(4) *John Brown at Harper's Ferry and Charlestown*	2500
(5) *What Happened at Harper's Ferry?*	

(Figuratively, that is—in the larger sense.
Include the Charlestown period in your scope.)   2500

TOPICS FOR LIBRARY RESEARCH

INSTRUCTIONS: The documents of this book stop with the end of the century, with the passing of most of the people who participated in the Raid, witnessed it, or felt its influence directly. But since 1900 have appeared literally hundreds of additions to the John Brown story—from full-length books to mere squibs. A partial bibliography of them, as well as of 1859-1900 documents for which no room could be found in the present collection, appears in Oswald Garrison Villard's *John Brown: A Biography Fifty Years After* (1910; 1943); this can be brought up to date from the various indexes (of books, essays, magazine and newspaper articles) in the reference room of your library.

As your instructor directs, select one or more of these documents; then write a report, documented or not, fitting the new material into the John Brown story where this book leaves off.

BIBLIOGRAPHY

Compile a bibliography of the documents used in this book, arranging them methodically, according to Books, Magazine Articles, etc.